P9-DFX-315
"A SONG IS BORN"
Soul
Music by
HOAGY CARMICHAEL
en - slave me
Oft
I'm Hans Christian Andersen
From the Samuel Goldwyn Production "Hans Christian Andersen"
Moderato
(broadly)
Piano
By FRANK LOESSER
Chorus
Pompously
1. I'M HANS CHRIS-TIAN AN - DER-SEN, I've man - y a tale to tell And
HANS CHRIS-TIAN AN - DER-SEN, I bring you a fa - ble rare There
HANS CHRIS-TIAN AN - DER-SEN, My pen's like a bab-bling brook Per -
I tell them rath - er well I'll
"Oh how I'd love a chair" And
my ver - y la - test book Now
Excerpt from Act I Scene II of "THE MOST HAPPY FELLA"
The Most Happy Fella
Joyously, with vigor
By FRANK LOESSER
TONY and ENSEMBLE:
Piano
f (ben marcato)
I'm The
the whole Na -
Lord
Ammunition!
Words and Music by
FRANK LOESSER
- let was his fate
Once In Love With Amy
From the Musical Production "Where's Charley?"
Slow and easy soft shoe
Verse
I caught you, sir, hav-ing a look at her as she went stro
heart beat boom, boom, boom, boom, boom and
I warn you, sir, don't start to dream o
gone Or it - 'll be boom,
Sung by Marlene Dietrich in the New Universal Picture "DESTRY RIDES AGAIN"
THE BOYS IN THE BACKROOM
Lyric by
FRANK LOESSER
Music by
FREDERICK HOLLANDER
Moderately
See what The Boys In The Back-room will have And

A MOST REMARKABLE FELLA

On the Paramount lot.

A MOST REMARKABLE FELLA

Frank Loesser and the Guys and Dolls in His Life

A Portrait by His Daughter

Susan Loesser

DONALD I. FINE, INC.
NEW YORK

 Published in the United States of America by Donald L. Fine, Inc. and in Canada by General Publishing Company Limited.

Library of Congress Cataloging-in-Publication Data

Loesser, Susan.
A most remarkable fella : Frank Loesser and the guys and dolls in his life : a portrait by his daughter / Susan Loesser.
p. cm.
Includes bibliographical references and index.
ISBN 1-55611-364-1
1. Loesser, Frank, 1910–1969. 2. Composers—United States—Biography. I. Title.
ML410.L7984L6 1993
782.1'4'092—dc20
[B] 92-54985
CIP
MN

Manufactured in the United States of America

10 9 8 7 6 5 4 3 2 1

For Jordan and Gracie

Contents

Acknowledgments

Most grateful acknowledgment is given:

To Sam Vaughan, who championed the first draft of this book as though it were a diamond in the rough, and whose sensitive analysis and suggestions for the finished product were given from the goodness of his heart.

To Frank Campbell, retired Chief of the Music Division at the Library of the Performing Arts of the New York Public Library, who not only personally guided me through my extensive research at that institution, but also spent many hours with me in discussions of my father's work, giving me inspiration, ideas, and friendship.

To the Library of the Performing Arts, without whose incomparable collection of manuscripts, clipping files, and statistics this book could not have been written.

To Abba Bogin, who so generously gave me many hours of his time, both in interviews and in painstaking critical notes on the manuscript as it evolved. His special knowledge of my father's working methods and madnesses were invaluable to me.

To Jack Gallahue, with whom I first discussed my idea to write this book, and who challenged and encouraged me throughout the process.

To my cousin Ted Loesser Drachman, who helped me research our family history, provided me with anecdotes and information, and made many valuable and creative suggestions, most of which I have incorporated.

To Renni Browne and Dave King of The Editorial Department, who copyedited the first draft with intelligence and wit and gave me a writing course in the process.

Everyone who is quoted in these pages was generous and accessible to a degree that touched and surprised me. I am grateful to them all.

Introduction

Sometimes I can smell my father. Sometimes as I walk down the street, or when I get in an elevator, ride a bus, enter a lobby, I catch a wisp of his scent. Dominated by the glassy green pomade he wore in his hair, spiced with his cologne (Shalimar), sweetened by his crisp, laundered shirts, the fragrance curls around my awareness and, always startled, I look for him in the crowd. I never even find the perpetrator with the stolen aroma, which is fine with me. I like to think that my father visits me at these moments, is saying hello, is checking in with me to see how I'm doing.

I know I should remember him smelling like cigarettes. I certainly have no memories of him without a cigarette smoldering, an ashtray brimming. And he must have smelled the way people do who smoke three packs a day. Maybe it's because I smoked them too and had no awareness of that odor. Whatever the reason, when I smell my father now he smells clean and crisp and good, and I feel wistful and melancholy and happy, too, to remember him.

Here in the summer of 1992, it is hard not to be thinking of him all the time. Broadway is Loesserland lately. The two-piano revival of *The Most Happy Fella* and the big and brassy production of *Guys and Dolls* are mentioned almost daily in the New York press. Both shows opened to rave reviews. *Guys and Dolls* has a huge advance sale and is expected to run for years. Both shows have just released cast albums. There is talk about a new first-class production of *How to Succeed in Business Without Really Trying.* His music is everywhere—in movies, on the radio, even in the supermarket. Frank Loesser is as big a name this year as he ever was when he was alive. Perhaps bigger.

I wonder if he's aware of all this as he wisps into the world on his visits. He always said he didn't write for posterity. He said he wasn't interested in what future generations thought of him. He was a person of the present who cared deeply what his peers thought, who needed success and respect, who reveled in his hits and mourned his failures, and who never talked about what the public's opinion about him might be after he was gone. He didn't care.

But I care, along with my brother and stepmother and the rest of what's left of our family. We all care about his reputation and his fame and whatever portion of his fortune we've inherited. We're all very proud and pleased to see this renaissance, and I, for one, feel just a little smug that the hottest show on Broadway this year is not by Andrew Lloyd Webber, nice as he might be.

I began this book in 1988. I had two reasons. The first was that there was no book exclusively about my father, and I felt there should be and that I would probably be the appropriate author. The second reason, and the one I wasn't consciously aware of for some time, was that I never *really* knew my father, and I wanted to find out more about him, to see if I could snuggle my mind up to his and discover some of the person behind the personality that dominated so much of my life.

I read letters and manuscripts, I talked to many of his friends and colleagues, I revisited his songs and his shows, and I cut holes in the frozen lake of my memories and went ice fishing. The experience was joyful as well as painful, frustrating as well as rewarding. I realized that I had never talked with him about his feelings, or even about his goals or regrets. When we were together, he did most of the talking, and he talked about concrete things. About a show ("It's a crime about *Candide,* such a brilliant show"), about the Mets ("Let's Go, Mets!"), about my current boyfriend ("You've got another date with that pimplefarm?"). He didn't give himself away, and I didn't ask him to. By the time I was a teenager we lived in separate households, and when I saw him I was a guest. There was a physical distance, and also a mutual reserve. We had our roles. He was the entertainer. I was the entertainee. I once asked him why he left my mother, and he said he had gotten tired of waiting for her. It amazes me now that I let him leave it at that. But it also satisfies me now that I've figured it out, more or less, and I know it wouldn't have crystallized for me at all if I hadn't written this book.

I never thought very much about his relationships with his mother and half brother. I knew I wasn't very fond of them, and I sensed that it would hurt him if he knew that for a fact. Now I think I understand what was painful and what was joyful for him to be a member of that family.

I've learned a good deal more about my father, and I wish now he'd visit with a little more of himself than his scent, so we could finally talk about how it felt to be connected to each other by such a fragile bond.

Singers had a strong effect on my father. He reviled them or he adored them or he married them. He pestered them, badgered them, coached them to tears. He once briefly walked off a show over a stubborn star. Fought a verbal duel over style with Frank Sinatra that left them lifelong enemies. Got so mad at one leading lady that he hauled off and hit her. Fell so madly in love with another soprano that he left my mother (also a singer) for her.

To some extent he must have viewed the singer as simply the instrument through which he spoke to his audience, and as such, the singer was not to interpret or show off or indulge in any quirks that might detract from the pure song pouring forth. My father expected singers to perform his songs clearly, meticulously, enunciating every word—with no deviation, no extra notes, no frivolous embellishments ("Singers love to vocalize beyond the sense of a lyric," he'd say. "They're always so sure you want to hear their goddamned *tones!*")—and he wanted it *loud.* If you couldn't project to the last row of the balcony without benefit of microphone, you had better not bother to audition for Frank Loesser.

I once sang for my father. It was a humiliating experience. I was thirteen. Among the many career choices I made frequently and feverishly in my teenage years, singing was—briefly—a favorite.

"Pop, I want to be a singer," I announced one day.

"Really! Do you really want to sing? Or do you just 'want to be a singer?' If you *really* want to sing, it has to be because you can't stand *not* singing. You'll never be any good if you want to be a singer just because you think it's a nice idea."

My heart had already begun to sink. I defensively asserted my deep love for the sound of my own voice in glee club. I told him I really loved to sing (which, in fact, I did—sort of).

"Okay, why don't you come down to my office and audition for me tomorrow afternoon, after school," he said.

An audition! That was not what I had in mind. I had thought he'd suggest lessons, or give some mild encouragement. But my father had taken me all too seriously, and he challenged me the way he challenged everyone who came to him. "Show me your stuff. If you're good, I'll help you."

So, full of trepidation, the next day I stood and sang the Christmas carol I had selected while he accompanied me on the piano.

"Again. And louder," he said. And then, "Do it again in this higher key. And you're not projecting."

And so forth, for about two years, it seemed.

"I don't think you really have a gut love for this," he finally said. "And besides, you're nowhere near loud enough."

Even early in his career, when he was a struggling lyricist in Hollywood, my father raged and raved and carried on about how singers should sing. Eventually he found the phrase to crystallize his feelings. "Loud is Good," he announced to the cast of *The Most Happy Fella.* He had a sign made, and the maxim became Loesser dogma. It was audacious and outrageous and funny. It was just like him.

It was just like him to terrorize the men's chorus at a *Guys and Dolls* rehearsal, chewing them out for saving their voices, screaming and swearing at them. And it was just like him to end his diatribe by walking out of the theater and into the ice cream store, buying a double scoop and strolling peacefully back to his hotel room.

Actually, he didn't stop with the men's chorus. And he didn't stop at screaming. During a tantrum that became a Broadway insiders' legend, he actually slapped Isabel Bigley (who played Sarah Brown) in the face when she failed to sing his way. Like his explosion at the chorus, his attack on Isabel was over in a flash. Overcome with remorse, this time he did not casually walk away with an ice cream, but begged forgiveness (which was not immediately forthcoming). Again, it was just like him—flammable, mercurial, and able to realize when he had gone too far.

Although he had already had a success with *Where's Charley?*, my father still based his life in California, where he continued to write for Hollywood. But in his heart he was a New Yorker, and so he was delighted to return to Manhattan and join with several cronies of similar persuasions to put together the show that would become the quintessential Broadway musical. *Guys and Dolls* is peopled with Broadway characters on the stage and created by Broadway characters behind it. Frank Loesser, Abe Burrows (book), Cy Feuer (of Feuer and Martin, producers), and Michael Kidd (choreographer) all spoke and acted like tough guys, like people who got their education on the street or at the school of hard knocks. They *were* tough. And they were loud and profane and, shall we say, indelicate. All of them were fierce anti-snobs, and you would be surprised to learn that Abe had been a Latin scholar, that Cy was a serious musician, or that my father had been brought up in a genteel, intellectual, German immigrant family, the son of a Prussian piano teacher.

Nothing in *Guys and Dolls* even hints at the intellectual or cultural roots of its creators. And this suited my father just fine. By then he had completed his self-styling as a Tin Pan Alley wunderkind, a squall of a man with a hot talent and a hot temper and a Broadway background. His personality, as well as his work, was as far as he could get it from his heritage. Everything about him suggested otherwise, but it was upper Broadway, not the lower East Side, that was his childhood neighborhood. It was Goethe his mother read him at bedtime, not Sholom Aleichem. And it was serious music that filled the air at home. In the rarefied intellectual atmosphere of West 107th Street, popular songs—when noticed at all—were scorned as base entertainments for the lower classes. No, though they loved him dearly, my father's family neither nurtured nor cherished his talents and ambitions. Not by a long shot.

1

Beginnings

My grandmother Julia almost always looked old. Long before I knew her—and she was in her early sixties when I was born—she was matronly. Her long gray hair was pushed into a bun, her plump old-fashioned figure arranged into old-fashioned rayon dresses with small prints and matching jackets. She gazes out at me from the old photographs in the family album. There's one of her and my father (who also looks older than his twenty-five years) with their beloved dog Whoopee, taken about 1935. And another taken in 1937 in which she sits by a window somewhere, smiling benevolently. The very oldest photos discover her as a young, attractive woman in her twenties, but by the time my father turned five she had become the woman I remember, who barely changed again in all her many years thereafter.

Julia Ehrlich Loesser was not a cuddly grandmother. Although her soft figure promised warmth and comfort, she was actually stern and proud and exacting. "Eat your green peppers," she would say. "Don't forget the little girl who didn't eat and wasted away until her parents couldn't find her." This story, which she never tired of telling, frightened me terribly. The little girl became thinner and thinner, until she was no bigger than a thread. Eventually, her parents couldn't see her at all and so they couldn't save her from starving to death. I vividly

Julia, Frank, and Whoopee.

Julia in 1937.

imagined the little wisp of a thread sitting at the table, crying for her parents, who were looking past her, calling, "Susan, where are you?" And of course I was told the one about the little girl who played with matches and burned up and when her parents came home they found a little pile of ashes.

She used to take me to Times Square to feed the pigeons. God knows why we had to travel from her apartment on East 82nd Street all the way to Times Square to feed pigeons, but whenever I visited New York we went to Times Square. The birds would flutter all over us, landing on our heads and shoulders, pecking peanuts out of our hands. Looking back, I find it hard to believe that this fastidious matron would have any interest in traveling to 42nd Street—even then—and letting pigeons poop on her. Among my memories of Nana these little journeys stand out as curious exceptions to her generally ironclad rules of behavior.

More in character were our frequent visits to the Metropolitan Museum, where she would guide my malleable taste with meticulous concern and then take me to lunch on little sandwiches in the elegant fountained cafeteria. Or we would go to the Museum of Modern Art, where on each occasion I was steered away from my favorite painting, Tchelitchew's *Hide and Seek,* and planted firmly in front of a Renoir. I would return to the great canvas of a tree crazy with scenes of heaven and hell, of children consumed by flames and children soaring into space, of apparitions fearful and wonderful among the roots and branches and leaves. The painting fascinated me, and it disgusted Nana. I couldn't get enough of it; she couldn't get me far enough away from it. It was a small but ongoing battle that I felt justified in fighting. Being the daughter of extremely outspoken parents, I figured out early on that censorship was not okay.

From the time I was five or six until we all moved to New York when I was twelve, my parents brought me with them from California on some of their frequent East Coast trips. They would deposit me at Nana's upper East Side apartment, and although they would take me out from time to time, I was mostly under my grandmother's care, and mostly I felt abandoned and wary. I missed my California friends, my nurse, my house. I hated green peppers and I wasn't crazy about my grandmother. But being in the big city was exciting, and going out with my parents to the theater or to restaurants made me feel very grown up. It almost compensated for Nana's iron hand.

"No, no, no. You're not going to wear that ugly dress when you go out with your mother. She wouldn't want to be seen with you in that thing. Where in the world did it come from?"

"But Nana, Mommy bought me this dress. What's wrong with it?"

"Well, if you *must* wear it, then go ahead. But it's a dreadful frock, and I'm sure your mother will be embarrassed to be with you looking like that. Really, you should wear *this* dress. This one is much nicer."

I don't remember the outcome of that little skirmish. I only remember that my grandmother, as usual, made me feel like a poor relation, a second-class citizen, her ward.

My mother, or father, would pick me up and we would go out somewhere wonderful, and I would complain about Nana.

"It couldn't be so terrible, Susan. Your grandmother loves you. And she takes such good care of you."

"But I want to be with you. She makes me eat things I don't like and she makes me take baths instead of showers and she tells me scary stories and she even hates the clothes you buy me."

"You have to make allowances for her. She's an older lady and she's kind of set in her ways. But she loves you very much and she takes very good care of you."

"She hates me. She's bossy and mean."

And so she was. She was bossy and mean and so self-controlled—and controlling—so formal and awesome a presence that it is hard to imagine that she was once a young, pretty, adventurous teenager, freshly arrived in New York from Bohemia and madly in love—virtually upon arrival—with her sister's husband.

Julia was the eleventh and last child of her mother (also Julia), who died in the process. My great-grandfather Josef—undaunted by this threat to the continued production of his progeny—immediately remarried a peasant woman named Rosa, by whom he had five more children. (Josef, in his handwritten genealogical list, refers to his wives simply as "first mother" and "second mother," which illustrates his attitudes toward women rather clearly.) Julia—along with her sisters—was educated in a convent school, ostensibly because it offered a better curriculum for girls than the local public school. The Ehrlichs were Jewish by blood, but not by thought or deed. No religion was practiced at home. (However, Julia kept the little pictures of the saints given her at the convent and always had a soft spot for things Catholic.)

Although all of Rosa's children apparently remained in Europe, most of the "first mother's" children emigrated to America. Siegmund, the second oldest and first to arrive, came to the United States to escape being drafted into the Austrian army. In his frequent letters home, he referred to his new country as a land of economic opportunity where "nobody bothers you." One by one, most of his siblings followed him over.

Julia's sister Bertha, eleven years her senior, worked as a bookkeeper in a pharmaceutical firm and lived in a boarding house in the German-oriented Yorkville section of Manhattan. It was there that she met Henry Loesser, who had come from Prussia in the 1880s to avoid both military service and the family banking business. Henry was also of Jewish blood, but his only spiritual life was involved with the rites and rituals of the Freemasons, a secret, fraternal, and allegedly ancient brotherhood, more like a medieval guild than anything else. Like the Ehrlichs, Henry Loesser cultivated intellectual, not theological, fields. His mother had been a good amateur pianist, and Henry supplemented his income as a grocer with odd jobs playing the piano. When he and Bertha married in 1892, they moved to West 107th Street and he began teaching piano full-time. They had their first child, Arthur, in 1894. When Julia and her older brother Eddie arrived in 1898, they moved in with Henry and Bertha. Julia was seventeen.

According to my aunt Grace, Julia and Henry fell in love on the spot. Julia also fell for little Arthur, whom she helped take care of. But her developing romance with Henry apparently led Bertha to send her to Washington, D.C., to live with another brother who had children her age. She wasn't there long before Bertha died, of septicemia, after her second stillborn child. Henry asked Julia to return—ostensibly to keep house for him and Arthur—and married her in January of 1907. My aunt Grace was born in December of the same year; my father on June 29, 1910. But Arthur, although not really ever hers, remained Julia's special child, her favorite always.

Arthur was a child prodigy. He began giving concert tours at eighteen, eventually became the head of the piano department at the Cleveland Institute of Music, and remained a highly regarded pianist, critic, and musicologist his whole life. Arthur cast a long shadow over my father and Grace as they grew up.

> Arthur was kept out of kindergarten and public school until the age of seven [Grace wrote], when he entered P.S. 165, which he romped through. Apparently the study of reading, math, languages, and geography was recreation to him. School was a breeze—even through college.
>
> Once Arthur got to a party, it wasn't just conviviality that kept him out past two A.M. First, people would get him to play—and I've never known him to refuse or even to tire. The other factor that made a nightowl out of him was his conversational prowess. Ask him a question and he'd start at the beginning and give you the works. "Arthur starts with the egg" was a family saying, referring not to what he had for breakfast but to his need and desire to dig down to first causes.[1]

Arthur began calling Julia "Mama" shortly after she came to stay, and she always thought of him as her son. My father and Grace thought of him simply as their brother, despite the fact that he was more than a decade older than they were. By the time Grace and Frank reached their teens, Arthur was a grown man, often away on concert tours and always the family

Julia and Arthur.

model of intellectual success—the only kind that counted chez Loesser.

My father grew up in a house full of music and seething with intellects. But he was a rebel from the beginning. At two years of age he refused to speak German, the family's language of choice for many years after their emigration. As Arthur once put it, "German was the vehicle of culture and loftier thought; English was the medium suitable for purchasing vegetables."[2] "Frank is getting to be more and more charming," Henry wrote in 1912. "He is very musical, especially as far as singing is concerned, but is absolutely unwilling to speak German. If forced to do it, he sounds as if he were the son of exotic—but not German—parents."[3]

My father spent much of his childhood in trouble. Julia would routinely tell Grace to "Go see what Frankie is doing and tell him he mustn't." Like his brother Arthur, he was too bright for school; but unlike Arthur, he didn't breeze through it. He was accepted at Townsend Harris, a three-year high school for gifted children, but expelled before graduation because he put more of his creative energy into practical jokes than into his studies. At fifteen he was accepted without a high school diploma at City College of New York, then expelled again, shortly after entering—for failing every subject but English and gym, and for polishing the nose of a bronze statue.

Grace was often his partner in crime. They invented many practical jokes together. One year they worked out an elaborate telephone scam in which a selected victim was led to expect the imminent arrival of an unsolicited pet from "Cousin Max in Ohio." On one occasion they went so far as to produce the dog. When their scheme backfired, the Loesser family acquired the Maltese puppy they named Whoopee, whom they treasured and spoiled for the next fifteen years.

Henry was a fear-inspiring little man (barely five feet two inches) who wore a beard, yelled at his students Teutonically, and commanded respect, if not affection, from those around him. The few people still alive who knew Henry speak of staying out of his way and feeling sorry for his students. They remember his fiery temper and his loud didactic voice behind the parlor door. They remember that they didn't like him. Yet within the bosom of his family he was dearly and unconditionally loved. His children and his wife adored him. And the few surviving letters from him to her are tender and affectionate.

Now there is no one left who loved him. No one to tell me about his charms, his warmth, perhaps even his sense of humor or his calm wisdom. In the old pictures the bearded little man looks practically demented, his eyes wild, his face gaunt. I can imagine him flaring with rage. I can imagine him stiff and formal at the piano. I can't imagine loving him.

Although he taught piano to his pupils all day long, Henry never taught my father. It is not clear which of them was responsible for this omission, but my father certainly had little patience for lessons of any kind, and Henry must have had little patience with my father. However, since he was a natural musician surrounded by music from birth, he had no trouble picking

The fierce Henry with Grace and my father.

Henry at the piano.

out tunes by ear. In 1914 Henry wrote to Arthur that four-year-old Frankie was "developing more and more into a musical genius. He plays any tune he's heard and can spend an enormous amount of time at the piano. Always he wants attention and an audience."[4]

Grace did study piano with Henry. She loved music intensely but was never a particularly good pianist. Even when she slaved over a piece she often failed to master it, whereas her little brother would play it "like an angel," having learned it easily by ear while listening to her struggles.

Most people who are self-taught simply had no alternatives. My father was self-taught—in music and in everything else—despite his alternatives. He chose to go in his own direction very early on, and his path was the lowbrow one. Arthur could dazzle the European gentry with his virtuoso piano performances and his erudition. Frank was smitten with entertainment, pure and simple. He began writing song lyrics in his teens, and from the beginning he had confidence that he would succeed. His family was entertained but not impressed by what they considered his pedestrian pursuits. They were amused by him when he was young and brash. And when he became older and brasher and successful in a world they basically disdained, they were still amused, and often patronizing. But along with the intellectual snobbery and the genteel tastes that Henry, Julia, and Arthur affected went a genuine fondness for one another, including Grace and Frank. They loved and adored Little Frankie—they couldn't help it—and somehow, despite their attitudes, they must have helped him find his own unique way.

I look through the photos of my very young father and his sister, looking for clues. Were they happy children? I never asked them directly. Their reminiscences were always affectionate, never bitter or sad. They grew up in a generation that didn't question such things, barring outright abuse or gross neglect. But I do believe Henry Loesser's family was basically stable and happy. I think the conflicts of style and taste that arose between my father and his elders did so in an atmosphere healthy enough for him to give full, unfettered expression to

Julia with Little Frankie in the family "baby dress." If I didn't know better I'd think this was a Christening dress.

My father the toddler.

Grace and Frank.

his persona. Not that the conflicts didn't cause him pain—but I'm getting ahead of myself.

Right now I'm looking at my father when he was three years old. He's wearing a hand-knitted sweater, leggings, and a pointy hat. He looks like a little winter pixie, with his half smile and his slightly downcast eyes. I could say I see the creative genius shining forth, but I can't, really. When I look at this child what I think is that this little guy grew up and became my father, and how amazing it is to see him across the gulf of almost eighty years.

On the evening of July 20, 1926, Henry (who was sixty-nine) died quite suddenly after dinner. (Melon was pronounced the culprit and summarily banned from the table for years thereafter.)

The family was devastated. Grace wept for weeks, and my sixteen-year-old father walked the streets day after day, brooding and silent. Julia, although cruelly bereft and deeply grieving, kept her back straight and her lip stiff, and carried on.

In fact, they did not have the luxury of mourning actively for long. When Henry died, his income simply stopped—no pension, no life insurance, no Social Security, no savings. Julia's friends rallied to her support by hiring her to give lectures on contemporary literature, a job she no doubt enjoyed as much for the prestige it brought her as for the bread it put on the table. But most of the family income came from Arthur, who gave up his concert tours and accepted a steady teaching job at the Cleveland Institute of Music in order to provide for Julia, Grace, and Frank.

At this point my father began a long series of odd jobs which, interspersed with a little money from his early songwriting efforts, also helped keep the family afloat. He sold classified ads for the *Herald Tribune.* He was knit-goods editor for *Women's Wear.* He drew political cartoons for the *Tuckahoe Record.* At eighteen he became city editor of the short-lived *New Rochelle News.* He also screwed lids on insecticide cans, was a process server, and worked for his meals as a restaurant spotter (the restaurant chain paid seventy-five cents plus the cost of a meal for reports on the food and service).

His goal was to make it in Tin Pan Alley, located in those days on 49th Street, in and around the famous Brill Building. Tin Pan Alley was the home of the established New York City popular music publishers—M. Witmark, T.B. Harms, Dresser, Leo Feist, among others. Writers took their songs to the publishers, who auditioned them. A publisher who decided not only to publish but to promote a song would send a song plugger around to nightclubs, vaudeville performers, and radio stations. If a song became popular, the public would buy the sheet music.

In those days sheet music sales were where the music industry made its money—recordings were still a novelty. You could go to the music section of a department store like Macy's and ask the piano player who demonstrated songs to play the one you heard Rudy Vallee sing last week. If you still liked it, you'd buy the music, which was displayed on the shelves. Of course it was the song pluggers who determined just which songs were offered to leading entertainers and thereby introduced to the public. The music business was tough, political, and fickle. My father wanted in.

In his late teens he began writing song lyrics. His earliest collaborators were a group of his friends who hung out at the In Old Algiers restaurant on upper Broadway and tossed song ideas around while they socialized. One of these was a kid named Joe Brandfonbrenner, and he and my father took some songs they wrote down to Leo Feist, where they managed to come away with a year's $100 a week contract for all the songs they could write. Little Frankie had his $100 advance changed into singles, burst into the house, and merrily scattered bills all over the living room to the raised eyebrows of his mother.

Joe shortened his name to Brandfon, and he and my father set to work as a team. A year later they had written dozens of songs, none of which Feist wanted to publish. Not a lyric survives from this earliest work.

My father formed a more significant partnership in the early

1930s—in between newspaper and insecticide stints—with his friend William Schuman. Bill grew up to become one of this country's most esteemed classical composers; but in those days Bill and Frank, just out of their teens, were bursting with hot ideas for popular songs and eager to have them performed.

Sometimes they were hired as "special material writers" for someone's act. They wrote some special material for a comedienne called Violet Carlson, who had appeared in Jerome Kern's *Sweet Adeline,* and they worked out a way to write two songs at the same time. First they would outline the two songs, and then Bill would work out a tune for the first idea on his piano while my father worked on the lyrics for the second song in the other room. When they each had a composition they would switch off. Bill would set the music to my father's lyrics and my father would set the lyrics to Bill's tune.

> We were writing all these songs and had modest success [Bill remembered], got very little money, not enough to live on but enough to pay our expenses. We once started on an operetta based on the life of da Vinci and Frank had some wonderful lyrics. Then a few years ago I wrote a choral work, in which I wanted to bring in some old American tunes. I felt I ought to have a waltz, and suddenly a waltz tune I had written with Frank for the da Vinci show came to mind. The work was first performed by the New York Philharmonic. There they were playing the waltz—a rousing tune—and I'll tell you what the real words were: "Here comes that drunken da Vinci again, all filled with highballs, stewed to the eyeballs."[5]

Bill and Frank hung around the Leo Feist offices and presented their songs persistently enough to be given a room to work in. But having an office did not guarantee success. Their one published song, "In Love with a Memory of You," was a flop.

My father said of those days, "I had a rendezvous with failure." But he wasn't discouraged. In 1933 he expressed his optimism (not to mention his prescience) in a letter to Arthur:

> Enclosed you will find your check to Mama—which I think is about the most vital evidence of our impending good fortune in business. To put it in words, Mama has been doing a little better than she expected with her lectures, and I have managed to gather in enough funds out of the song business to keep the roof on and even real cream in the coffee. I never have said anything directly to you about how awfully swell I thought you were to keep us going these years—but I have been doing a lot of thinking about it. Now, the quicker I try to relieve you of the burden we must be, the better and more effectively I can say thanks.
>
> And so I have gone back to the song business. Although I have been writing them five years or more, I have never stuck to the trade for more than a year at a time. Not because I got tired of it, but because every once in a while some "money-making" idea comes up (process-serving, for example) which takes me off the track, in the hope that I can make a better living in it than with music. But in every month off Broadway, I lose a year's trade. I said "trade." It is no art. I found that out. It is all contact, salesmanship, handshaking, etc.—not a bit different from cloaks and suits or any other industry. This time I am a salesman and a handshaker (still a little genteel for Broadway, but going Broadway fast). This will bring success. I know it, and am going to stick to it.
>
> Hopes, with a capital H, are of course coming thick and fast. A play I have adapted for the American stage (was a hit in Vienna)—various songs, acts, etc. Even a movie idea. One out of every ten of these MAY come near realization. The entire industry (entertainment) is improving. I had a talk with Mr. Bitner, President of Leo Feist Inc., who showed me figures on 1933, for sale of educational music as well as new piano sales based on major jobbers' reports. Educational music is up 30 percent (in number of pianos sold). This means a lot to me and my popular songs. The more pianos sold, the more sheet music (popular), and the more educational music this year, the greater the piano sales next year. Popular songs are already at about a third of the gross figures for record high years (1924–5–6)—which someday will make me a millionaire.[6]

"Going Broadway fast," indeed. Early on he cultivated a brassy new York blue-collar accent, sprinkled with a little Yid-

An early Hollywood publicity photo.

dish for ethnic flavor in a family that had no religious or cultural ties to their Jewish heritage. If anything, they were embarrassed by it. Not so my father. Tin Pan Alley was dominated by New York Jews, and he embraced their world, adding its spice to his already well-developed style. And the spice quickly permeated his personality, until you (and he) could have sworn he had grown up in a traditional Lower East Side milieu. By the time he was twenty-five, much to Julia's dismay, he had perfected a self-styled background blend: Jewish, urban, working class, and street smart. He still refused to speak German—at least in whole sentences. He enjoyed peppering his speech with Yiddish, and he would occasionally add a dash of Deutsch as well. He would also often spell a German word phonetically, making it look silly and exaggerated. He didn't seem to misspell the Yiddish.

Two songs he wrote with Joseph Meyer in 1934 have actually not only survived, they've become less obscure than when they were written. "Junk Man," originally introduced by Benny Goodman and quickly forgotten, has appeared in several albums in recent years and was performed memorably by Debby Shapiro in the 1980 revue, *Perfectly Frank.*

The other song, written with Meyer and Edgar de Lange, is a little charmer called "I Wish I Were Twins":

I wish that I were twins,
You great big babykins,
So I could love you twice as much as I do.
I'd have four loving arms to embrace you,
Four eyes to idolize you each time I face you.
I'd feel no jealousy, if you kissed both of me,
'Cause both of me would only want you (to double your pleasure).
I wish that I were twins, you great big babykins,
So I could love you twice as much as I do.

This one was first recorded by Fats Waller in 1934 and reissued in a 1986 Waller collection. In 1982 Zoot Sims performed it on an album by the same name. But I've heard the best version: a tape of my father singing it himself.

When they weren't working on their music or for a living, the young people in my father's crowd went dancing, went to speakeasies, went to vaudeville shows every Saturday, went to the theater at every opportunity. The highest price for a Broadway play was $2.20. But at Gray's Drugstore in Times Square you could buy a discount ticket and sit in the orchestra for fifty-five cents. For a dollar you could make an evening of it: ten cents for the subway, thirty-five cents for a meal at Schrafft's (remember Schrafft's?), fifty-five cents for the theater ticket. They saw everything. My father loved the theater, especially musical theater, and he longed for a chance to write for a real Broadway show.

He got it. He had written some vaudeville numbers for Lita Grey Chaplin, whose accompanist, Irving Actman, became another of his early collaborators. In 1935 they were playing their songs at a club called the Back Drop, on West 52nd Street. It was an intimate little club, warmed by a potbellied stove and furnished with an old upright piano, at which Loesser and Actman performed nightly. One night a well-known Broadway press agent named Tom Weatherly was in the audience, and, impressed with the young men, he promised to use some of their songs when he acquired the right property.

> There was an annual show put on by the Society of Illustrators [my mother wrote], a bawdy affair that always got a lot of publicity because it was put on in New York City by artists, and of course everybody knows that artists use nude models and have no morals. You couldn't get in to see the one performance of the show unless you belonged to the Society or were invited. The word around town was that everybody went to a gigantic orgy after the show was over. The columnists always wrote that they had been there and couldn't give a full report of the goings-on, but wowie!
>
> Well, in 1936, the talk about the upcoming show reached someone at City Hall who wanted to enhance his reputation as a pillar of civic morality. After 174 minutes of its scheduled 180-minute single performance, the show was raided by the New York City police. The ensuing headlines were a publicist's dream. Tom Weatherly rushed to the Society of Illustrators and made them an offer to produce their show on Broadway.
>
> The first thing he discovered when he took a good look at his purchase was that he had bought a title, period! There was not one song, joke, costume, scenic design, or jailed naked woman to flesh out his package and ride the wave of publicity the raid had engineered.
>
> Tom remembered Frank and Irving and sent for them. He

> chose two of their already written songs and hired them to write the finale. The show opened on January 20th and closed on the 25th. The reviews were devastating, but some of them said nice things about the Loesser and Actman songs.[7]

One of the "nice things" was written by John Mason Brown in the *New York Evening Post:* "No doubt it is the police who must be blamed for last night's production of *The Illustrator's Show.* If they had not stopped it when it was playing uptown at a private performance, Tom Weatherly would probably never have had the unfortunate idea of assembling a new edition of it and making it public downtown at the Forty-eighth Street Theater . . . As 'Bang-the Bell Rang' is the only song that stands out at all, and as even the numbers that threaten to be amusing end up by being amateurish, there is little or nothing that can be said for the evening." Brooks Atkinson didn't even mention the Loesser-Actman songs in his *New York Times* review: "Of course it may be that illustrators are easily entertained. What is known as *The Illustrator's Show* arrived at the Forty-eighth Street Theater last evening with a squadron of lean models in parsimonious costumes and a stageful of intelligible innuendoes. These are the shrunken remains of the private show which the constabulary rudely interrupted some weeks ago, much to the astonishment of the libertines who had paid generously to ogle a Bohemian debauch."

Loesser and Actman returned to the Back Drop. It was, after all, a friendly place. You might even meet your mate there.

My mother was born Mary Alice Blankenbaker in 1917 in Terre Haute, Indiana—the only child of an advertising copywriter, Ralph, and his wife, Florence. In 1935, having dreamed of being on the stage all her young life, Mary Alice changed her name to Lynn Garland and came to New York looking for singing jobs. One evening she found herself at the Back Drop with a group of friends. One of the proprietors announced, "Ladies and gentlemen, I take great pleasure in presenting to you Frank Loesser and Irving Actman, two young songwriters I know will be the writers of many future Broadway musical hits!"

> She directed our gaze to the two young men at an old upright piano that matched the antiquity of the potbellied stove at the back of the room. The one at the piano was of medium height, rather stolidly built, wearing eyeglasses and a genial, benign expression on his face. The other young man was leaning on the lid of the old upright, his right elbow and hand supporting the weight of his head. He was short, slim and dark; his expression was intense, challenging, sardonic. His brown eyes commanded attention as they audaciously scanned the audience.
>
> "All I did was look at you, you gorgeous thing, and bang-the bell rang!" sang the short, dark, intense young man looking straight into *my* eyes.[8]

Short, dark, intense, a ready laugh—and, she soon noticed, an even readier temper, which he displayed with the same flair and flamboyance as the rest of his personality.

Perhaps he inherited that awesome temper of his from the fierce little Henry. When my father was angry his wrath bubbled over. He shouted and swore passionately. His language was appalling. For him, yelling "Fuck you!" was just a warm-up. He would rant. He would curse. He would jump up and down, pouring forth a steady stream of dirty words like an obscene Rumpelstiltskin.

And then, just as suddenly as it arose, the storm would be over and, as far as he was concerned, forgotten.

Strange to say, there are people who knew my father well and who never experienced his temper. I can't imagine how they missed it, how or if he hid it from them. He certainly didn't hide it from my mother, who accepted it readily as part of the package—a package that delighted her. She fell in love with him immediately, deeply, and permanently. They spent their first few months of courtship in New York, meeting for coffee in the afternoons, taking long bus rides and longer walks, holding hands and singing in harmony—school songs, nursery rhymes, folk songs, Loesser-Actman songs, operetta, made-up operatic dialogue. They always ended with "The Isle of Capri," which made them laugh. It became their song.

One evening, instead of getting on a bus, they got on the subway and made the long trip to West 143rd Street, where my father lived with his mother. Lynn had been invited to meet the family over after-dinner coffee and cake.

> Julia Loesser welcomed me and introduced me to Arthur and his wife. They were all short, dark, and erudite. I was tall, blonde, and naive. It was a tortured evening for me. We all tried desperately to make conversation. The one thing I could speak of with authority was my belief in Frank's talent. I resented the attitude of impatient tolerance that seemed to emanate from his mother and brother. It was as if he were a naughty little boy who hadn't yet faced up to the seriousness of life.[9]

Julia, for her part, when asked by the Schumans to describe Frankie's new girl, said, "Well, she has a face like an egg."[10]

My mother eventually did manage to endear herself to my grandmother—a mission she undertook with determination and good will. In the meantime, Loesser and Actman had been discovered by a movie studio scout, and by the time my father left for California, my mother had become a regular caller at Julia's. In the first few months of my father's new career in Hollywood, it was the egg who brought Julia tidings of Little Frankie.

2

Early Hollywood Years

In April 1936, the songwriting team of Loesser and Actman got a six-month contract with Universal Studios. The contract was a typical agreement between a Hollywood studio and "employees-for-hire." For $200 a week, Frank Loesser and Irving Actman became employees of the studio, which was deemed the author, owner of all copyrights, and sole owner of all proceeds resulting from the contract. Universal had the right to "adapt, arrange, change, transpose, add to or subtract from" any song written. The composers could be loaned out to another studio at any time for a fee paid to Universal, but they could not accept any other job on their own.

They agreed to conduct themselves with "due regard to public conventions and morals" and to refrain from "any act or thing that will tend to degrade them in society or bring them into public hatred, contempt, scorn or ridicule, or that will tend to shock, insult or offend the community or ridicule public morals or decency." If their songs were published, they were to give a third of the royalties paid by the publisher to the studio. If a "substantial" part of their musical compositions were used in a movie, they would get on-screen credit. The company had the option to extend the contract for three six-month periods followed by five one-year periods. If the studio decided not to exercise its option, it would furnish the composers airplane tickets to return to New York—provided they left town within one week and made no stops en route.

The terms of this contract may seem rather feudal today, but at the time any father was happy to have a contract at all. Even in 1936, earning $200 a week in the movie industry put him near the bottom of the local socio-economic ladder, but a man who had been pounding the pavements in New York and singing for his supper at the Back Drop could look at this modest success with some pride.

I'm sure he was proud of himself. But his letters to my mother were more entertaining than self-congratulatory:

> William Powell and Carole Lombard are making a picture on a sound stage across the back yard from our bungalow at the studio. Neither one of them has a chin in real life.

> The movie I saw last night was pretty bad, probably the fault of most of the company, notably Otto Kruger who takes too long to die, and makes very stagey love. Edith Barrett was swell though, and also a couple of others. Remember the guy in "Sweet Aloes" who looked like he was made of ice? The nasty tall man with the clipped speech like cubes popping out of a rubber tray? Well, he was in it too. Up to his neck he was in it.

> Right now Irving and I are in the throes, trying to knock off a hit out of a situation where the producer orders a certain title, the musical director orders a certain rhythm, the dance director orders a certain number of bars and the composers order a certain number of aspirins.

> The first picture of ours to be released is an utter stinker. The only redeeming feature is the orchestrations and recording of the music which we watched like hawks at every step. "Don't Let Me Love You" is in it at every possible moment, during bank robberies, flood scenes, dance hall sequences and a long shot of the Bronx Zoo, It is also sung by a guy and Pat Ellis,

> very mournfully indeed, while they dance. God, why didn't I stay in the process-serving business.[1]

But he was clearly high on Hollywood. The town was in its heyday in the late 1930s. People in all facets of the movie business were making and spending big money, building expensive houses, throwing lavish parties, and living outrageous lifestyles. It was all glamor and glitter, and my father relished being part of it.

> Dear Brother Arthur,
>
> It looks as if the seven lean years have passed. I only hope there are as many fat ones ahead . . .
>
> I have seen all (or almost all) the "lots" of the big companies out here. They would interest you. My firm is situated on so great an expanse of real estate that it has been made into an incorporated city, with its own police force and post office. There are acres and acres, devoted to permanent exterior settings—facades of buildings—early Italian or Vermont log cabin. Saloon doorways, reproduction Versailles Palace complete with fountain (working), model bridges, skyscrapers, entire jungle villages . . .
>
> I haven't been here long enough to inquire much into the technique of making pictures, but the sound and camera machinery is impressive. I'll learn.
>
> You know what the climate is around these parts. (I remember your having been here.) Well I am thriving on it. Two days after I arrived I had a tan. I also have a car—or rather a half-interest in one with my new partner. Brand new Plymouth Coupe. I had a driving lesson today. Will be tearing around Los Angeles (red-light district of course) with one arm around a hoyden (tight) and the other on the wheel (loose) in another two days.[2]

In September of that year Loesser and Actman learned that their option was not going to be renewed. They did continue to work for the studio on a nonexclusive basis for a while, but they were paid only by the songs, which were bought sporadically. My father, finding himself poor once again, for some reason chose this time to propose to my mother. He did it with a combination of hints, warnings, demands, and cajolery:

> I've given up making specific plans because it's too hard to stick to them—I mean about WHEN I'll send for you—it depends on a lot of things that haven't happened yet, so I'm shutting up. Only be ready. Also be ready to be broke when you get out here.
>
> Enclosed please find 150 bucks, for which please hurry and buy a railroad ticket (something like 73 dollars) and a lower berth (about 18) and a suitcase (cheap please) and food on the train (about 25 bucks)—and get the hell out here. . . . Get on the train quick, because any day now I may be awfully busy—and right now I have the time to buy you a second-hand broken-down flivver, and bring you to the offices where we can make some contacts for you—and get married (which takes time and travel)—and get you some clothes, and show you some scenery and friends—which would be impossible if you came too late. So kiss the folks chastely goodbye, darling, and take a chance on little Frankie please please please.[3]

How romantic—who could resist? Out she came, and married they got. The wedding was in a judge's office. My mother and father both wore gray suits. Irving Actman and my mother's new California friend Polly Rowles served as witnesses and guests. When the bride started to giggle in the middle of the brief ceremony, Polly kicked her. There was no photographer, no flowers, no reception. The foursome did go to a local restaurant afterwards to drink champagne.

Loesser and Actman continued to write songs for Universal, but there was no contract and the work wasn't steady. The movies included such unforgettable classics as *Turkey Dinner, Postal Inspector,* and *Freshman Year.* Julia, predictably, wrote to my father advising him against his chosen career, reminding him of his current failure, and urging him to "get interested in some other activity before it's too late."

In July 1937, Burton Lane, who was under contract to Paramount, heard a couple of songs my father had written with Manning Sherwin. "And I was bowled over by Frank's lyrics. I thought the tunes were nice—but the lyrics were sensational."[4]

My father with Irving Actman and an unknown starlett.

Lane contacted Lew Gensler, a Paramount producer, and persuaded him to hear the songs. The result was a ten-week contract for Loesser and Sherwin—fortuitous indeed, since my parents were poor to the point of desperation. Just before he signed with Paramount, my father invited Lane to come by and hear some lyrics.

> They were living off Sunset Boulevard, and I had to walk up a block of steps to get to their apartment. I got there around 8:30. They were about to have dinner, and Lynn asked me if I'd like to join them. I said no, I had already eaten. What they had was a can of baked beans—and an apple. One apple.

> They were going to share that with me. I was shocked at how he had been struggling.[5]

My father's first contract with Paramount was similar in spirit to his six-month indenture at Universal. He and Manning Sherwin became employees of the studio, which became sole author and copyright owner. The composers were paid a flat $1,500 (divided between them) to write songs for one specified movie, *Blossoms on Broadway*. There was no options clause, but on October 1 my father landed an individual contract with the studio, which by then was interested enough to provide itself with three one-year renewal options. His starting salary was $166.66 a week, with all the standard employee-for-hire clauses.

For a writer of hit songs, this type of agreement did have one bright spot: it allowed him to earn royalties based on sheet music and records sold. At three cents per copy for sheet music and one-third of the studio's income from recordings (now becoming a significant force), a successful songwriter could make some real money. As my father's songs became more popular, his income grew. After 1937 he was never poor again, although he continued to worry about money. Julia could criticize his lifestyle, his taste, and his lowbrow behavior, but she could no longer needle him about his lack of success. This pleased him immensely, and he supported his mother with glee all his life.

He remained under contract to Paramount until 1949, even during the war. And from 1941 on, the terms of his contracts improved steadily.

In those days the Hollywood film industry produced two basic types of movie, A and B:

> The "major" studios [my mother wrote] specialized in highly expensive star-studded vehicles photographed on very shiny film. Rhinestone pendants sent out four glittering rays from their centers each time the heroine took a breath. Crystal droplets of rain splashed into glistening puddles and hurricane winds disturbed only one stray lock of feminine hair. All was beauty. These gossamer films were the A products of Metro-Goldwyn-Mayer, RKO, Warner Brothers, Columbia, and

> Paramount. The echelon of *A* producers had wall to wall carpeting in their offices and reserved tables in the Executive Lunch Room, which was entered through a door marked "PRIVATE" at the back of the Studio Commissary. The parade in and out of that door was watched eagerly by the common diners, and many a business and/or personal rumor started at lunch and wound up the next morning as a hot "What's New" item in the *Hollywood Reporter.*
>
> The major studios also produced *B* films, small-budget pictures shot faster than the speed of light with do-it-yourself-at-home-quality film. There were no reserved commissary tables or office carpeting for the producers of the *B*s, though very often it was the financial success of the *B* films that made it possible for a big studio to produce its glossy extravaganzas. In fact, there were many times when the *B*s saved a studio from bankruptcy. Audiences followed the *B*s (referred to as second features) the way they follow television series today. They would fall in love with a character like Charlie Chan or Hopalong Cassidy and not give a damn what else was playing on the bill. Most movie houses ran double features (an *A* and a *B*—two for the price of one) and gave away dishes. The minor studios, like Republic and Monogram, made lots of *B*s and lots of money.[6]

The Hurricane was an *A* movie starring Jon Hall, Mary Astor, Raymond Massey, and Dorothy Lamour. My father and Alfred Newman were loaned out to MGM to write a song for Ms. Lamour.

> The moon of Manakoora filled the night
> With magic Polynesian charms,
> The moon of Manakoora came in sight,
> And brought you to my eager arms.
>
> The moon of Manakoora soon will rise
> Again above the island shore.
> Then I'll behold it in your dusky eyes,
> And you'll be in my arms once more.

Lamour recorded "The Moon of Manakoora" but did not, in fact, sing it on screen in the movie. The music was used for some of the underscoring, but the words were heard only during intermission, when the recording was played. Still, it became a hit—my father's first solid hit in Hollywood—or anywhere, for that matter.

Another song he wrote in 1937 (with Harry Akst) was eventually called "Blame It on the Danube." He wrote my mother about it:

> Going off the lot we ran into Dave Dreyer, who asked in his usual high tension hurry-up manner whether we have a continental type of waltz for Ida Lupino and John Boles—a melody that is easy enough for Lupino to yawp, and good enough to sound all right with Boles singing it. We said we would whip one up, which we proceeded to do this afternoon at Akst's house. This is about it:
>
> If we should kiss
> While dancing like this
> Let's blame it on Vienna
>
> If muted strings
> Say heavenly things
> Let's blame it on Vienna
>
> If I get gay
> On too much Tokay
> And foolishly say:
> "Be mine!"
>
> And if you answer yes
> Let's blame it on Vienna
> For making this night so divine!
>
> I get home and call Akst. They don't like Vienna. It happens to take place in Budapest—and they want to settle on a song TOMORROW. So last night Akst and I worked—and worked and worked until three.
>
> No results.
>
> This morning, we met at seven. No results. The date at RKO is for nine thirty.
>
> We go—ready to stall and play the tune. Al Lewis the director and some others including Dreyer hear the tune. For fun, I sing the old Vienna lyric which wasn't bad. They love it! Only we're to change the locale from Vienna to the Danube. Half conscious from my lack of sleep and their lack of taste and brains, I make a few highly unsubtle changes to the Danube of all things and up we go to Briskin, who okays the song, and that's that.[7]

With Hoagy Carmichael he wrote "Small Fry" for Bing Crosby (who sang it to the young Donald O'Connor in *Sing You Sinners*), "Two Sleepy People," and "Heart and Soul." When I was a kid my friends and I would play the piano at parties—easy things, like "Chopsticks" and "Heart and Soul." I never knew my father wrote "Heart and Soul." I thought whoever wrote "Chopsticks" had written it.

"Two Sleepy People" was written one dawn at Hoagy Carmichael's house. The Carmichaels had been entertaining the Loessers and Hoagy and my father had been trying unsuccessfully all evening to come up with a new song. Finally, around three in the morning, the exhausted foursome decided to call it a night. At the door my mother said, "Look at us: four sleepy people." My father and Hoagy looked at each other, said, "That's it!" and went back into the house. When the song was published the sheet music noted, "Title suggested by Lynn Garland."

He wrote a number of songs with Burton Lane, including "How'd Ya Like to Love Me," "Says My Heart," "The Lady's in Love with You," and "I Hear Music." Burton told me that my father "had a funny way of working."

> You know, in those days we did things differently. Today when you work with a lyric writer you make a cassette of the melody and he takes it home and plays it over and over. In those days the composer would have to sit at the piano and play it. Till ya hated it. We were going through this process of writing songs, and Frank was very secretive. He would sit across the room from me with a pad of paper up in front of his face. And he'd write. And he wouldn't tell me what he was writing, you know? He wouldn't give me any clue. He'd smile, and I'd say, "Tell me, what are you working on? What's making you smile?" I was impatient. He wouldn't tell me. And when he got through he'd put the lyric on the piano. He had terrible handwriting. And he'd say, all right, now sing it. So I'd start to sing it, but I couldn't read his writing. So I would break up, you know? He'd say, "Goddammit, can't you read?!"[8]

He wrote "The Boys in the Backroom" with Frederick Hollander for Marlene Dietrich in *Destry Rides Again*. He and Victor Schertzinger wrote "Sand in My Shoes" and "Kiss the Boys

Goodbye" (both from *Kiss the Boys Goodbye*). In addition to these and other familiar titles, the Frank Loesser ASCAP catalogue lists over a hundred songs written for the movies with various people between 1936 and 1942. Some of the songs are obscure indeed: "I Like Humped-Backed Salmon" written with Burton Lane for a movie called *Spawn of the North*, "I Get the Neck of the Chicken," written with Jimmy McHugh for *Seven Days Leave*. ("Can't Get Out of This Mood" was also in that movie.) He wrote a song with Lawrence Welk and Bob Calame called "Bubbles in the Wine" that is on a discount Lawrence Welk cassette currently being sold at the check-out counter of my local supermarket.

In the late 1930s the goal of every songwriter was to make the "Lucky Strike Hit Parade." Broadcast once a week from coast to coast on NBC radio (later it moved to television), the hour-long program ran through the ten most popular songs judged on the basis of number of performances and sales of sheet music and records.

> The fact that each and every song was performed in the same tempo [my mother wrote] did not detract from the prestige. It was said by those behind the scene that the insistence on the constancy of the tempo came from the president of the American Tobacco Company, George Washington Hill. Mr. Hill was a foot tapper who liked a steady upbeat tempo and got very upset at any change of pace.[9]

Between 1937 and 1938, eight of my father's songs made the "Hit Parade": "How'd Ya Like to Love Me," "I Fall in Love with You Every Day," "Small Fry," "Heart and Soul," "Two Sleepy People," "The Lady's in Love with You," "Strange Enchantment," and "Says My Heart." My parents' letters to each other frequently mention listening to the "Hit Parade," as well as checking out who was at the Brown Derby restaurant, both pastimes that were all in a day's work.

The Brown Derby (actually there were several branches, but the one at Hollywood and Vine was the mother lode) was *the* restaurant for the famous and the would-be famous to socialize and do business. It was said that Clark Gable courted Carole Lombard at the Derby (where they usually occupied booth five). Depending on your rank, which naturally fluctuated with your current success or lack thereof, you were assigned to different tables or booths in separate and unequal sections of the restaurant. My father frequented the Derby regularly in his Hollywood days and was accorded the rights and privileges of the more successful denizens of the town. One evening after a late night supper there, he wrote my mother that Jane Wyman had been at the next table "with her new husband, what's-his-name. I knew it a minute ago—oh yes, Ronald Regan" [*sic*].

My father had a hard time sitting still. While working he was a pacer, a doodler, a smoker—always on the move with nervous energy. Perhaps for this reason he liked to compose while driving around in a car, but he got so involved in his thoughts that he would drive through red lights, sit through green ones, turn the wrong way on one-way streets, drive past his house when coming home, and generally behave like an absent-minded highway menace. Fully aware of his liabilities, he chose the passenger's seat as often as possible. Either my mother or a friend would be strong-armed into driving him around, sometimes until all hours of the night, so he could compose. My mother never enjoyed being pressed into duty. He paid no attention to her while they drove—just stared out the window, drumming his fingers on the seat or the dashboard.

During these years my mother was still trying to make it as a singer. She never did get very far—a few walk-on roles, a couple of radio shows, and a lot of promises—and she eventually gave up and had me, after which her performances were limited to demonstrating my father's songs (something she loved doing). But early on she made several career-minded trips to New York, for which she would be away for months at a time. Some of my parents' friends made unwelcome, suggestive comments about these separations, but their bond was in fact strong at the time. They wrote to each other every day during these separations, sometimes twice a day. His letters indicate that my father loyally supported my mother's quest, although he did express some impatience with her. And for good reason. She was a procrastinator her whole life long, even when seeking her own fortune.

> Now look [he wrote]: I listen to all the raised-eyebrow people who ask me how you are with the same disgust. It happens to me all the time . . . The only thing that constitutes a real challenge from these idle people with their cocks in their hands is their attitude toward why we aren't together. The more they suspect, the more necessary it will become for you to be somewhere before you quit. The personal reflections don't mean a thing. Laugh them off, like I do. Only I'd just a little rather they didn't think we were damn fools to go through all this. So don't start trying to justify your position by sitting home or ducking dates with people you like. Justify it by, for Christ's sake, going to work.
>
> P.S. Suggested shortcuts in dialog between you and our inquisitive friends:
>
> "Aw go fuck yourself" (from *Barber of Seville*)
>
> "Kindly shit in the lake" (Act 2, Scene 4, *Richard the Turd*)
>
> "Kiss my ass" (Ibid)
>
> "Piss on you" (from *30 Years Before the Mast*)[10]

His strong opinions about singing and singers, consistent throughout his life, were already well developed. His letters were sprinkled with advice:

> Don't sustain notes—any notes, I don't care if it's grand opera you're doing—beyond the point where they stop making sense, or beyond the safety limit of your wind or nervous system. Breathe your head off any time you want. Don't sing over-long phrases in one breath, because even a Kenny Baker can't do it without making the next passage suffer from lack of control. It beautifies nothing except your own private opinion of your vocal prowess—which is not what the public wants. They want entertainment.

> Remember to tell the story and let God take care of the tones.

> Singers love to vocalize beyond the sense of a lyric—just like some ham actors. I wish there were an operatic Orson Welles. But that's expecting too much from trained singers. They are always so sure you want to hear their God damned tones.[11]

At least one letter a day in each direction flew across the country when my mother was in New York. All airmail (remember when you had to specify?), some special delivery as well, the letters chronicle their separated lives. My mother spent her time working with singing coaches and socializing with people in the music business, hoping to advance both her career and my father's. She plugged his songs and she worked on her singing and she looked for gigs. My father, his success growing steadily, kept her up to date on his activities, and kept her laughing.

> Paul and I want to a movie last night: "Stand Up and Fight." Subtitle: For Your Money Back.

> Yesterday we auditioned the Veronica Lake song [I think this was "Jitterbug's Lullaby" or "Need I Speak," written with Harold Spina for "True to the Army"], and the producer and director took exception to part of it (the good part as usual) and I'm very low . . . [Next day] Yesterday Harold and I rewrote the Veronica Lake song for the shit-ass producer and director, according to <u>their</u> ideas, putting in a few big words (one French) so they'd think it was smart (Clifton Webb, 1928) and we hope we don't vomit at the demonstration this afternoon.

> [On an ASCAP meeting] The meeting was the usual thing—Ira Gershwin fell asleep—Mack Gordon shouted louder than anybody, and Arthur Schwartz read a lot of legal stuff from a piece of paper. Arthur Freed raved about his own pictures. Johnny Mercer read a magazine, and Harold Arlen kept looking in the bar mirror, as if any minute his face would become bearable and then he'd start enjoying it.

> I miss you like Grant took Richmond
> I Miss you as *X* is to *Y*
> I miss you, I miss you, I that you, I this you
> Oh hark, how the similes fly![12]

My father took his fondness for pranks with him to Hollywood. In 1938 he created TUC, Inc, or the Throw Up Club. The music room at Paramount was a long, high-ceilinged room full of secretaries' desks, off of which the writers had their smaller offices. A few inches below the ceiling a four-inch wide molding ran all around the room. My father began by throwing pennies up onto the molding but soon moved on to pencils, glue pots, bottles of ink, ashtrays, and other sundry office supplies. The secretaries learned to grab their things whenever he came into the room, but almost nothing was safe. One day he threw up all their raincoats (on their hangers). Shoes and umbrellas also ended up on the molding from time to time. Once he tossed an ice cube onto the molding above Joe Lilley's door and managed to get Lilley into a long conversation in the doorway. The ice began to drip, and Lilley kept rubbing his head with a puzzled look on his face. That Christmas my father gave each secretary a leather-bound note pad inscribed in gold, "Charter Member of TUC, Inc." But a far more welcome gift came from one of the music cutters: a long pole with a hook on the end of it.[13]

By 1939 my father was doing very well. The sign on his office door now read "Frank Loe$$er," and my parents could now afford to have housekeeping help—not one but *two* servants:

> Evelyn is doing better all the time [my father wrote my mother]. No style but some very good solid cooking—Jerry (OUR BUTLER) has been listening to me swearing on the phone and to myself and to him and his wife, and has now picked up the habit. He approaches the table now, saying things like "the goddamned peaches had us fooled. They're green. But we have a sonofabitch of a cantaloupe." You'll love him.[14]

He combined a lifelong concern about having enough money with an equally long-lived appreciation of luxury. Even when they were living at the top of a block of steps and eating beans and apples, they had a cleaning lady once a week. And Burton Lane told me that the morning after my father signed with Paramount he found him in his office being fitted for a new suit. "He was off and running."[15]

He was feeling good. A few weeks before Christmas that year he started talking about getting a dog. My mother, who wanted a dog about as much as she wanted the flu, didn't voice her objections very strenuously. He kept talking about a dog, and she kept getting more and more nervous. As Christmas loomed he began hinting at the wonderful surprise he had in store for her, and her fears mounted. Christmas morning he woke her and took her out to the back yard, in the middle of which a doghouse had appeared overnight. My father pointed to the little bit of fur that stuck out of the opening: "He's yours—call him. His name is Fido." Now in tears, my mother whispered, "Here, Fido." Whereupon my father gently led her to the doghouse and lifted the little piece of fur. It was the sleeve of a mink coat.

My father met Jule Styne in 1940. Jule was working at Republic studios, mostly doing vocal arrangements, and he tells me it was only because of John Wayne that he got to work with Frank Loesser.

> There was a lot of trading between studios. Republic did all those westerns and we had John Wayne. Paramount borrowed John Wayne to do *Stagecoach,* and I asked for Frank Loesser in return. The head of Republic said we had to pay a lot for Frank, so I could only have him for three weeks.
>
> He hated going to Republic. He thought it demeaned him. He said, "It's bad enough on my own lot—Johnny Mercer gets all the big pictures. And now this is adding insult to injury. They're sending me out to a cowboy studio to write.[16]

At their first session at Republic, Jule played my father the tune to "I Don't Want to Walk Without You,, Baby," a song he had been working on with another lyricist. "I play about eight bars of it, and he says, 'Sh! Don't ever play that around here again. We'll take it to Paramount and write it over there.'" Which they did.

> I don't want to walk without you, Baby,
> Walk without my arm about you, Baby.
> I thought the day you left me behind,

I'd take a stroll and get you right off my mind,
But now I find that
I don't want to walk without the sunshine.
Why'd you have to turn off all that sunshine?
Oh, Baby, please come back
Or you'll break my heart for me,
'Cause I don't want to walk without you, Nosiree.

Sometimes they would goof around and write sea chanties. Their favorite was "Ahoy, Minnie."

Oh, whatever became of Minnie—Ahoy, Minnie!
Oh, whatever became of Minnie J. McGee?
Oh, the admiral married Minnie—Ahoy, Minnie!
And I hope she did for him what she did for me!

They used to begin their day with a chorus of "Ahoy, Minnie." "No one in the world was as sophisticated as the two of us sitting there singing 'Ahoy, Minnie' like a couple of Peck's Bad Boys."[17]

In 1940 my father and Hoagy Carmichael went to Miami to write songs for a cartoon feature, *Mr. Bug Goes to Town.* He developed an instant hatred for Florida—calling it the "sweat state" and "crotch of the Southland," among other things.

> They really are lazy down here. I mean mentally. The crew of artists, writers, and idea men admit they accomplish about half a day's work compared to what they'd do in a day in California or New York. None of them like it down here, and there is a tendency to quit on their part, whenever the slightest personal annoyance comes up. That's why the bosses are nice guys. There isn't much in the way of replacement manpower down here.
>
> Once in a while there is a bright spot. For instance last night we went to a place called the Carousel and had VEGETABLES with our roast beef. Of course they were frozen, but that's better than grits and gravy and fried potatoes.[18]

His anger shows up in many of the letters he wrote during the two months he spent in Miami. I can picture him jumping up and down and screaming before and after he scrawled "FUCK ALL PENS" across the middle of a letter in which his pen kept giving out. He and Hoagy Carmichael had a hard time of it working together under the subtropical circumstances. Eventually Carmichael left and my father labored to finish the job. Finally, at the end of a blistering August, he wired my mother: "HOLD YOUR BREATH AND CROSS YOUR FINGERS THE JOB IS DONE IF THIS LAST TUNE LINGERS."

He was writing lyric after lyric, for which he was getting better and better known. Back in Hollywood, he wrote my mother about "[I've Got Spurs That] Jingle Jangle Jingle": "Last night I worked at Joe Lilley's house and out came one of the cutest things I've ever done. A good record can make it a big hit and a real novelty." A few days later: "Today I sneaked out on Arthur [Schwartz] to join Joe [Lilley] in a visit to Decca where we knocked Jack Kapp on his ass with 'Jingle Jangle Jingle'—which he <u>immediately</u> assigned to the Merry Macs for recording." On "We're the Couple in the Castle" (with Hoagy Carmichael): "One of the things I did last night was listen to the Hit Parade. 'Couple' was No. 8, and announced as being by Carmichael the Master Songwriter—of course they neglected to say the Master held the tune in his pocket 4 years before he could get a lyric which would sell it for him." And when "I Don't Want to Walk Without You Baby" (with Jule Styne) was published: "Irving Berlin came in today and spent a solid hour telling me that 'Walk' is the best song he ever heard. I was flattered. He played and sang it over, bar by bar, explaining <u>why</u> it's the best song he ever heard. I was flattered like crazy, then. Maybe he'll take an ad in *Variety* about it."

My father had no great interest in sports, though he did enjoy swimming, walking, and horseback riding. He began riding in 1941, and even owned a horse briefly before shying from the responsibility. For several years it was his favorite recreation.

> Last night I got a <u>THRILL</u>! I went riding with Johnny Johnston—at eight o'clock, after a Chinese dinner somewhere in the valley. We picked up his girlfriend and the three of us rode over the hills in the bright moonlight—in spots they use

> for locations—we couldn't even see telegraph poles or wires or anything—and live wild deer leaping around us from out of the trees. It was beeoootiful.
>
> [December 8, 1941] Of course the war is preoccupying everybody, including me. I heard about it on the bridal path yesterday. A lot of soldiers on leave were riding. I got up on a trail on a mountain overlooking the whole section—and watched the news spread—and could see the soldiers turning their horses around and making for the stables.[19]

World War II provided my father with a rich source of material for his creativity. The first song for which he wrote both music and lyrics was inspired by the war: "Praise the Lord and Pass the Ammunition."

3

War Songs

By the time the war was over, my father was well established as a composer of both words and music. For years he had been writing "dummy tunes," music used simply to set the lyrics until the real tunes were composed. Some of these dummy tunes were very good, and my mother and others encouraged him to keep the songs as he wrote them. But he had never felt secure enough about his musical abilities to do that.

In April 1942 he wrote my mother, "I have a title—'Praise the Lord and Pass the Ammunition'—which is a quotation from a news story a few months ago—a sentence supposedly spoken by a brave army chaplain. Joe Lilley and I are on it." But Joe Lilley never got involved. When my father wrote the dummy tune to establish the rhythm and sang it for his friends, they all thought the music was perfect. So he let it stand as it was. And it was a smash.

Schoolchildren sang it in assembly; housewives hummed it while they ironed; the Office of War Information, concerned that the public might tire of it prematurely, limited its performance to once every four hours. To quote David Ewen: "In his haphazard and casual way, Loesser had created a song that had an American hymnlike character, rich with folk flavor. It was not the kind of melody a Tin Pan Alley troubador was likely to regard as commercial, and that was its inherent strength; for it was the only kind of melody demanded by the unusual lyric."[1] For months the song was on everyone's lips.

> Praise the Lord and pass the ammunition!
> Praise the Lord and pass the ammunition!
> Praise the Lord and pass the ammunition,
> And we'll all stay free!
> Praise the Lord and swing into position.
> Can't afford to sit around a-wishin'.
> Praise the Lord; we're all between perdition
> And the deep blue sea!

It sold over two million records and a million copies of sheet music.

Although he continued to collaborate for a few years, the success of "Praise the Lord and Pass the Ammunition" gave him the confidence to write more and more of his own music, using the war effort to hone his newfound talent.

In the spring of 1940 my mother met another young singer, Gwyn Conger, who quickly became a close friend. One of the first things my mother learned about Gwyn was that she was having an affair with John Steinbeck, who was already internationally known, as well as already married. John would get divorced and marry Gwyn a couple of years later, but at the time Gwyn and my mother were sharing confidences, the romance was a secret. When my mother met John she immediately sensed that he and my father would like each other, but between the difficulties of geography and the sensitivity of the situation, it took the better part of a year to get the two men together. When they finally did meet, in December of that year, John and Frank quickly became thick as thieves.

From the beginning of their thirty-year friendship until John's death not long before my father's, the two planned countless collaborations, not one of which ever bore fruit. They read each other's manuscripts, gave each other encouragement and advice, plotted and dreamed, and served as mutual cheering sections. When they weren't talking business they played together like perennial adolescents.

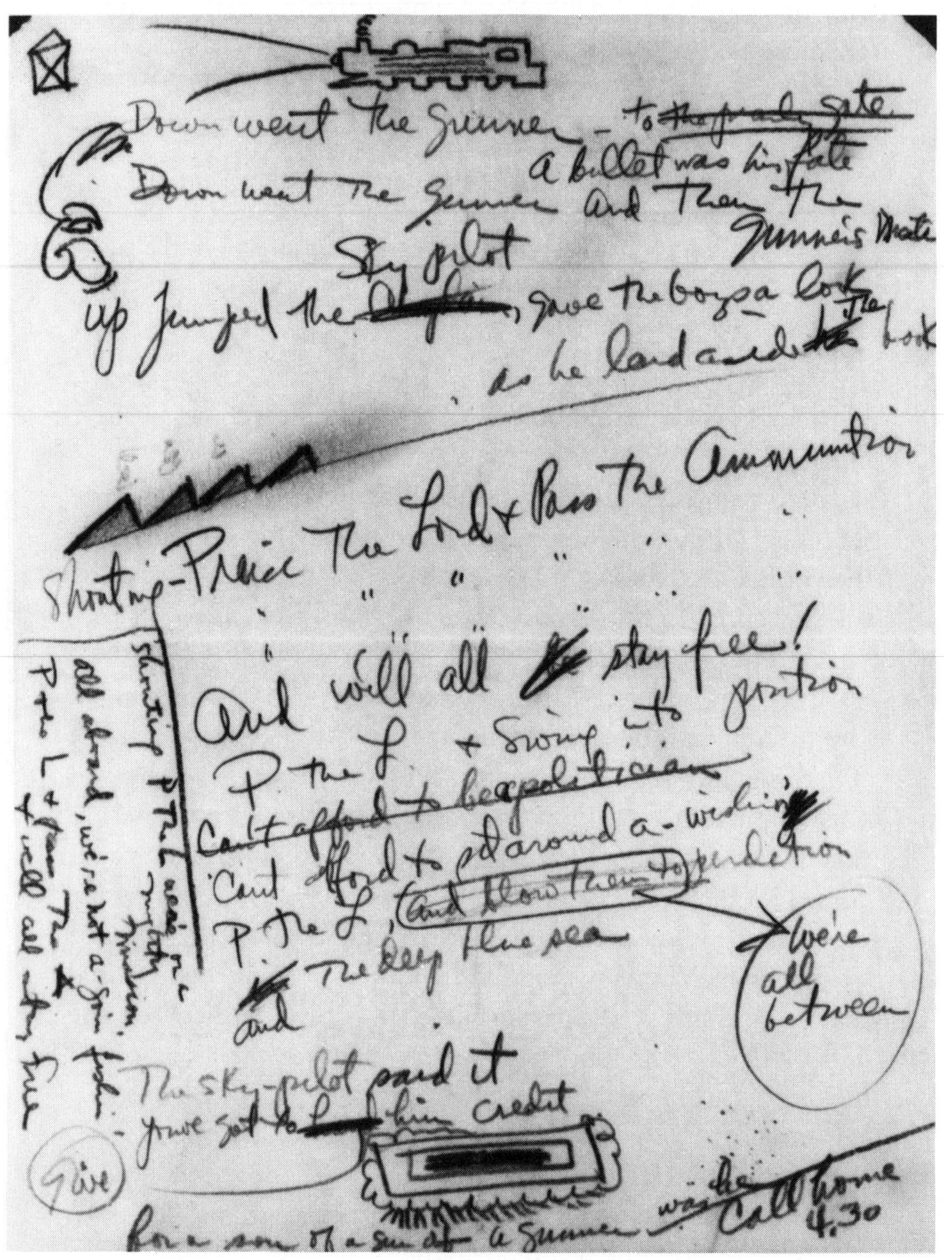

Down went the gunner — to gate
a bullet was his fate
Down went the gunner and then the gunner's mate
Sky pilot
Up jumped the , gave the boys a look
as he laid aside the book
Praise the Lord & Pass the Ammunition
Shouting—Praise the Lord & Pass the Ammunition
And we'll all stay free!
P. the L. & swing into position
Can't afford to sit around a-wishin'
P. the L.
the deep blue sea
we're all between
The sky-pilot said it
you've got to give him credit
Give
For a son of a gun of a gunner was he
Call home 4.30

Working out the lyrics for "Praise the Lord and Pass the Ammunition."

The only Steinbeck/Loesser venture that came close to getting anywhere was the first. In 1942 my father read *The Moon Is Down,* John's recently published short novel about the War in Norway, and proposed to write what he called an oratorio.

> I didn't really write it, Steinbeck did, all I did was to make it rhyme. I'll show it to Joe Lilley today and have him write the music—which he'll do beautifully. Then we'll produce it on a record, for baritone and 8 voices (mixed), organ, and sound effects. When the music is done, and I have a real idea of how the whole thing sounds, and I still like it, I'm going to mail the poem to JS to see what he thinks. I'm a little self-conscious about it—like first long pants—from Poppa, and too big in the waist.[2]

As it turned out, Arthur Schwartz wrote the music, and a lengthy struggle to get a demo made ensued.

> There are only a dozen singers in the country who could really do it well—Robeson, Keast, Tibbett, Rise Stevens, Marian Anderson . . . Anything less than 40 musicians in the orchestra will make it sound like whorehouse music. . . . Today we're finding out (we hope) how to get that god damned record made. It's as important to get the right sample as anything else in the whole set-up. Even Rise Stevens won't actually do it correctly, I'm sure. . . . I am organizing Dave Rose' Band, KHJ and its executives, Joe Lilley, Walter Scharf, two copyists, a print-shop and various press representatives—all free for nothing, and correspondingly touchy and tough to handle—for that Saturday recording.[3]

A record was finally made. John loved it, but the song was never published. Jonathan Schwartz remembers that it sounded rather pompous, with an operatic voice—possibly Tibbet's—singing a "dark" melody. I've never heard it myself, and the demo seems to be lost, but here are the lyrics, hot off the archives:

> People of Norway, listen
> People of Holland, listen
> People of France, people of Java, listen, listen. . . .

Your nights of despair are not without number
You live without life—you sleep without slumber
But nights of despair are not without number

People of Poland, listen
People of Belgium, listen, listen. . . .

The moon is down
The moon that was life in our eyes
Now the wind that was full of our song
Only cries, only mournfully cries—yet even so—
There is light from the moon that is down
There is fear in the conqueror's heart
There is death in the streets of the town
That the music of freedom may start
And the song will be whispered along
From the doomed and the dead, to the young
And the young will be mighty and strong
And the song once again will be sung—will be sung
—in the light will be sung

The moon is down
The moon that gave promise of day
Now the night will be endlessly long
On its way, on its ominous way . . . Yet even so—

There is light from the moon that has fled
In the sparks where the barracks have burned
In the blood that is gleaming so red
On the knife in a back that was turned
And the song will be whispered along
From the doomed and the dead, to the young
And the young will be mighty and strong
And the song once again will be sung—will be sung
—in the light will be sung!

The moon is down
The moon that was life in our eyes
The moon is down, yet even so . . . the moon will rise!

That fall my father decided to enlist in the army. An Army Air Force base in Santa Ana housed something called the Radio Productions Unit, organized so the army could produce recruiting shows on its own rather than use the more expensive option of buying commercials. The RPU was headed by Colonel Eddie

Dunstedter, a featured radio organist, in-house organist at MGM, and local character/musician at the Pig 'N Whistle restaurant in Hollywood. (Celebities took their kids to the Pig 'N Whistle because there were special children's menus, drinks, portions, even special children's organ music, played by Eddie Dunstedter—Hollywood day care.)

Besides an eighty-man orchestra, the RPU consisted of writers, producers, actors, and singers, all of whom Dunstedter skimmed from the cream of Hollywood talent as they enlisted or were drafted. Because of the caliber of the unit, and because Dunstedter already knew most of the celebrities in Hollywood, it was easy to attract well-known guest stars, including Jack Benny, Bing Crosby, Danny Kaye, Dinah Shore, and Rosalind Russell. The RPU produced some of the finest radio programs of the era.

The RPU crew broadcast two live shows a day five days a week—one at 5:00 A.M. to reach the East Coast, and another later in the morning for the West Coast—using the program to plug whatever they were told to plug ("become a WAC" or "enlist in the Air Force"). They rehearsed and broadcast the shows from the Santa Ana American Legion hall, starting at 3:00 A.M. in order to perform at 5:00 A.M. Thanks to the odd hours, they were allowed—even encouraged—to live off base, which suited them just fine. Hal Bourne, a pianist with the unit, had rented a house in a Santa Ana orange grove, and my father and Peter Lind Hayes moved in with him.

Peter and his wife, Mary Healy, were already nightclub personalities before the war. While he was with the RPU, Peter wrote songs and skits and scripts for the daily shows, many of them with my father.

They had good times there in the orange grove. My mother and Mary would come down on weekends, bringing an assortment of musicians and entertainers with whom they would play poker and party. After a while Mary and my mother moved in permanently. Hal Bourne got to feeling that his little house was getting too crowded, so, Mary told me, they moved him out.

The only musical instrument in that house was a little electric organ, and my father took to it right away. Always an early riser, he would already be pounding away on the muted keyboard when Mary came downstairs at 6:00 A.M. She would bring him coffee, which he appreciated so much that he wrote a song for her: "Once in Love with Mary." Six years later it became Ray Bolger's show-stopper, "Once in Love with Amy," in *Where's Charley?*[4]

Another orange-grove song took twenty years to reemerge. When Peter left the RPU in 1943 to perform in Moss Hart's *Winged Victory,* my father bought Peter's half of "Why Do They Call a Private a Private." He liked the melody and wanted to be free to write a new lyric for it, should the occasion arise. The occasion arose with "Happy to Keep His Dinner Warm" in *How to Succeed.*

When my father went into the army Jule Styne had given him a tune to work with. It was a big Irish ballad. He called Jule one day and told him to go stand outside the Chinese Theater at a certain time when the army band would be parading. The band came by playing the ballad, which was now in march time. Jule laughed. "That son of a bitch, I said. I'll get even with him!"

> So in 1947 I've got this hit show on Broadway, *High Button Shoes.* And Frank wants to come. "Sure, anytime," I say. The place is sold out and the only seat I've got for him is a front box seat. Now in this show there are various cameo vignettes: the thieves on the beach, the flirting lifeguard, and so forth. One of them is of these two pretty girls, all dressed up with big hats, who pick up a fellow. And for this vignette I put in that song, the one Frank had turned into a march. But now I've turned it into a gavotte. Only one person in the audience makes a sound. From the front box, Frank goes, "HA, HA, HA."[5]

One of the most talented musicians in the RPU was a Milton DeLugg, the accordionist with Matty Malneck's orchestra before enlisting in Eddie Dunstedter's unit. He was also a composer and arranger, and the early helpful influence of his skills on my father's talent was the beginning of a long professional association and friendship between them. They wrote several songs for the army together, and Milton became my father's first musical secretary, writing down the music that my father composed in his head and played (fairly primitively) on the piano.

> He always had an idea of the melody in his head [Milton told me], but actually couldn't notate it at all—not for many years. He'd plunk a little bit out on the piano and sing it to me. I would sit and write down what he was singing. And then we'd discuss maybe changing a chord—because when you first start writing, you write the world's simplest chords. And sometimes we'd even change the melodies a little bit. He caught on very fast.[6]

Later, Milton and my father wrote "Hoop Dee Doo" together. This polka was so popular that they followed it with "Just Another Polka," then a joke song called "Crying Polka." "Nobody treated that one with any respect," Milton told me, "and nobody bought it." (Nevertheless, in the first six months of 1988 the song made forty-four cents in royalties for my father's estate.)

In 1943, my father was transferred to the army's Special Services Unit in New York, where he helped write a series of "Blueprint Specials." These packaged shows, according to the Army pamphlet introduction to *About Face,* were "complete in all details for speedy and simple production by soldier entertainers, be they showwise professionals or the most inexperienced amateurs." They consisted of scripts, sheet music, sketches, and complete instructions for making costumes and sets out of whatever odds and ends were on hand at most any base.

Like the members of the RPU, members of the Special Services Unit in New York were allowed to live off base. In fact, the "base" was in midtown Manhattan, in a number of different buildings between 42nd and 45th streets—the heart of the theater district. My father commuted from his suites at the Navarro Hotel on 59th Street to his "base" office on 45th Street, across from Zero Mostel's brownstone. Mostel and my father used to communicate by yelling to each other across the street. My father, who was downright well-to-do by this time, kept no less than three suites at the Navarro—one for him and my mother; one for my mother's mother, whom they were looking after; and one for my nurse and me. (I was born in 1944 and spent my first year and a half, like Eloise, at a posh New York hotel.)

Although he reported to work every day, Private Frank Loesser often snuck out of his office in the afternoons to come home for a nap. He rarely slept more than five or six hours at night and liked to nap several times a day. But the army, while allowing him to wear personally tailored uniforms, stopped short of providing him a couch to nap on. My mother used to stand by in case the army came looking for him, but once, when she was out and he had left a message with the hotel's switchboard not to be disturbed for any reason, the general called. And was told that Private Frank Loesser could not be disturbed. And left his own message that if the private weren't back at his post within fifteen minutes he would face a court-martial. He made it back—thanks to the switchboard operator, who was brave enough to wake him and his temper.

Yes, he had his uniforms tailored. He was a most dapper little private. There is a story that when he met General Romulo of the Philippines in the Stork Club, the general saluted him. He was so taken by Private Loesser's tailoring that my father, judging correctly that they were the same size, had a couple of uniforms made up for him.

And yes, he remained a private. Despite his elegant taste in haberdashery, he had no desire to rise through the ranks. He relished the romantic idea of being a famous but ordinary soldier, and, according to my mother, "He was furious when he was made Private First Class. He said he wanted no responsibility whatsoever, and he really meant it." He managed to evade further promotion for the duration of his army career.

My father loved to express his individuality through his clothes, sometimes by being expensively and tastefully dressed and at other times by sporting the most flamboyant outfits (I have always suspected that he invented the Hawaiian shirt). Sometimes he'd do both at the same time—an impeccably cut, understated suit would be set off by a garish tie. We kept him supplied with loud, ugly ties every Christmas, which he would delight in wearing. He had an enormous collection of "hideosities."

His best buddy in Special Services was Willie Stein, with whom he wrote "Wave to Me, My Lady." They worked together on the Blueprint Specials, on original songs for Harry Salter's Hit Kits, and on special material for the *Army Navy Screen Magazine.* But they had just as much fun playing together. At noontime they celebrated "Frank and Willie's Hour" by eating lunch, taking walks, visiting the zoo, and making newspaper parachutes—from which paper cups of water dangled—sailing them out of the 14th floor window. As they glided down to street level, concerned wartime pedestrians would ask the cop on the corner for an explanation. But the cop was too busy picking up the coins that kept landing mysteriously at his feet to pay the parachutes any mind.

In addition to the Blueprint Specials, my father wrote songs for various branches of the armed forces, including "The Sad Bombardier," "WAC Hymn," "Salute to the Army Service Forces," "The One Pip Wonder" (for the Canadian Tankmen), and "What Do You Do in the Infantry?" This last is a "gripe" song, expressing the feelings of the ordinary infantry private. The first verse:

What do you do in the infantry?
You march, you march, you march.
What do you do when your pack has got
Your back as stiff as starch?
There's many a fall in the cavalry,
But never a fallen arch—
And what do you do in the infantry?
You march, you march, you march.

The infantry had asked for the song, but after they heard it, they turned it down. Not uplifting, they said. My father had it published elsewhere, and it became very popular, especially among foot soldiers.

Another "gripe" song, written with Ted Grouya in 1943 for

Frank Loesser joins the army and tries a pipe.

See Here, Private Hargrove, was "In My Arms," in which a soldier sings of his urgent desire to be holding something other than a rifle.

In my arms, in my arms
Ain't I ever gonna get a girl in my arms?
In my arms, in my arms
Ain't I never gonna get a bundle of charms?
Comes the dawn, I'll be gone
And I thank you for the many letters you'll write.
As for something nice and cute and female
I'll never get it in the V-mail
Gimme a girl in my arms tonight.

The NBC censor at the time, offended by the word "female," chased my father down by phone at the Brown Derby and asked him to change it. My father said there was nothing wrong with it—after all, his very own mother was a female.

The censor gave in, but the infantry kept after my father

for a "proper" infantry song. Finally he decided to write a ballad about a Medal of Honor recipient and got hold of a list of World War II "winners" to search for a name that would scan. He came upon the name Rodger Young, liked the sound of it, and thus was born one of the most memorable songs of World War II.

The infantry loved the ballad enough to put together a public relations campaign to promote it, and the campaign director asked my father for some background. This presented him with a problem, since you can't very well say you went through a list of Medal of Honor recipients until you came to a name you thought would sing well. As it happened, my parents' friend Larry Adler had just returned from entertaining the troops in the South Pacific. Larry is probably the world's best-known harmonica player, and Rodger Young was a harmonica player, so Larry was asked if he could have told my father about a brave, harmonica-playing soldier who was killed on the island of New Georgia in the Solomons. Larry allowed as how he *could* have, and the story was made official. My mother told me that my father always felt rather guilty about the cold-blooded reality of the evolution of the song as well as its packaging. But the song itself is surely moving and Rodger Young was a genuine hero despite the fact that he was immortalized while hundreds of other war heroes remained unsung because their names didn't scan well.

> Oh, they've got no time for glory in the Infantry,
> Oh, they've got no use for praises loudly sung,
> But in ev'ry soldier's heart in all the Infantry
> Shines the name, shines the name of Rodger Young.
> Shines the name, Rodger Young—
> Fought and died for the men he marched among.
> To the everlasting glory of the Infantry
> Lives the story of Private Rodger Young.

The ballad goes on to tell the true story of the heroic private who, when his platoon was ambushed, volunteered to draw the fire of the Japanese machine guns, sacrificing his life and enabling the rest of the platoon to retreat safely.

(*L to R*) Mayor Bowron of Los Angeles, Mrs. Young (Rodger's mother), Gov. Earl Warren of California, and my father.

The song premiered to much hoopla in March 1945. The governor of Ohio proclaimed March 11 "Rodger Young Day." The hero's parents were photographed listening to the song's first broadcast on the "Stage Door Canteen" radio program and attending dedications of several public places in memory of their son. One of these was the Rodger Young Village in Griffith Park, near Los Angeles—government-sponsored emergency housing for veterans and their families, Quonset huts for them to live in until good, permanent housing could be built. My father, sporting one of his hideosities—a checkered bow-tie—was at the opening ceremonies as well, along with Jack Benny, Dennis Day, and Bette Davis.

The proceeds from the song were donated to charities of Mrs. Young's choice. My father kept a special "Ammunition Account" from which the money he made from his war songs flowed to the war effort and war-related charities. He had originally intended to donate the copyright of any war song he wrote to the government, but the government didn't want copyrights. Then, as now, they wanted taxes. They were quite happy to tax my father handsomely on all his profits, war-related or not. So my father, not wanting to make money from the war, resorted to some very complicated bookkeeping (delegated to my mother and a tax accountant) so that the profits from his war songs, *after* taxes, could be given to charity.

A month earlier he had presented President Truman with the original manuscript of "Rodger Young." As the *Chicago Times* said later:

> When the President, himself a musician of note, first glanced at the battered manuscript, the puzzled expression on his face indicated he couldn't quite make it out. Loesser hastily explained that he is far removed from the old school of music writers who took great pains to turn out manuscripts with a flourish. He pointed out that he half-writes, half-types his works, which partly accounts for their sloppy appearance. He also explained that he is a doodler and pointed his finger to the odd drawings on the manuscript that indicated what he was thinking at the time.[7]

He *was* quite a doodler—a doodler extraordinaire, in fact. He experimented with number-two pencils, colored pencils, charcoal, and fountain pens, but he was particularly fond of ballpoint pens. He developed a rather painterly style with them, using intricate little squiggles for shading. He was, he explained, a ballpointillist. But he didn't limit himself to one medium. He would draw with whatever was around, and draw well. I have a large crayon portrait he did of me when I was five or six, and there is a self-portrait in oil of him saying "Shh," with index finger to lips, which he used to post outside his door before napping. One of my treasures is his pencil portrait of my mother the year they got married.

He drew, I think, for the same reason that he smoked—mainly to keep his hands busy. The fact that he was a fine draftsman (self-taught, of course) just didn't impress him the way it impressed others—it had little creative significance for

Pla 7-3352

Ci 7-6700

Shoreham Hotel

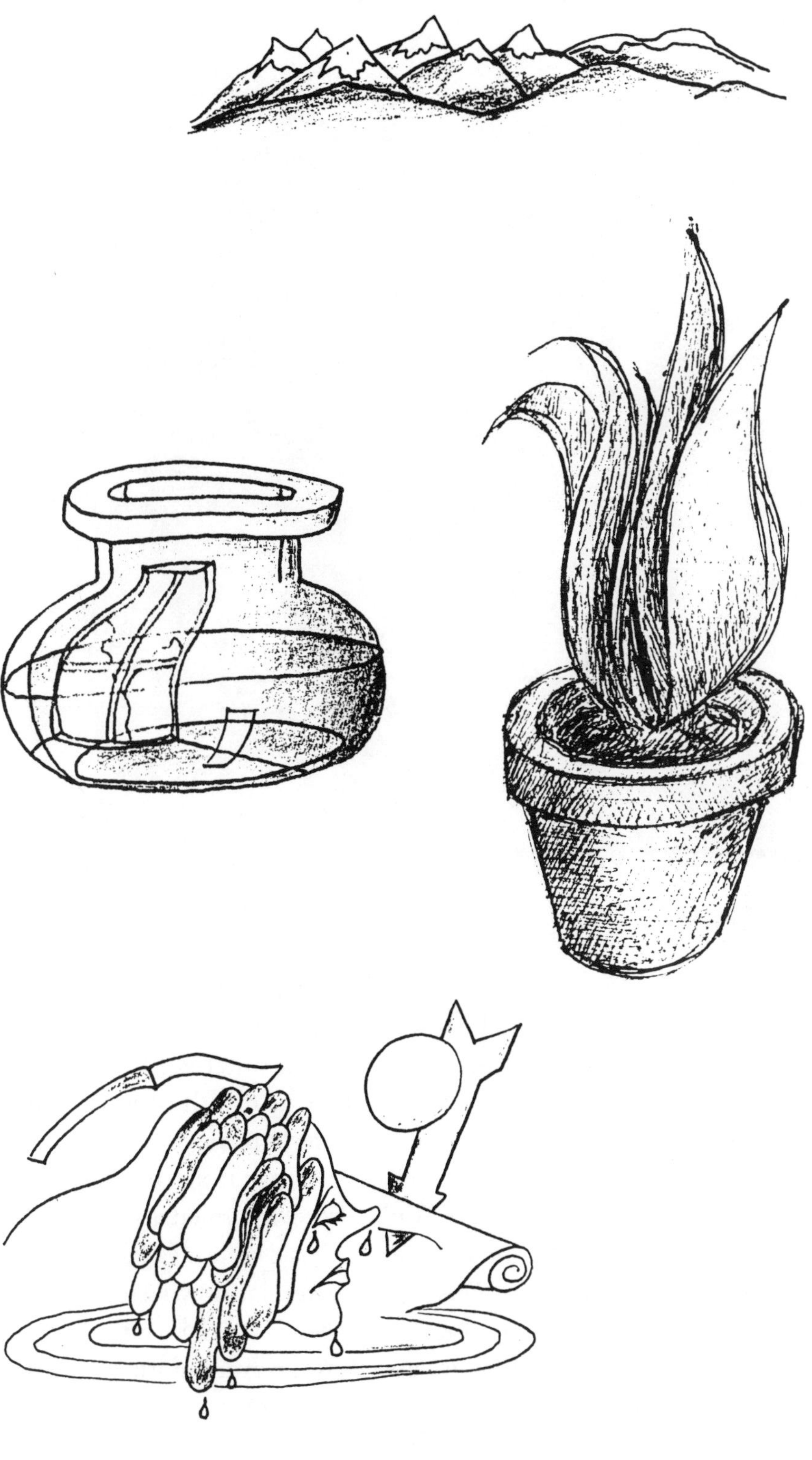

My father's pencil drawing of my mother shortly after they were married in 1936.

him. Some of my clearest memories of times with my father are of sitting beside his desk in a huge leather armchair, talking with him—mostly listening to him—and watching him draw. He would toss his stuff in the trash regularly throughout the conversation, and I would just as regularly retrieve it.

Shortly before they were to be discharged from the Army in April 1945, my father and Willie were informed that it was high time they had their six weeks of basic training. Packed off by train to Camp Lee in Petersburg, Virginia, they were met by a large contingent of the local press, who wanted to interview the author of "Praise the Lord and Pass the Ammunition." This was years before the likes of Elvis Presley, and it was still unusual to find a celebrity serving as a private in the U.S. Army. The next day the front page of the local newspaper heralded the arrival of the songwriting buddies from New York.

During his first week of training—and his last, according to my mother—my father caught a cold, which turned into pneumonia and landed him in the hospital. He was visited by the commanding general, who was as solicitous as a concerned headwaiter hoping for a big tip. (Is everything all right? Are you being treated well? How's the food?)

Actually, he found that the hospital was run just about the way you'd imagine an army bureaucracy would do it.

> One guy here is a really sad case. He was sent in because of a retching cough. He is *vomiting.* Only nothing comes out because he doesn't eat anything. He has tried to explain to *everybody* that he has, and always has had, a nervous stomach, and that's that. So they give him cough medicine and aspirin, which irritates his stomach—which in turn makes him vomit—which is construed as a cough. I don't know how long he's been here (he was here when I arrived), and I shudder to think how long he'll stay on.
>
> The army nurses and the student nurses are just like civilian ones. The only change in their behavior is their walk. It has become military. The ward boys are medical students of army age, deferred for the purpose and continuing their "study" by this experience, which consists of pushing wheel-hampers of dirty laundry and mopping up ward floors etc.
>
> Saturday is inspection day, just like in the barracks. The hospital C.O. marches through and looks us over. We are standing at attention by our beds—we have remade our beds with nice new sheets, folded over exactly 4½ inches, and blanket folded twice on the long axis, with only the rounded edges showing. Also we have swept and mopped the ward floor, which is fucked up all week with big gray clots of wool from the hospital blankets which shed all the time. This shit has blown around the floor all week getting into everybody's lungs and keeping all the coughing and sneezing up to par. But on Saturday all is serene.[8]

As soon as he recovered he was discharged and sent home. Six months later, it was back to California.

4

Back to Hollywood

My father by no means lost touch with Hollywood while he served in the army. From 1941 through 1945 he wrote songs for over twenty motion pictures, nearly all of them Paramount's, although RKO, MGM, Warner Bros., Universal, Columbia, and Republic were served as well. His first Academy Award nomination was for the 1941 song "Dolores," written with Louis Alter for *Las Vegas Nights* (Paramount). He sent the certificate of nomination to my mother in New York with the note "Always a bridesmaid" on it. He paired up with Arthur Schwartz for *Thank Your Lucky Stars* (Warners, 1943), one of Hollywood's wartime all-star reviews. Of the nine songs they wrote for this movie, three have become standards: "Love Isn't Born, It's Made," "How Sweet You Are," and "They're Either Too Young or Too Old." This last song, immortalized by Bette Davis in the film and also nominated for an Oscar, comments on the shortage of eligible men at home during the war and the consequent enforced fidelity of the women to their far-flung lovers:

They're either too young or too old,
They're either too gray or too grassy green,

With Arthur Schwartz.

The pickin's are poor and the crop is lean.
What's good is in the army,
What's left will never harm me.

. . . .

I'll never, never fail ya,
While you are in Australia,
Or out in the Aleutians,
Or off among the Rooshians
And flying over Egypt,
Your heart will never be gypped,

. . . .

And when you get to India,
I'll still be what I've been to ya.

For *Happy Go Lucky* (Paramount, 1943) he and Jimmy McHugh wrote several songs, including "Murder, He Says," and a satire on exotic-island ditties called "Sing a Tropical Song."

Upon the Island from which we come
We have a national characteristic which is very strong—
Because we put the accent upon the wrong syl-LA-ble
And we sing a tropical song.
Upon the Island from which we come
The point of interest, beside the coconut and the sarong
Is that we put the accent upon the wrong syl-LA-ble
And we sing a tropical song.

And so forth.

A tropical-island song had propelled him onto the "Hit Parade" in 1937 with "Moon of Manakoora." But after that one—followed by "Hawaii Sang Me to Sleep," "Palms of Paradise," "Moon Over Burma," and, God help him, "White Blossoms of Tah-Ni" (from *Aloma of the South Seas*)—he must have been more than ready to parody the genre. I have heard a fuzzy old recording of him singing it, as only he could. When he demonstrated his songs, he was always the brilliant entertainer, his face lively with expression, his gravelly tenor voice obviously, disarmingly untrained, sticking to his rules about telling the story and letting God take care of the tones. In this case he sings in an Island accent, emphasizing the wrong syl-LA-bles and adopting a whiny, obsequious tone presumably suitable to the proprietor of a small Caribbean resort.

More and more throughout the forties he was writing both lyrics and music, and the songs that were completely his own turned out to be the most popular and the longest lived. "Have I Stayed Away Too Long" (1943), country-western flavored and smoothly laconic, was written for Paramount but did not appear in a film. "Spring Will Be a Little Late This Year" (1944) was featured in a long-forgotten movie, *Christmas Holiday* (Universal).

January and February were never so empty and gray.
Tragic'lly I feel like crying

"Without you, my darling, I'm dying."
But let's rather put it this way:
Spring will be
A little late this year,
A little slow arriving
In my lonely world over here.
For you have left me, and where is our April of old?
You have left me, and winter continues cold,
As if to say
Spring will be
A little slow to start,
A little slow reviving
That music it made in my heart.
Yes, time heals all things,
So I needn't cling to this fear,
It's merely that
Spring will be
A little late this year.

This song is one of his few melancholy ones, but it is not without hope. Nor does it lack a clear-eyed sense of reality. Frank Loesser lyrics are rarely up in the clouds. Usually they are true to the way people actually think and talk, and often they include a dimension of self-observation. In this one, the analogy of the coming of spring with the return of happiness is hardly innovative. What makes it a Loesser song is the idea of the season's slow start. It doesn't make the mood less sad, but it makes it clever at the same time.

In 1947 he wrote "I Wish I Didn't Love You So" (which got him another Oscar nomination—but no award: a bridesmaid once more), "Poppa Don't Preach to Me," and "What Are You Doing New Year's Eve?" It is early spring in this last song; the singer, madly in love, is making a (possibly rash) commitment far into the future. ("Maybe it's much too early in the game. Ah, but I thought I'd ask you just the same—What are you doing New Year's, New Year's Eve?") It always annoyed my father when the song was sung *during* the holidays.

"Bloop Bleep" (1947) is a song about a man tossing and turning to the music of a leaky faucet.

Bloop, Bleep,
Bloop, bleep, bloop, bleep,
The faucet keeps a-dripping and I can't sleep.
Bleep, Bloop,
Bleep, bloop, bleep, bloop,
I guess I never should have ordered clam soup.
Bloop, Bleep,
Bloop, bleep, bloop, bleep,
I wonder where to go to buy a car cheap.
Bleep, Bloop,
Bleep, bloop, bleep, bloop,
What is it with the babe next door?
What is it she does to me?
What mad kind of thrill do I find,
Looking at her walking, just walking by?
Don't know I'm alive, and she's driving me out of my—
Bloop, Bleep,
Bloop, bleep, bloop, bleep,
The faucet keeps a-dripping and I just can't sleep.

This was another song my father made a record of. (It was released commercially by MGM.) The performance, again, is wonderful, charged with the rat-a-tat thoughts of a tosser and turner who's wired and irritable.

"I'd like to get you on a slow boat to China" was a well-known phrase among poker players, referring to a person who lost steadily and handsomely. My father turned it into a romantic song, placing the title in the mainstream of catch-phrases in 1947. There it has remained to this day, often appearing in a newspaper headline for some story or other about a long, romantic, or otherwise memorable voyage.

Although both of my parents preferred New York—adored New York—they reluctantly returned to California early in 1946. My father's contract with Paramount was so very generous: they were paying him a handsome salary while allowing him to take a leave at any time "to render services to others in connection with motion pictures and stage." And my father was, as always, concerned about financial security, so, although my mother urged him to stay in New York and try his hand at a Broadway show, he chose to take the sure bet in Hollywood

My father and me.

for the time being, and he went ahead out to the Coast to look for a house.

As it turned out, Veronica Lake was selling her house in Beverly Hills. (Remember her? The girl with the peekaboo hair? Née Constance Ockelman. In her *New York Times* obituary in 1973 it was remembered that during the war she cut her hair at the government's request because so many women were getting theirs caught in factory machinery.) My father looked at the house, liked it well enough, and bought it while my mother was still organizing our move out of the Navarro. I don't think she saw the house until it was ours and we were there and it was too late to back out, because she never liked it very much.

Me, I loved it. It was Southern California Spanish—white stucco with a red tile roof, an abundance of large rooms, nooks and crannies, and secret, out-of-the-way places. It had doors all over the place—a front door, a patio door, a kitchen door, a screen porch door—and two outdoor staircases leading in one case to the "sewing room" and in the other to my nurse, Ida Bennett's room, nestled next to mine and handily accessible from indoors and out.

We Beverly Hills kids all had nurses. They were the people who were there for the skinned knees and the fear of the dark. They were our companions, our confidantes, our disciplinarians. Ida put me to bed at night, woke me up in the morning, got me off to school. She cooked my meals, which we ate together in the upstairs "nursery" kitchen while listening to soap operas on the radio (Can a young girl from a small mining town in Ohio find happiness as the wife . . .).

When Ida came to us as a young woman she already had the demeanor of an old maid. She was a simple person with conservative values and opinions. She was poorly educated, not very interesting, and had little imagination. But she was loving and kind, and she was always there. She chauffeured and chaperoned my social activities while she enjoyed her own social life with the other nurses. She told me she had been left at the altar as a young woman, and to my knowledge she never had another date with a man. Her hair was prematurely white. She wore thick glasses. She could touch the end of her nose with the tip of her tongue. She had a nervous stomach and various skin conditions. Her only living relatives were a brother and his family who lived in an early lower-middle-class development in New Jersey, and she took me to visit them once when we were in New York. I was enchanted that the neighbor's house across the street was identical in layout and thought it was a marvelous coincidence.

My nurse, Ida—the most significant adult in my world. Unlike my parents, she was always there.

My father used to say that Ida was provincial and stupid and that by the time I was five years old I knew more than she did. Maybe so. My parents were grateful for her loyal and consistent caretaking but viewed her with benign condescension. They assumed that I did too. I didn't. I viewed her as the mainstay of my life. I loved her and depended on her. And, most important, I knew without a doubt that she loved me. My parents never really understood what a kindness they bestowed when they assigned the day-to-day care of their children to this unfortunate and affectionate woman. Without her we would have grown up bereft indeed.

Our parents, on the other hand, were glamorous acquaintances, viewed with awe. We loved them, too, but mostly we were concerned with their approval, and most of the time we spent with them was special time—little glistening nuggets embedded in our days. To me, my mother was a golden goddess and my father a fierce and funny god.

Watching my father at work on his little electric organ. It's probably around eight o'clock in the morning, so he's probably been up since four A.M. and is just about ready for his morning nap. (*John Swope*, Life *Magazine*)

I used to visit with him on my way downstairs from breakfast. He'd be sitting in his office, in his maroon plaid armchair with the arms rubbed down to the stuffing—smoking, drinking coffee, coughing, tapping his fingers, and getting up every once in a while to pace back and forth or to play a phrase or two on the little electric organ, a descendent of the original orange grove instrument.

"What are you doing, Poppy?"

"I'm working."

That seemed such a funny thing to say. If that was work, it was certainly well disguised. But then, few of my friends' parents "worked" according to the definitions we were taught in school. What most grownups did in Hollywood seemed far more like play.

There was Vicky James's father, Harry, for instance. He

played the trumpet for a living. And her mother, Betty Grable, apparently spent her time having her legs cast in cement. Vicky had the longest, thickest, reddest hair in our first grade class, and I supposed that when she grew up she'd have a job showing off her pony tail. (For all I know, she does!)

Candy Bergen's father was a caretaker to a wooden dummy, whom I used to watch on television sometimes but never met personally when I went with the other girls to ballet class at Candy's house. Melinda Marx's father clowned around with his three brothers in the movies and played word games with a duck on TV. He must have also played golf, because Melinda and I used to take long walks together on a golf course somewhere, our excitement at the adventure somewhat tempered by our mutual fear of being struck by a flying golf ball. Liza Minnelli's mother was the most mysterious. Liza and I used to play together—the sandbox was our favorite locale—and we attended each other's birthday parties. At one of hers we saw *The Wizard of Oz.* I remember looking back and forth from Judy-the-mother to Judy-Dorothy on the screen, and not being able to figure it out. This was Hollywood, where fantasy and reality blurred, where play was work, where entertainment was life, and vice versa.

My father and I occasionally went on adventures together. Only later did I realize how special it was to go out in a car with him. He actually drove on those outings (they are the only times I remember him behind the wheel), and he couldn't possibly have been working on his songs—not with me along, chattering away, all excited about the playground or the beach or the roller-skating rink we were headed for. We loved to roller-skate together. My father taught me tricks—skating backwards, spinning your partner—that seemed Olympian in their virtuosity.

One of our favorite destinations was Griffith Park, where we would first visit the observatory, marvel over the perpetual pendulum they had (we never caught it at rest), and then explore the park itself. Once we buried some treasure there, gleaned from my mother's vast collection of costume jewelry and my father's pocketed pennies. We made a map so we could return years later, find the treasure, and dig it up. We never did, but I like to think that someone prospecting with a metal detector has since found our cache.

"Who's the boss?" he'd demand as we got into the car.

"I am," I would tease.

Then he would glare at me. "WHO is the boss?"

I would giggle and say, "You are. But why are *you* always the boss?"

"Because it's my house and I'm bigger." And that was the final word.

We also played in our own back yard. We roller-skated on the badminton court when the net was down, played badminton when it was up. Every time we played he would tell the same joke about the bird flying south who gets caught up in a badminton game, and it was funny every time.

My favorite little game was called "This-a-way or That-a-way," in which he would take my arm and pull me in one direction. "This-a-way?"

"No, that-a-way" (pulling him the other way).

Then he'd alternate directions. Around and around we would whirl. "*This*-a-way? or *That*-a-way?" I would get deliriously dizzy, but never too tired to go on. I'd pull on his arm, briefly changing our direction, but he would always prevail, propelling me in giddy circles all around the yard. Giggle heaven.

However—I would have jumped into a cageful of tigers rather than consciously cross him, or confront him, or fight him. Although his easily-aroused ire was not directed at me all that often when I was little, when it was, it was devastating. Like the monster creatures who swoop down at you in the House of Horrors rides, memories of my father's rages still jump out from their dark corners and frighten me again, all these years later. Once he slapped me on the hand for teasing the dog. The slap didn't hurt at all. The fury of his face and voice as he said, among other things, "Don't *ever* do that again!" left me mortified.

A variation on "This-a-way or That-a-way." (*John Swipe*, Life *Magazine*)

My father in one of his favorite shirts, serving up a badminton birdie in our Beverly Hills back yard. The shirt was a shirt of many colors—primary stripes on a black background. For its day, it was very tacky.

Another time, the worst time, I was trying to make a phone call—I was six or seven—when I inadvertently called him on the intercom and woke him from a nap. I heard words I had never heard before—as well as words I did know in new and horrible contexts.

"Oh, Poppy! Did I wake you?"

"You bet your bleeding ass you did, goddammit! What the fuck do you want?!"

"It was a mistake—I'm sorry—"

I hung up and collapsed to the floor in shame and fear. To my amazement, when I saw him later that day he acted as though nothing had happened. He was neither angry nor contrite. At the time I felt reprieved and grateful to be on his good side once more. But when I think of the incident now I am angry with him. He was inexcusably terrible to me, and he should have apologized.

Incurring my father's wrath was dangerous beyond rationality. It meant annihilation—my life and soul and spirit completely extinguished by his rage. Because he was, in effect, a visitor on my planet, it took me a long time to learn that his temper would quickly burn itself out and the offense be forgotten. Each time he exploded I felt sure I was being blown to bits. And each time I would survive it after all, my father would resume being funny and entertaining, and there would be more badminton, and roller-skating, and "This-a-way or That-a-way."

In our house we had a storeroom with shelves of canned goods, crates of oranges and apples, and a huge freezer containing miles of meat and ice cream. I don't know if this hoarding was just one of those quaint Beverly Hills customs or the result of some sort of siege mentality. After all, these were the early years of the Cold War, in the middle of which was injected the Korean War, and there was a pervasive sense of anxiety about "the Commies" and the possibility of attack. At school we were trained to curl up under our desks with our sweaters pulled over our heads at the sound of the alarm. At home we installed "blackout shades" on all the windows. Some of our neighbors even built fallout shelters. So maybe the storeroom gave us a sense of security against starvation in case of a hot war at home. Or maybe it was simply so we would always be ready to entertain. I suspect the latter.

Our laundry room was also the cats' room. On a walk after dinner one night my father spied a black-and-white kitten, skinny and obviously homeless, its long hair matted and dirty. He called it. It ignored him. He jingled his keys. It ignored him. He jingled the change in his pocket. In an instant the kitten was at his feet, sinuously making friends with his right leg. He laughed, said, "Looks like you're my kind of cat," and brought him home. We were all delighted. My mother had him neutered and named him Christine Jorgensen, which she had fun explaining to me. Chrissie was the first of our many cats, all of whom hung out in the laundry room, snoozing on the piles of dirty laundry.

Our house was immense when I was a child. We even had two living rooms, although one of them was called the playroom for some obscure reason. For a back yard we had an entire park in which I went on safaris with our weekly gardener, Mack. But some time between then and 1986, when I passed through the area again, our house had shrunk to a miniature replica of itself. Even the olive trees that I used to climb so bravely had shrunk. In fact, the whole neighborhood has been transformed from a world of wonders into a grid of closely packed Southern California suburban upper-middle-class dwellings. Yet this was and is one of the most desirable neighborhoods in the Los Angeles area. (Not that there aren't real mansions nearby with real parks for yards. But they are not the norm, and they certainly aren't on my old street.)

From the beginning the house was a disappointment to my mother. She disliked it on sight, especially the modern sliding glass doors and windows inserted in the traditional stucco walls and apparently never used, since they could not be opened. She had them replaced, planted a peach tree and a walnut tree, heaved a sigh of resignation, and settled down to party.

They were friends with *everybody*. Humphrey Bogart and

Lauren (or Betty, as she was known to her friends). Bacall, Danny Kaye, Abe Burrows, Lena Horne, Tony Quinn, Fred Allen, Judy Garland, Jack Benny, Bob Hope, Groucho Marx, Steve Allen, Betty Furness, James Mason, Ethel Merman, William Holden, Walter Winchell, William Saroyan, and many others famous then or now were all in their circle. They were invited to parties at the Arthur Rubensteins', the Otto Premingers', the Alfred Hitchcocks'—and on one occasion at "Pickfair," where they drank and chatted with Mary Pickford herself.

The Steinbecks were frequent houseguests in the late 1940s. They would come with their two sons, Thom—a few months older than I—and John, two years younger. Thom and Johnny and I would play various toddler games like "Knock Her Down with the Wagon" and "Bite Him on the Butt" while our nurses watched over us, occasionally intervening when things got too rough. (In later years the three of us had a more sophisticated friendship.)

Meanwhile our parents would also be socializing—my father and John pursuing those elusive collaborations or planning practical jokes for the next party, like the one at Irving Lazar's, where they sewed his entire wardrobe together.

My mother and Gwyn Steinbeck enjoyed cooking together, and when they finished preparing one of their light-as-a-soufflé meatloafs or multi-layered spaghetti casseroles they would meet their spouses in the bar to whet their appetites on a series of cocktails.

Drinking, of course, was a major social activity. In those days and in that crowd people consumed vast quantities of liquor. A friend of my parents recalled with amazement that when she reviewed her diary for those years she discovered the word "hangover" in virtually every entry. Recently I listened to a tape recording of my parents and several unidentified guests cocktailing it up one evening and was thoroughly disappointed to hear, not scintillating conversation, but a series of non sequiturs punctuated by "Let me freshen that up for you." But despite all the alcohol, the festive atmosphere did often produce clever, creative entertainment.

Some of the many parties were at our house. Occasionally a large tent would be erected in the back yard, and I would help blow up the hundreds of balloons my mother insisted were the key decorative elements for a successful fête. In exchange I would be allowed to attend the party for the first hour or so and have a "pink drink" before politely excusing myself. My parents and their friends would perform, a band would play, and the fun would continue all night. Performances at these events were practically mandatory. Almost everyone invited to a party came with a routine of some kind. Usually the entertainment was musical, and although often ad-libbed, it was usually first class.

The most trivial occasion could trigger a party. Jack and Mary Benny would have carpeting installed, and the next day fifty of their friends would be at their door, celebrating the new broadloom with gifts, food and drink, song and dance. The visit of a friend from the East Coast or the return of a colleague from a business trip would inspire a splendid catered evening of wining and dining. Parties were the center of the social and business lives of Hollywood denizens. Their world revolved around them. And my parents were well known as two of the most gracious and creative hosts in that world.

Two of their best friends were Benay Venuta and Armand Deutsch. Ardie—the grandson of Julius Rosenwald, a great philanthropist and president of Sears Roebuck—was a very rich Hollywood and Broadway producer. Benay was a musical comedy actress and singer. The two couples gave a memorable party for Howard Lindsay and his wife, Dorothy Stickney, who had come to the Coast on business. (Howard Lindsay wrote many memorable shows with his partner, Russel Crouse—*State of the Union* (1934), *Call Me Madam* (1936), *The Sound of Music* (1959)—but his most famous venture was *Life with Father* (1939), which he wrote with Crouse and starred in for seven years, while his wife, Dorothy Stickney, starred as his wife.)

> Benay and Ardie had the walk from the curb to their house lit with spotlights [my mother wrote], and everyone made an entrance up to the house carrying a present for the guests of honor. People had a ball finding gifts. Stuffed and mounted

> birds and fish were among the most popular items, along with department store dummies and model ships in full sail. Busts of obscure historical figures were also good. The Charles Brachmans had the most spectacular gift—a stuffed eagle with its wings fully spread. The donors wrote speeches which they read to Howard and Dorothy, and Frank wrote a new lyric to our favorite round, "Hi, Ho, Anybody Home": "Sing ye, sing with all your hearts/ To a lady and gentleman of parts/ Dorothy and Howard Lindsay!/ Sing ye, sing with all your hearts!"[1]

They used to cast their parties, Benay has reminded me: "We'd say, let's invite so-and-so, because she can go on second. And then we'll do the madrigal parody, and Marc Connelly will do his opera thing, and so on."[2] Connelly (who died twelve years ago at ninety), was known as a great raconteur, a member of the group of literary wits who used to gather at the Algonquin Round Table, and a Pulitzer Prize-winning playwright *(The Green Pastures)*. "Bald, portly, merry, avuncular, he sang for his supper by regaling his hosts with anecdotes, mimicry, and aphorisms struck off at the moment."[3] For parties he would create mock operas, which he and my father and Abe Burrows would act out.

Hollywood parties were not confined to adults. In fact, the children's parties had a spectacular life of their own. My mother, although she participated in the mandatory children's extravaganza, viewed the custom with contempt:

> The thing about the children's parties in Hollywood is that they weren't really for the children. The most important rating of a party came from the children's nurses.
>
> The first guest list was made up by the child's mother—I don't believe Mama ever consulted Papa on the list. Mama did consult her four-year-old child, in the following fashion: "Elizabeth, Mommy and Daddy are giving you a birthday party and I'd like to read you the list of your guests." Elizabeth: "I want a soda fountain." Mama: "We'll see about that, dear, but just now I want to read you your guest list." Elizabeth: "And a horse." Mama: "We'll see."
>
> The second guest list was made up by the child's nurse, who consulted no one. "Mrs. Hollywood, there will be twenty children and twenty-four nurses at the party—that includes

A Beverly Hills birthday party. One of mine, in fact. This is our back yard. I'm sitting front row center, on another kid's lap. As is evident, these parties were well attended by nurses. Many of them were also well attended by celebrities. In this case, Judy Garland is sitting in a small group in the background, Liza on her knee, Vincent Minnelli behind them. I think that's Bette Davis on the right. I don't know the woman Judy is talking to. Is she, as they say, "somebody"?

> the relief nurses." Mother: "Oh." Nurse: "Yes, and I thought it would be nice if we had smoked salmon instead of cucumber sandwiches." Mother: "Oh." Nurse: "All the girls are tired of cucumber sandwiches. I've made out the invitations, if you'd like to see them. And by the way, what have you booked for entertainment this year? The clown at the Barstow's scared poor Nanny Smyth's child something terrible. I hear Mrs. Bigstar has booked Walt Disney's recent rejects for a world premiere for their party. And what about favors? I know the nannies would like those cigarette cases with the built-in mirrors."[4]

After a few years of this, my mother chose the relatively bourgeois option of renting the local Beverly Hills amusement park for a day.

More frequently than at large parties, my parents entertained at small social gatherings centered around the bar off the playroom. Its walls were hung with the work of Abner Dean, a close friend and a delightful cartoonist. My father somehow discovered that the filter end of a Parliament cigarette, when moistened appropriately, would stick fast to a flat surface. The glass covering Abner's cartoons was the first item to be so decorated, but my father, perhaps recalling fond memories of the Throw Up Club, didn't stop there. He learned that if you tossed them just right, the cigarettes would also stick to the ceiling. Everybody played the game, and the bar was soon transformed. Cigarettes studded every available surface—the ceiling, the walls, the bar, the moldings, the lamps, the end tables. Abner's cartoons were all but obliterated. It only worked with Parliaments, and it never worked for me. Every time I was allowed to hobnob with the adults at the bar I would try the cigarette trick. I would watch my parents and their friends toss their Parliaments to the ceiling. I would study their wrist action, their moistening techniques, their degree of thrust. Then, once again I would pluck a Parliament out of its container, lick the filter, and shoot. And once again the cigarette would bounce off the ceiling and land at my feet.

My father snuck into the host's bathroom at one party and filled the tub with Jell-O. For a time, he kept a hidden phonograph in our powder room that automatically played the "Laughing Record" when the toilet seat was raised. On one occasion he painstakingly layered clear nail polish onto a long nasal hair until it formed a great pendulous pseudobooger, then took my mother and some acquaintances out to dinner. My father sat across the table from his guests, quietly breathing this thing in and out of his nose as he ate. No one ventured to mention it. The emperor's new booger.

On the occasions when I was allowed into my parents' world I was struck by the unbelievably strong personality of every adult I met. Grownups were so clever and entertaining and self-assured. And each one had a distinct but seemingly careless charm, as though the scintillating personality lounging in the playroom had effortlessly evolved, as though a magical and natural development had simply taken place. Every word, every gesture, every mood was perfectly performed and together composed a unique and attractive and successful adult. Success

My father walking me down our front path to the school bus (which was a wood-paneled station wagon). This was not an ordinary occurrence. In fact, my father never put me on the bus. This was staged for a magazine photographer.

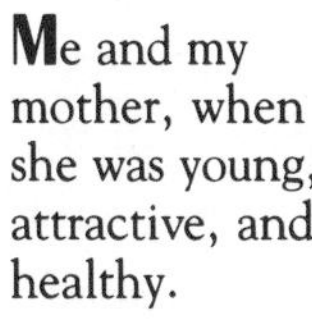

Me and my mother, when she was young, attractive, and healthy.

meant that everyone else would pay attention to you, be entertained by you. And the ticket to this success lay simply in the display of these naturally acquired grown-up characteristics. Like wisdom teeth, these personalities came out of hiding when you were old enough.

Everyone was famous, or near famous, or the mainstay behind someone famous. And even if they weren't, they all acted that way. They were stars. I wanted to be one too. And I knew that to be a star all I'd have to do was grow up and show off my wisdom teeth. No one ever told me anything different. In fact, as a child I was told I was charming, adorable, smart, and special. I remember talking one day with an adult who acted very impressed with me. "You have a very big vocabulary for a little girl," he said. I said, "What's a vocabulary?" and that just broke him up. I remember his loud and long laughter, but I have no idea who he was.

My father loved to tell people about the time I sat down at the bar, got my "pink drink" (I was four or five), raised my glass and toasted the group with, "Well, Suppository!"—the longest word I knew. (I don't remember that one personally, but I trust it happened.)

Well, yes, I was a cute kid. And the feedback I got reinforced my notion that I was simply destined effortlessly to become a star like all the adults I observed.

Oh sure, my father used to tell me about working. He'd say, "You have to earn what you get in this world. Nothing is free. You have to earn everything." He said those words frequently. But what I saw was parties and cocktail hours and performing. I never realized that when I heard him at the piano repeating the same musical phrase over and over again, sometimes all day long, he was working. And working hard. In later years, when I saw him at his office, I still didn't see the part that was work. He was always being entertaining or being entertained.

My mother never told me about work at all. And though she too worked in her fashion, I certainly never saw it. I saw her blow up balloons and I saw her at the hairdressers and in the kitchen. I saw her getting dressed for a fancy evening, and I saw her singing with my father. But I never saw her struggle with anything. When, in later years, I saw her in pain, it didn't have to do with work, but with the cruel blows that she felt life was dealing her. My mother taught me how to tweeze my eyebrows and how to mix a drink. She told me that taupe was the only flattering color for stockings and that pearls lost their lustre if you didn't wear them often. But she never said anything about work.

All the adults thought I was a charming little girl. I knew I was well on my way to becoming a charming adult, a star. I developed, quite naturally I thought, a kind of pseudo-soulfelt "honesty" with which I entertained the grownups, and which my parents encouraged. I was outspoken with the opinions I thought might turn heads. I became very emotional about what was "right" and "fair." I imitated my father and had tantrums when I thought they were appropriate. The problem was that I hadn't a clue about a couple of basic things: what was really appropriate and what I was really feeling. While I was still a child I got away with it. Later, it got to be fairly uncharming. Much later, I began to see the empty little dollhouse I had built for myself, and in its (still ongoing) dismantling came my first appreciation of real work.

"The Isle of Capri" was no longer my parents' song. My father had written "Baby, It's Cold Outside" in 1944, in New York. Shortly after my parents moved into the Navarro Hotel, they decided to give themselves a housewarming party, including the requisite performances. When their turn came, Lynn and Frank went to the piano and introduced "Baby, It's Cold Outside" to their friends.

> Well, the room just fell apart [my mother remembered]. I don't think either of us realized the impact of what we'd sung. We had to do it over and over again and we became instant parlor room stars. We got invited to all the best parties for years on the basis of "Baby." It was our ticket to caviar and truffles. Parties were built around our being the closing act.[5]

For several years my father held on to the song, which he and my mother performed regularly at parties on both coasts. They would sit together at the piano and act out the lyrics with great charm. They even made a recording of it—then, as now, a collector's item.

My mother treasured that song. She loved performing it. She loved the fact that it was theirs alone to perform for adoring audiences. Then, in 1948, my father decided to sell it to MGM for the film *Neptune's Daughter,* starring Esther Williams and Ricardo Montalban.

> I felt as betrayed as if I'd caught him in bed with another woman. I kept saying "Esther Williams and Ricardo Montalban!!!" He finally sat me down and said, "If I don't let go of 'Baby' I'll begin to think I can never write another song as good as I think this one is." He had to let go of it.[6]

Letting go was, of course, the best thing he could have done with the song. It won an Academy Award in 1948 (at last—a bride!) and it remains a standard. Many stars recorded it. Dinah Shore and Buddy Clarke made one of the first (1948) records. In 1949 Margaret Whiting and Johnny Mercer recorded it in the Capitol Records lounge, with my father conducting them from behind the bar. (After they finished they stayed at the bar and had cocktails.)[7] Ella Fitzgerald and Louis Jordan made a Decca recording in 1949. Louis Armstrong and Velma Middleton recorded the song on Decca in 1952. Pearl Bailey and Hot Lips Page. Carmen McRae and Sammy Davis, Jr., Al Hirt and Ann-Margret. Ray Charles and Betty Carter. The title phrase has a life of its own. Not a winter goes by without a couple of "Baby, It's Cold Outside" newspaper headlines. "Baby, It's Cold Outside" was his first contrapuntal duet, a form he particularly liked and used many times again:

> The Mouse: I really can't stay.
> The Wolf: But, Baby, it's cold outside!
> The Mouse: I've got to go 'way.
> The Wolf: But, Baby, it's cold outside!
> The Mouse: This evening has been
> The Wolf: Been hoping that you'd drop in!

The Mouse: so very nice.
The Wolf: I'll hold your hands, they're just like ice.
The Mouse: My mother will start to worry.
The Wolf: Beautiful, what's your hurry?
The Mouse: And Father will be pacing the floor!
The Wolf: Listen to the fireplace roar!
The Mouse: So really, I'd better scurry.
The Wolf: Beautiful, please don't hurry.
The Mouse: Well, maybe just a half a drink more.
The Wolf: Put some records on while I pour.
The Mouse: The neighbors might think—
The Wolf: But, Baby, it's bad out there.
The Mouse: Say, what's in this drink?
The Wolf: No cabs to be had out there.
The Mouse: I wish I knew how
The Wolf: Your eyes are like starlight now.
The Mouse: To break the spell.
The Wolf: I'll take your hat—your hair looks swell.
The Mouse: I ought to say no, no, no sir!
The Wolf: Mind if I move in closer?
The Mouse: At least I'm gonna say that I tried.
The Wolf: What's the sense of hurting my pride?
The Mouse: I really can't stay—
The Wolf: Oh, Baby, don't hold out,
Both: Ah, but it's cold outside.

"The mouse" and "the wolf" have a second verse. Also delightful. Many people consider this delicious song his best.

My father must have been proud of his Oscar on some level, but he treated it as a kind of joke. He gave it to me to play with after he received it, and I had it enshrined in my room for several years. Following my parents' divorce in 1956 and our move to New York, I couldn't find it. I discovered that he had taken it back only when he dragged it out one day, laughing, to use it as a doorstop. "I knew I'd find a use for this thing," he said. (Still, he did take it back.)

Another song my father wrote for himself and my mother to perform together at parties was a novelty number called "The Delicatessen of My Dreams." It is typically playful and at the same time nostalgic:

He: Join me, my sweet, for a bite to eat,
In the delicatessen of my dreams.
She: Tempt me, my prince, with a handmade blintz
In the land where the Russian dressing gleams.
Both: Where salamis are endlessly long and lovely
And the liverwurst is bursting at the seams.
He: You will be mine
She: By the Kosher sign
Both: In the delicatessen of my dreams!

She: Lead me, my love, to that realm above
To the delicatessen of my dreams.
He: Help me, my mate, to a heaping plate
Where the celery tonic gently streams.
Both: Where the herring are patiently marinating
As the hot pastrami sits around and steams.
He: We shall return
She: For one sweet heartburn
Both: To the delicatessen of my dreams.

My father's love of New York bordered on the chauvinistic. Southern California had its charms, but truly his heart belonged to Broadway. Although my brother, John (born in 1950) and I lived full-time in Beverly Hills until 1956, my parents often made trips to New York when my father was working on a show, and sometimes we got to go along. (Before Johnny was born I'd be deposited at Nana's. Afterwards, Ida would come with us and we'd all stay in the Warwick Hotel.) I remember spending time with my father in *his* city—I remember him pointing out the snow in the park (snow!), the people hurrying and hustling everywhere, a man vocalizing as he walked down the street ("See him? He's working on his way to work"), hansom cabs, taxi cabs ("Look. You can get anywhere, any time!"), the shops, the theaters, the delicatessens—the pace that so suited him, the varied climate, the food, the twenty-four hour availability of *everything.* I remember the way he beamed with excitement and pride as he showed his daughter a *real* city, a thriving, throbbing environment, a far cry from the endless suburban summer of Beverly Hills.

Throughout the forties my father wrote for Hollywood,

under contract to Paramount, subject to their benevolent but constant control. They not only held the copyrights to most of his songs, they dictated and censored his work. He was not unhappy—he was becoming well known and well heeled—but he was itching for full control of his artistic (and fiscal) life. By 1948 he was more than ready to try his hand at Broadway and creative freedom, when opportunity, in the form of Cy Feuer and Ernest Martin, knocked.

5

Where's Charley?

My father had met Cy Feuer early in his Hollywood days when Cy was head of the Music Department at Republic Studios. In 1948, Cy and Ernie Martin—who had started as an usher with CBS in 1942, rising quickly through the ranks to become a producer—formed a partnership to produce a Broadway show, a musical version of Brandon Thomas's *Charley's Aunt*. The play, variously known as "that old British warhorse,"[1] "the undying British antique,"[2] and "that venerable and indestructible comedy,"[3] is an 1892 British farce in which two undergraduates at Oxford, Jack Chesney and Charley Wykeham, have invited their sweethearts to lunch in order to meet Charley's aunt, Donna Lucia, a wealthy widow from Brazil ("where the nuts come from") whom Charley has never actually met.

When the aunt is delayed and the boys need a chaperone, Charley and Jack persuade another classmate, Sir Fancourt Babberley, to impersonate her, dressing him in petticoats, black satin, a wig, and a fan. As Charley's aunt he is introduced first to the two young ladies, Amy Spettigue and Kitty Verdun, then to Jack's impoverished father and to Mr. Spettigue, Amy's uncle as well as Kitty's guardian. The two older men, hoping to improve their financial positions, compete for the hand of the "aunt." Babberley leads old Spettigue a merry chase, eventually tricking him into consenting to the marriages of Jack and Kitty, Charley and Amy.

The real aunt, who happens to be the long-lost love of Jack's father, turns up in the midst of this chaos and assumes a pseudonym in order to better observe the goings on. She is accompanied by a young woman—who, it turns out is Babberley's lost love. When the true identities of all the characters are sorted out, four happy couples take their bows.

In *Where's Charley?*, George Abbott's adaptation, the plot is simpler. The Babberley character is eliminated, and Charley impersonates the aunt himself, madly racing on and off stage, changing costume as the occasion demands and getting himself into various amusing situations.

George Abbott had agreed to write the book and direct, Ray Bolger to play the lead. Feuer and Martin wanted Harold Arlen to write the music and Frank Loesser to write the lyrics. "I didn't even consider Frank for the music," Cy told me. "I wanted Harold Arlen. He would have been totally wrong for that show, but what the hell did I know in those days?"[4] Although my father wanted to write both music and lyrics—having had, after all, considerable recent success with his tunes—he was prepared to collaborate. But then Harold Arlen's house burned down, and he was suddenly too busy putting his life back together to think about writing for a while. Cy and Ernie decided to give my father a chance—subject, of course, to Mr. Abbott's approval.

> George Abbott was a magic name to us [my mother wrote]. In fact, at that time, he was a god to us. Cy and Ernie persuaded him to fly to California with them to meet Frank and hear his songs. He came to our house and we sang "Baby, It's Cold Outside" and all the songs Frank had written with Broadway in mind. He agreed that Frank should write the music. He made Frank and me feel so at ease we called him George. It seems that everybody else in the world calls him "Mr. Abbott."[5]

Well, everybody but Cy. When Abbott agreed to travel to the West Coast to meet my father and hear his music, he made it clear that he expected the producers to pay his first-class accommodations on the train and put him up at the Sunset Plaza. Cy said to Ernie, "When I'm paying a guy's transportation and room rent, I ain't calling him Mr. Abbott. He asks me for a per diem—he's George to me."[6]

Everything agreed upon, the show began to take shape. My father wrote a delightful score for *Where's Charley?*, old-fashioned and innovative at the same time. Romantic ballads ("My Darling, My Darling," "Lovelier than Ever"); a waltz ("At the Red Rose Cotillion"); a "traditional" school song ("All the Years Before Us"); and a march ("pompous"), "The New Ashmolean Marching Society and Students' Conservatory Band":

> Here they come with the sunlight on the trumpets.
> Here they come with the banners flying high.
> In my throat I've a lumpy sort of feeling
> And a bright gleam of pride is in my eye.
> Here they come with the clarinets a-wailing.
> Here they come rather bravely up the square.
> And I know in a moment I'll be cheering
> And my fine Sunday hat will be high in the air for the
> New Ashmolean Marching Society and Students'
> Conservatory Band.

Among my father's manuscripts for *Where's Charley?* is a similar song, apparently rejected in favor of "The New Ashmolean." It's called "Your Own College Band":

> On Friday night you venture forth
> To hear a symphony play
> And then you come away
> With highly critical
> Analytical
> Things to say.
>
> "The interpretation wasn't quite inspired.
> The performance left a lot to be desired.
> The second movement could stand improvement
> And it hurts so
> To hear the scherzo
> Done dirt so
> By the percussion

Which was just too vehemently—Russian!"

. . . .

But when it's your own college band,
Isn't it great? Isn't it grand?
What if they flat every note.
Feel the immense, tense, lump in your throat!
And as they come marching by
There is a proud gleam in your eye.
The dismal din of drum and cymbal crashes
Might just as well be somebody hauling ashes.
But isn't it great? Isn't it grand?
When it's your own college band.

He also wrote a delightful duet, "Make a Miracle," similar in its counterpoint to "Baby, It's Cold Outside." Amy, who is reading a book about the future, sings about the miraculous inventions to come in the twentieth century, while Charley tries to get her attention on a more important matter. The voices overlap conversationally, and the lively, dynamic song blends social commentary, history, and humor. And, as my father would remind you, it all rhymes:

Amy: I've just read a book on what's to be expected
They'll have wireless telegraphy perfected,
Electric lights, and fountain pens,
And machines by which a lie can be detected.
Charley: (Spoken) Amy, what about us?
Amy: Horseless carriages, on the road,
Breakfast cereals that explode.
Charley: (Spoken) I know. I know. I know, I know, I know.
Someday they'll have horseless carriages that fly
Amy: Horseless carriages that fly
Charley: Horseless carriages and
Someday they'll be roaring all about the sky
Amy: Spelling out slogans: "Buy a beer at Hogan's"
Charley: But who knows when that age of miracles will come to be
So meanwhile, darling, make a miracle
And marry me.

He wrote a song set in a ladies room ("The Gossips") that can be easily read as if it were spoken dialogue. In "The Woman in his Room," which he called "a musical soliloquy for a soprano momentarily in despair," the mood swings from outrage to forgiveness to renewed trust to renewed outrage as Amy tortures herself over a picture on Charley's mantle of a scantily clad woman.

Another novelty number, "Serenade with Asides," is sung by Spettigue while he pursues the false Donna Lucia:

> If there's one thing that I hate
> It's the thought of acquiring a mate.
> Especially one with a face like a hatchet,
> A voice like a duck and a figure to match it!
> Short of sight and long of tooth
> With a walk that's decidedly funny.
> And yet, and yet,
> If there's one thing I love—it's money.

They had George Abbott and Frank Loesser, and they had George Balanchine as choreographer. Sets and costumes were by David Ffolkes. Edward Simons was the musical director. They had Allyn Ann McLerie, Byron Palmer, and Doretta Morrow. But their greatest asset was Ray Bolger, a star who guaranteed an advance sale, a star whose following was so big that, even if the show were to open to disastrous reviews, he alone could keep it running. And, in fact, he did.

The show was shaky on the road in Philadelphia. My mother described it as

> a hornet's nest of feuds, illicit love affairs, unrehearsed ballets, unfinished orchestrations, and an overall fury at Feuer and Martin. They were not easy. This was their first show, and they were determined to bring it into New York as cheaply as possible. They were not familiar with Broadway producers' codes of conduct. Their manners were atrocious. Everything seemed wrong with the show in Philly. George Balanchine had no classical ballet dancers to work with, and the ballet in "The Red Rose Cotillion" came off as a parody. Feuer and Martin, not known for extravagance, had purchased the most artificial red roses ever crafted, which didn't help. Frank was upset and impossible.
>
> Balanchine came over to me one night when I was stand-

> ing in front of the theater after the show, kissed my hand, and said, "Goodbye. I'm going to New York." "When will you be back?" "Oh, I'm not coming back. I have a real ballet to do." "My God, George, how can you leave with 'The Red Rose Cotillion' in this shape?" "Oh, it doesn't matter." "What do you mean it doesn't matter? Don't you care that your name is on the program as the creator of that dreadful mess?" "It doesn't matter," George said. "Everybody knows I just do these things for the money so I can afford to do real ballet." Off he went to New York, and he didn't come back. He left one of the dancers in charge and the number never improved.[7]

In such an environment, my father had ample opportunities to unleash his temper. Opening night in Philadelphia, Bolger went all-out. The audience was warm, but there was no spark. He worked himself into a frenzy. By the middle of the second act he was exhausted, and after the curtain he had to be helped to his dressing room, where he languished, his wife Gwen barring the door. There was a loud knock, then, "This is Frank. Let me in!" When they opened the door, a small raging madman stormed in, yelling "Jesus Christ! What happened to you? You lay down in the second act! How can you do this to me?"

"Once in Love with Amy" was a perfect song for Ray Bolger. He did it as a soft-shoe routine "down-in-one." (A scene "in-one" or "down-in-one" is played at the footlights in front of a curtain which hides the scenery change going on behind it. In my mother's words, "It was always an awkard interruption of the story line, even when you just had the merry villagers dancing somersaults and chasing balloons across the stage on their way to the palace." Nowadays, with the high tech scenery on Broadway, the device is seldom used.) The number was expected to stop the show and the audiences were expected to demand several encores. But that wasn't happening in Philadelphia, and it didn't happen in New York either. The audiences liked the number well enough, but it was no show-stopper, even with the soft-shoe routine. Then one day a couple of weeks after the opening, Cy Feuer's seven-year-old son Bobby attended the Saturday matinee with a friend—but I'll let Cy tell the story:

> Bobby knew Ray, who used to come to the house. We had Frank's demos for the show, the old acetate kind, and we used to play them all the time. And you know, a seven-year-old can listen to a record a hundred and twenty times. So Bobby knew the demo of "Amy" by heart. At that time the number ran about three minutes—just a song and a dance.
>
> This performance, Ray somehow forgot the start of the second verse. To cover, he gestured wildly to the conductor, saying, "Hold it, hold it, Mr. Conductor, let's start that again. Now how does it go? 'Once in love with Amy'?"—and Bobby gets up and gives him the next line. And the audience laughs. "Oh, good," Ray says, "You know the song? You want to join me?" He doesn't know who the hell it is, and he's irritated. "Yes, Ray," Bobby says.
>
> And they start to sing, but it's awkward. So Bolger turns to the audience and says, "Okay, everybody, let's all sing." They sang, all right, but when he got off stage he was pissed. "How can people let kids—" And I said, "Ray, that was Bobby."[8]

After he cooled off, he said, "You know, maybe I can do something with that community singing. I got a feeling there for a minute." Cy thought he was crazy, but Bolger wanted to try it, and he snuck it into the Wednesday matinee. From then on he did it at matinees until he had it rolling, and then he did it at night. He developed it and embellished it and played games with the orchestra. "Ray could conduct [Cy continued]. They would go on and on and come to a musical climax, and then start all over again. The audiences loved it. On closing night the number ran twenty-five minutes."[9]

Still, *Where's Charley?* had opened on October 11, 1948, to quite a bit of damnation and only faint praise. Howard Barnes of the *Herald Tribune:* "On the whole, this is a heavy-handed and witless entertainment. The sturdy slapstick of the 1890 is rarely funny in George Abbott's libretto, while the Frank Loesser songs do little to compensate for the loss of laughter." Brooks Atkinson of the *New York Times:* "In *Where's Charley?*, Ray Bolger is great enough to make a mediocre musical show seem thoroughly enjoyable . . . Even with a musical background it is a pretty stupid plot . . . Frank Loesser has scribbled off a lively score in a number of entertaining styles—Gilbert and Sullivan pastiche for the beginning, a marching song, a comic chorale for some female gossips, and standard romances in a pleasantly sentimental vein." Ward Morehouse of the *New York Sun:* "Ray Bolger. Very little else . . . There is a routine score from Frank Loesser with only a bright spot here and there." Robert Garland of the *Journal American:* "An amusing musical." Richard Watts of the *New York Post:* "Mr. Loesser's score has several pleasant numbers, but it is, in general, both commonplace and unexhilarating, and it lacks the touch that had been expected of him." And Robert Coleman's headline in the *New York Daily Mirror* read, "Ray Bolger's Big Hit, But Where's Charley?" The night our friends Bob Wright and Chet Forrest saw it, they told me they left the theater behind a very beautiful young woman and her much older escort.

"Darling," the man said. "How did you like it?"

"Well," she said, "I liked it a lot better than *Medea.*"

The only really good review came from William Hawkins of the *New York World Telegram:* "There is no point in fooling around about the fact. *Where's Charley?* is a sublimely satisfactory evening . . . Frank Loesser wrote a score that is brisk and fresh without being deliberately tricky." My father threw Hawkins a party, which helped a little—only a little—to lift everyone's spirits. But then Bolger found himself in his "Amy" number, and at just about the same time Rodgers and Hammerstein went to see the show and loved it. They told their friends. They told their acquaintances. Ads in the newspapers quoted their raves about the freshness and inventiveness of the songs. Word of mouth worked its magic: it was a good show after all. It ran for two years on Broadway, went on the road with the original cast, was made into a movie by Warner Brothers, and is still performed regularly in stock and amateur productions and revivals all over the world.

Thanks to a lengthy musicians' strike, a cast album of the original show was never made. There is a record of the British version from 1958 starring Norman Wisdom, which my father tried to block, since he was hoping to produce a revival and wanted to make the definitive cast recording himself. That Broadway revival didn't happen, and the British recording did. It's pleasant enough but doesn't capture the original flavor. And Ray Bolger is a tough act to follow.

Back in California my father wrote songs for several more movies, including "Why Fight the Feeling" from *Let's Dance* and "(Where Are You) Now That I Need You" (with Jimmy McHugh) from *Red, Hot, and Blue,* a Paramount movie starring Betty Hutton (he wrote lots of songs for her over the years) and Victor Mature. My father actually had a part in that one: he played Hair-Do Lempke, a piano-playing, scar-faced gangster. "Hey," Betty says, "you play pretty good—maybe you're in the wrong business."

It was 1949. By now, with songs on the "Hit Parade" every week, an Academy Award to his credit, and a successful Broadway show under his belt, you would think my father would finally have earned some respect and admiration from his mother and brother. In one of his letters, Arthur, who was doing very well for himself in Cleveland, still teaching at the Institute and writing music criticism and history, mentioned a piece he was planning on my father for the erudite little quarterly journal of the Music Library Association, *Notes.* My father replied, "It would be just dandy if you accepted the challenge from that fancy magazine to write about your brother. I would be very curious to see what you write."

This, in part, is what Arthur wrote:

> As one of the current leading practitioners of the song-writing "game," [Frank] has the keenest understanding of its underlying realities. He knows that popular songs are largely formulas without intrinsic distinction, that thousands of people can make songs that are just as "good" as the most successful, that a song is a flimsy, perishable article of merchandise whose success often depends on an immediate topicality and which is frequently cold-bloodedly tailored to the imponderables of a fleeting situation; furthermore, that songs do not make their way by any natural human process of communication, but that an expensive technique is used for ramming them down

On the set of the movie, *Red, Hot, and Blue,* with Betty Hutton, Victor Mature, and Frank Loesser.

> the ears of an abject public—that is, into the heads of the tens of millions of poor souls who have so little mental self-respect that they actually expose themselves to vomiting radios and pestilential juke boxes of their own "free" will. The interesting thing is that despite all this Frank has so many bright and amusing ideas . . . His success may be viewed in two ways. If one compares the huge amounts of money he has taken in with the amount of thought and labor he has expended on his products, his rewards might seem excessive. On the other hand, seen from a different angle, he is getting much less than he deserves. A hundred and forty million people, including newspaper editors and star politicians, docilely babble the words he puts into their mouths; but only a minor fraction of these persons knows that he is the author of their little pleasure. A relatively small number of people have ever heard of Frank Loesser; he is far less famous than his songs.
>
> He is not exceptional in this. There is something so common and so easy about a popular song that the ordinary thoughtless person does not associate it with the conscious efforts of a craftsman. All the more so nowadays, when people rarely see printed copies of songs, with their authors' names inscribed, but mostly get their music anonymously and mechanically, like a whiff of drugged air.[10]

This article is often cited to me as evidence of Arthur's fondness for his brother, and there is a fondness there. But the article offers far more eloquent testimony to the kind of withering snobbishness that both Arthur and Julia affected toward him and his craft. Arthur did love his little brother, and my father certainly loved Arthur. They were always happy to see each other and delighted in long animated conversations on anything from Bach to baseball. They shared an insatiable intellectual curiosity—both of them perused the *Oxford English Dictionary* for entertainment—yet their styles were completely different.

For instance, my father might say, "Did you ever notice that someone with a strong New York accent does *not* pronounce 33rd Street as 'toity-toid,' but as in the French *fauteuil* [armchair], or *feuille* [leaf]? That odd sort of back-of-the-mouth sound. 'Toity-toid' is a caricature—not the sound at all." And

Arthur would contribute a lengthy etymology of the French *euil* words, or relate the sound to Japanese, which he spoke fluently. The two of them would talk for hours like that—my father interested in the earthy aspects, Arthur in the cerebral.

When I was a kid I saw Arthur and his wife, Jean, as a boring old couple who were to be tolerated and kissed on the cheek when they came to visit because they were related to us. (Every Christmas until I was well into my teens I would get a card from Jean with a check for five dollars and the words, "Dear Susan, Please do our Christmas shopping for us.") I assumed, because my father was so much more exciting and interesting (to me) that he tolerated Arthur as well. To my mind, anyone who wasn't "on" all the time was either a servant, a child, or an inconsequential old fogey. I wasn't particularly interested in music, especially not classical music, so Arthur's prowess at the

Arthur in concert. (Actually, I don't think he ever really performed with a cigarette hanging out of his mouth. This must have been an added touch of "sophistication" for the photograph.)

piano was lost on me. I was oblivious to all the things he and my father shared together, and the only thing I noticed about their relationship was Arthur's cool condescension in the face of all that energy. He seemed to be somehow miscast in our living room.

My father never said a negative word to me about Arthur, and I never asked him directly, always sensing it was an untouchable subject. But my mother told me on many occasions that he felt intellectually and creatively inferior. She told me that he strove for Arthur's (and his mother's) approval all his life and actually had bought the notion that, despite his increasingly successful career, underneath he was a failure.

Bill and Frankie Schuman also remembered Arthur's dark shadow over my father. When Frankie lived for a short time as a child at the Loessers', she recalled, "Arthur was this toplofty creature who floated in and out. Everybody bowed and scraped, and I can still hear Frank saying, 'my brother Arthur, my brother Arthur.' But I'm happy to say that I lived to hear Arthur say, 'I am the brother of Frank Loesser'."

And Bill Schuman remembered that Arthur had been quite unkind to him: "When I was a very young composer," he said, "I took Arthur my first symphony. Traditionally one is kind and sympathetic to younger people in this profession, but Arthur was cruelly imperious to me. I never liked him for that."[11]

My stepmother, on the other hand, would disagree with these characterizations. She remembers the many times the two brothers spent all evening in close and stimulating conversation, the many times Arthur enchanted them at the piano.

"But didn't you see Arthur as patronizing?" I asked her recently.

"No, I didn't," she said. "They adored each other. Arthur was always wonderful with us. A delight."

Perhaps by the time she met him, my father had resolved any sense of inferiority he had had as a younger man, or perhaps he still and always felt constrained by his role as the baby of the family, the young prankster who always looked up—way up—to his much older brother. His reticence to speak about it notwithstanding, I am sure my father not only felt inferior to Arthur, but also was driven creatively by that feeling. Bursting from his genteel family like a peacock out of a swan's nest, he embraced popular culture and his popular art with a gusto and delight that can only be explained by his need to transcend his upbringing and give his mother and brother some lowbrow food for thought.

In 1949, with his Broadway career just beginning, my father must have been stung by Arthur's remarks in that article. I wonder, though, if he also saw the envy in it that I see. How dare you, Arthur seems to be saying, be making so much money writing such mindless drivel. Those of us who know anything about music know that what you're doing is formulaic and common.

Arthur, although highly regarded and certainly brilliant in his own right, was relegated early on to the role of a big fish in a small pond in Cleveland. He never made a lot of money, and, although he was admired by the cognoscenti, he was never famous. Since he was such a prodigy in his youth and spent so many of his young years on the concert circuit, I have to believe that he would have enjoyed a little fame and fortune very much indeed. Watching Little Frankie's career taking off in the forties must have been hard for him. And just as my father didn't speak directly of any bad feelings, neither did Arthur.

Julia, who, as far as I know, had no jealousy of my father, remained skeptical of his life and work. His success, which, in fact, was now maintaining her in her comfortable East Side, river-view apartment, was evident to her. But it was a success tainted by its very milieu—it had no class at all. And besides, he wasn't even musically literate. How long did he think he could get away with it? Worst of all, songwriting wasn't even steady work. Why couldn't he have taken up accounting?

Accounting was one of the few things my father never did take up, but cabinetmaking was one of the many things he did. In the late forties, my parents had some furniture made by a talented craftsman named William Fimpler. My father was so impressed by Mr. Fimpler's work that he asked him for lessons. He learned quickly, and before long he was turning out benches and tables and bookcases and sculptures. When our garage became too full of wood and tools to accommodate cars, the garden shed in the back yard was renovated and turned into his shop.

He made furniture for us and for his friends and just to learn. When our friend Benay asked him for a pair of candlesticks for her new breakfast room, she was put on the waiting list. "I've got a lot of orders ahead of you." One of his more amusing projects is best described by his friend Cynthia Lindsay: he constructed "with great craftsmanship the corner (just the corner) of a Regency desk, inlaid and perfectly finished. He then sent it to his friend John Steinbeck, a piece of notepaper attached with the printed words, 'FROM THE DESK OF FRANK LOESSER.'"[12]

Woodworking was one of my father's greatest pleasures. But in 1949, Feuer and Martin had reason to hope that my father would be spending a little less time with clear pine or bird's-eye maple for a while. Cy and Ernie had begun work early in the year on an idea for a new musical based on a Damon Runyon story, and they had my father firmly in mind for the score.

6

Guys and Dolls

In "The Idyll of Miss Sarah Brown," a story from the Damon Runyon collection *Guys and Dolls,* a Salvation Army sister from the Save-a-Soul Mission wins the heart (and saves the soul) of big-time gambler Sky Masterson. To this nucleus other Runyon characters and situations would be added—Nicely-Nicely Johnson, named after his response to a how-are-you; Big Julie, a rumble-voiced, gun-toting hoodlum from East Cicero, Illinois; dice players with names like Harry the Horse, Angie the Ox, Rusty Charlie, and Benny Southstreet; and Nathan Detroit, the proprietor of the oldest established permanent floating crap game in New York, engaged for fourteen years to the leading lady at the Hot Box club, the long-suffering Miss Adelaide (who apparently never had a last name to change, even in Damon Runyon's tale).

The rights to the story collection were held by Paramount, which had already made one movie from it—*Little Miss Marker,* starring Shirley Temple—and had plans for more. Feuer and Martin, faced with what looked like a tough fight over acquiring the stage rights, wanted Frank Loesser to write the songs. The team had already had a solid hit with *Where's Charley?,* and besides, Loesser's good relationship with Paramount might help them in their negotiations. It did. My father's agents at MCA worked out a deal between Feuer and Martin and Paramount in which Paramount released the property to them in return for first refusal of screen rights to the stage production. Feuer and Martin found a book writer in Jo Swerling, a Hollywood scenarist of note (his film credits included *Lifeboat* and *Pride of the Yankees*), and he and my father spent that spring and summer working together.

After a few months it became clear that all was not well. The songs were coming along, and the basic story was already there, but the book was not right. For one thing, it wasn't funny. For another, the dialogue didn't have the right Runyonesque flavor. Feuer and Martin began looking around for a new librettist.

My father had met Abe Burrows at a party (where else?) in 1943. At the time, Abe was the chief writer on the radio program "Duffy's Tavern," which began each week with Ed Gardner as Archie answering the phone: "Hello Duffy's Tavern where the elite meet to eat Archie speaking Duffy ain't here oh hello Duffy." Besides Archie, the show's cast of working-class New York characters included Miss Duffy, played by Shirley Booth with an impeccable Brooklyn accent; Crudface Clifford, a safecracker jailed for the first time at eleven years old (his mother lied about his age); and Clancy the cop.

Abe, who wrote dialogue for "Duffy's Tavern" for several years, also wrote parody songs that he tossed off at parties. The night he and my father met, they enchanted each other and the rest of the gathering for hours by ad-libbing songs at the piano. That evening was the beginning of a lifelong friendship, punctuated only twice by Broadway collaboration. Nonetheless, their perfectly meshed senses of humor and shared appreciation of language in action produced many smaller gems like the love song they wrote together for "Duffy's Tavern" called "Leave Us Face It":

> Leave us no longer pretend
> That you are merely a friend
> For it is wrote in the stars above
> Lovelight like in your two eyes

Could win the Pootziler Prize
Leave us face it, we're in love.

Most of the songs they wrote together were spawned at parties. I found one in a filing cabinet the other day called "You Haven't Got Cheeks Like Roses":

You haven't got cheeks like roses
You haven't got eyes like stars
Your sigh doesn't sound like music
The music of soft guitars
You haven't got lips like rubies
Your hair doesn't even curl
But, Baby, it makes no difference to me
'Cause you're not my girl.

Abe would sometimes write a particularly good song on the spot at a gathering, only to forget it by morning. But my father, who had written it down perspicaciously, would call Abe the next day to remind him of it, word for word. And so songs like "Memory Lane" ("I am strolling down Memory Lane without a single thing to remember") and "The Girl with the Three Blue Eyes" survived to be published and enjoyed by those not among the bi-coastal party set.

Abe and Frank respected each other's creativity as much as they enjoyed each other. So when Feuer and Martin found themselves with a turkey of a book, my father strongly suggested that they try Abe Burrows on for size. Abe, of course, turned out to be the perfect choice to bring out the show's essential Runyonesque quality. These are Broadway underworld characters who speak an unspeakable grammar with careful enunciation, dignity, and pride. These are adult delinquents who live by an ethical code that transcends street loyalties and expresses a universal morality. These tinhorns, these gamblers, these louts are also gallant and noble and loving—hence lovable. Abe, whose Duffy's Tavern characters were already in a similar league, warmed to his task. Feuer and Martin threw out Jo Swerling's script—not a word remains—and Abe wrote a new one. (Swerling's name appears in the credits because his contract said it had to.)

Abe wrote the new book around the songs already written, and my father wrote new songs around the new dialogue. Their synergistic writing continued until opening night in New York, each one feeding the other, refining, fixing, changing, adding and scratching songs, lines, scenes. Goddard Lieberson later described the score as "so perfectly integrated with [the book] that it was impossible, afterwards, to recall which was song and which was book in the furtherance of plot."[1] When Abe came up with a line about "the oldest established permanent floating crap game in New York," my father said, "That's got a great rhythm to it—let me have it, I have just the tune for it." And out came a Handelian cantata for what Stanley Green calls the "highminded low-lifes," the gamblers' ode to the crap game.

> Why, it's good old reliable Nathan—
> Nathan, Nathan, Nathan Detroit!
> If you're looking for action he'll furnish the spot,
> Even when the heat is on it's never too hot.
> Not for good old reliable Nathan,
> For it's always just a short walk
> To the oldest established permanent floating crap game
> in New York.

Raising money for a show that as yet had no director was not easy, and my parents found themselves auditioning the score for potential backers all summer long in 1950. Cy and Ernie wanted to get George Kaufman, that multifaceted giant of the theater, but he was difficult to approach at any time and was especially difficult then because he was in France. There wasn't much chance that they could prevail upon him from such a distance to direct a musical (he had never directed a musical, nor had he much interest in them) written by men whose work he didn't know and produced by two men he knew even less about. But Cy and Ernie knew Max Gordon, who had produced some seventy-five Broadway hits including *The Solid Gold Cadillac*, *My Sister Eileen*, and *Born Yesterday*. And Max Gordon was a friend of George Kaufman. My mother and father auditioned the score for him in their hotel room in New York on a rented piano, whereupon Gordon cabled Kaufman: "Heard score for *Guys and Dolls.* It is the best in years. Loesser wants to know immediately about you. Strongly advise you to do it."

Kaufman responded by flying back to New York to hear the score and read the book. My mother found him to be a "delightful, enthusiastic audience"—as well she might, since he enthusiastically agreed to direct. Now they could say that they not only had a director, they had George Kaufman himself. And now the money began to come in.

My father's close friend and one-time collaborator Irving Actman was brought on as the musical director for *Guys and Dolls,* Alvin Colt designed the spectacular costumes, and Michael Kidd was the choreographer. Jo Mielziner designed the sets and the lighting. The collaborative spirit behind this show was remarkable. The people involved all remember how exciting and rewarding it was to work with each other. Michael Kidd recalls it as

> by far the most complete, engrossing, absorbing experience I have ever had in the theater. We all worked so closely together. Many people have commented that it looked like one person had done the whole show. That's because we were all of similar minds. We had similar backgrounds, and we all thought alike. To be at one of our meetings was a unique experience, because we were all shouting at the tops of our lungs.[2]

My father was very involved in casting the show. At that time, one of his techniques for determining a singer's range was to have him or her sing "Blue Skies" over and over, higher and higher, louder and louder. (Later he switched to "Happy Birthday.") At the *Guys and Dolls* auditions, male singers had to sing a hot "Blue Skies," look like bums, and talk like gangsters. Aspiring Hot Box girls had to screech their lyrics in a parody of a cheap chorus line and, at the same time, make sure every word was clear. He even made the auditioning singers yell for help.

"Yell for help," he'd say. "Loud."

They'd say, "What do you mean?"

He would shout, "HELP!!! That's the way I want to hear it!"

The word at Actors' Equity was that the auditions were weird.

In those days, of course, shows were not miked. And even when the technology arrived on Broadway, my father—very much a purist—wanted no part of it. An unamplified voice should be heard easily from the back of the balcony. Later, during *The Most Happy Fella* rehearsals, "Loud Is Good" became his dictum, posted in prominent places, quoted frequently and vehemently, and obeyed—or else.

Vivian Blaine was cast as Miss Adelaide and Sam Levene as her gambling fiancé, Nathan Detroit. Isabel Bigley played Sarah Brown, and Robert Alda was the high-rolling Sky Masterson, who steals her heart while she reforms him. The role of Nicely-Nicely went to Stubby Kaye, who was to stop the show with "Sit Down, You're Rockin' the Boat," and Pat Rooney, Sr. played Sarah's grandfather, the old missionary Brother Arvide Abernathy.

At the time, you couldn't have an exclusive contract with a Broadway agent. Equity's rules were clear: The agent who gets you the job is the one you pay. This meant one agent could go and raid another agent's clients. Which they did.

There was no such thing as a casting director in those days either. Martin Baum and Abe Newborn were just starting out as theatrical agents. Thanks to Equity's rules, they had access to anybody and everybody, and they were highly enterprising. They went to Cy and Ernie and said, "You're two guys just starting out in the producing business, and we're two guys just starting out in the agent business. Give us the nod and we'll become your casting agents." Cy and Ernie figured why not, and Baum and Newborn ended up casting some fifteen roles in *Guys and Dolls.* One of them was Big Julie, the Chicago mobster with thirty-three arrests and no convictions.

B.S. Pully was one of Abe Newborn's clients [Cy recalled]. Abe came to us and said, "We've got a good client for Big

> Julie." "Well, bring him in," we said. "Uh, he won't be able to come for a couple of weeks." "A couple of weeks! What do you mean? Have him come in now." "Well, he can't come in now." "Why the hell not?" "Because he won't be getting out of jail for a couple of weeks. But really, he's very good."
>
> So we waited for him and after he got out of jail we went to see him perform at this terrible club in the village. They warned him to clean up his act, which was very dirty. He made his entrance from the men's room, flushing the toilet as he came out the door. He spoke in this low rumble: "Tonight is very important to me. There are two Broadway producers out there and I've been told to clean up my act and not to use the word FUCK."
>
> We thought he was perfect. We went to George Kaufman and said, "We've got just the right guy for Big Julie." Pully came to audition. Kaufman was on the stage, everything was very quiet, and Pully started bellowing from the wings, "Listen, I was told to be here and so I'm here. Now do we go on or what?" And Kaufman turns to me and says, "I think we've got Big Julie."[3]

Sam Levene, whose characterization of Nathan Detroit was ninety-nine percent triumph, had one small problem. He couldn't sing. Really, he couldn't. In "Sue Me," his only song, he would invariably come in on the wrong note, until my father put in "call a lawyer and," in an ascending five-note phrase, to give him the means to slide up to a relatively accurate starting point. When he was in a group number like "The Oldest Established," he was under strict orders to mouth the lyrics.[4]

My father had written "Traveling Light" for Nathan and Sky to sing together. It was a complicated song, in both 3/4 and 5/4 time, in which the free and easy characters of the two leads were to be established. Sam Levene simply couldn't learn it. He couldn't hear the rhythm and no one could find a key he could sing it in. In rehearsal after rehearsal Levene would stomp his foot midway into the first chorus and shout, "Stop! I don't know where I am!" At performances on the road in Philadelphia, Robert Alda would cover for him and everyone would wait, cringing, for the number to be over.

Cy said to himself, "We're going to have to take this song out. He can't do it."

George Kaufman said out loud, "Cut the number. He'll never be able to do it."

Still they persevered. Again and again Levene slogged his way through it—they all loved the song so much, they just couldn't let it go.

When previews started in New York, Abe said, "Let me try. I think I can get through to him." For twenty minutes he and Levene worked quietly together off in a corner. Abe came back. "Take it out. He'll never be able to do it."

Cy spoke to my father, who said, "Okay, goddammit. But *you* tell him. I don't want to hear his 'waddya cutting it for? You cutting it 'cause I can't do it? Leave it in. I'll *do* it!'"

The next day Cy assembled the entire cast on the stage and said, "As of tonight's performance, we're cutting 'Traveling Light.' It's *out.* Everybody readjust to it. 'Traveling Light' is OUT." And with his last word ringing in the air—before Levene could say a word—he ran out of the theater onto 46th Street, jumped into the cab he had waiting, and left. "Traveling Light" went into the trunk, where it remains.

My brother, John, was born at the end of September 1950, while *Guys and Dolls* was rehearsing in Philadelphia. My mother flew back to the Coast for his birth, but, unable to stay away from the show or my father for long, came back just three weeks later, returning me—and introducing my brand new brother—to the care of Ida.

I don't remember if it was just before he was born or just after, but it was because of my brother's birth that we built an addition to our house. The addition was for me, not him. I remember standing in the back yard watching the new upstairs wing being built over the screened porch and feeling pushed out of my room—out past the perimeters of the house—to make room for my brother. I didn't want a new room. I didn't care that my parents were having furniture specially made for my new room, that I would even have a little dressing room, just

The detested younger brother arrives.

like my mother had. All I could see was that they were pushing me away in favor of the new baby. My room became his. Now *he* was next door to Ida, and I was on the far side of the upstairs kitchen. Ida didn't love Johnny more than me, but the fact remained that now I had to share her and I hated it.

Johnny was an absolutely gorgeous baby with huge blue eyes and, within a year, glorious golden curls. I was just turning six when he was born, my stringy hair was getting browner and I wasn't pretty. I detested him for his adorableness, for his command of everybody's attention, for showing up in the first place. We didn't become friends for many years. There is a bunch of photos of me and my infant brother in my album. In most of them I look sweet and loving toward him. But there's one—and I vividly remember it being taken—of us both on the new rug on the floor of my new room with my new handmade dresser behind us. I'm kneeling and Johnny is propped up in front of me. His curls have not yet materialized, but he is plump and cute and clearly the focus of this set of pictures. My right hand is poised above the side of his head, thumb meeting middle finger, about to let it go and snap him one. I'm wearing a crafty, determined, rather thoughtful expression, and Johnny looks like he knows exactly what's coming. I got yelled at for it. But I knew he deserved it.

It was during the Philadelphia rehearsals that my father slapped Isabel Bigley. She had been working on a song, "If I Were a Bell," which Sarah sings after Sky gets her drunk in Havana. My father had been telling her—in detail—how he wanted it sung. She couldn't get it right. Over and over she couldn't get it right. My father jumped up on a riser to put him at her eye level, and slapped her in the face.

Everything stopped. Everyone, including my father, was horrified. Isabel went home. Some people remember that my father sent her flowers with his contrite note. Others remember a diamond bracelet. In either case, she returned, but she kept her distance from him, and "If I Were a Bell" still wasn't coming off right. They tried all sorts of things with the song, including having Vivian Blaine do it "down-in-one" during a set change.

When my mother saw the number after she came back, Blaine was lounging on a couch, singing the song into a telephone. The lyrics are appropriate to a young lady with "a quiet upbringing" who suddenly finds herself uninhibited and joyfully in love. Not a song for a well-worn chorus girl.

"What the hell is Miss Adelaide doing singing 'Bell' in that silly position?" my mother said. "Who in the name of God is she talking to—and why is *she* singing that song at all?"

"Isabel can't sing it," my father said.

"Who says she can't?"

"I say she can't."

"I say she can. You can teach her."

"She won't talk to me since I hit her."

Somehow my mother convinced my father to convince Isabel—without corporal punishment—to let him teach her the song the way he felt it should go. The next morning he was seen standing on two phone books, nose to nose with Isabel, coaching her through it. Not only did the coaching session cement their friendly readjustment, the song finally worked.

My father provided some background to "More I Cannot Wish You" (sung by the old missionary to his granddaughter Sarah) in a 1961 letter answering a question about the phrase, "standing there, gazing at you, with a sheep's eye, and a lickerish tooth."

> Sheep's eye is, just as you suspect, descriptive of amorous longing. I suppose the exact expression is "making sheep's eyes at." The color and sound of this was enough for me to hope that this passage of the song would describe the imagined lover's almost pitiable adoration of the girl. Now we come to "lickerish tooth." I decided that the sense of sheep's eye was a little too weak, however sympathetic, and did not truthfully reflect Grandfather Arvide's rooting interest in our leading man, Sky Masterson. At the point in the play where this song is sung both Arvide and the audience would already know a great deal about Masterson's resolute and forward character. Therefore sheep's eye was not enough. So I consulted Roget (grudgingly, because usually I know more than he does) to find that "covetous" (which was the key meaning in my mind) could be described as "lecherous." I then looked up lecherous for variations less apalling in sound to the modern ear. This I did by way of the *Oxford English Dictionary* (the big twelve-volume one) and found to my great delight two archaic spellings: one was licorice (somehow combining the literal sense of "sweet tooth" with the fundamental meaning of the word)—and the other "lickerish" which had a much more satisfying adjective suffix. In the exemplary material on these words I found "lickerish tooth," which fitted neatly with the notes in hand, and even more neatly with my sense of what the old man's mischief should sound like in the scene.
>
> I correct myself. It was not the old man originally but the elder brother of the young lady Roseanna McCoy, heroine

> and title character of a Sam Goldwyn movie. It was for a scene in which she sits beside her brother in the seat of a wagon. She is 16 and she is being taken to her first fair. Through the song her brother is wishing her good fortune in the heart. In the picture, of course, she meets a young Hatfield. This delays the heart's good fortune for several reels. Sam Goldwyn neither liked nor understood the song and asked me for another. This turned out to be "Roseanna" which gained certain broad popular approval and was quite right for the picture. I held on to the original and found quite proper use for it in *Guys and Dolls.*[5]

Then there's the story about "The Oldest Established," which Cy told me:

> The Erlanger Theater in Philadelphia was a long theater with a long orchestra and a long lobby that ran all the way to the street. Frank had the men rehearsing "The Oldest Established" for two days with the conductor. Then we had to stage it. Michael Kidd and I told them, "Listen, we're gonna have a long morning and a performance tonight, so save your voices while we block this."
>
> So they're walking through the song and in comes Frank, down the aisle, yelling "What the hell is going on here? Goddammit, we rehearsed all day yesterday, and now what do I hear? Nothing! This is the worst goddamn thing!" He's really burning. I say, "But Frank—" He says, "You stay the hell out of this!" Mike gets up. Frank says, "And you, too!"
>
> Mike's sitting in one end of the pit and I'm in the other end, and Frank says, "I want to hear the goddamned song the way I rehearsed it—and I want to hear it NOW." He's standing in the center aisle, and the guys start singing their hearts out. Frank starts backing up the aisle—backs up all the way to the back of the orchestra and just stands there listening to the guys singing their hearts out. Then he turns around and heads for the lobby, the guys keep singing, and I run up one aisle and Mike runs up the other and we open the doors and Frank is walking up the long corridor. The guys are still singing their hearts out. Frank walks out into the street, turns right, and goes next door to the ice cream store. We're watching him from the theater entrance as he buys an ice cream cone and walks on down the street to his hotel. Meanwhile, the guys are still singing.[6]

Ira Bernstein, who with Joseph Harris became a major Broadway company manager, was Feuer and Martin's assistant on *Guys and Dolls.* Just before the New York opening, Ira went to my father for his approval of the title page of the Playbill.

> And in those days [Ira recalled] the author's billing was small. Frank looked at the Playbill layout and said, "I'm billed smaller than Isabel Bigley. But that's okay, as long as I'm co-starred with Meyer Ecker" (the property man).[7]

Guys and Dolls opened on November 24, 1950 at the Forty-sixth Street Theatre in New York. (Orchestra seats cost $9.60.) No one was prepared for the immensity of its success. The show had gotten a warm but tentative response in Philadelphia, and new material and revisions had been incorporated up to the very last minute. Everyone was very nervous. While my father paced to and fro in the back of the house, Carin and Abe Burrows sat in the orchestra holding hands nervously.

> The overture was fine [Carin remembered]. The curtain went up. First there was the opening ballet, which went well enough. Then came the bugle call, and "A Fugue for Tinhorns." Well, there was such a reaction from the audience. It was like electricity. That's when we knew we had an enormous hit. You have to experience the opening night of a really major hit to know what it feels like. There's an electricity in the audience that is palpable. You know it right away.[8]

Richard Watts of the *New York Post* was so impressed he even took back his judgment on the *Where's Charley?* score:

> *Guys and Dolls* is just what it should be to celebrate the Runyon spirit, vigorous, noisy, humorous, tough on the surface and shamelessly sentimental underneath, filled with the salty characters and richly original language sacred to the memory of the Master, and a pleasure to all beholders. There can be no doubt that it is the town's newest hit . . . Mr. Loesser has long been recognized as a bright and resourceful song writer, and, with the scores for *Where's Charley?*, which I didn't at first properly appreciate, and now *Guys and Dolls,* there is no doubt that he is a valuable addition to American musical comedy.[9]

John McClain, in the *New York Journal American:* "From the minute the curtain rises, with a Broadway ballet which sets the mood and a song called "Fugue for Tinhorns," sung by three horse players, to the final reprise of "Guys and Dolls," there is scarcely a moment when you're not either laughing or humming . . . Run, don't walk, to the nearest ticket broker." *Variety:* "With the funniest musical book in years and a knockout score, *Guys and Dolls* is a whale of a show and apparently the top smash of the season." John Chapman in the *New York Daily News:* "Here is New York's own musical comedy—as bright as a dime in a subway grating . . . In all departments, *Guys and Dolls* is a perfect musical comedy." Brooks Atkinson in the *Times:* "Out of the pages of Damon Runyon, some able artisans have put together a musical play that Broadway can be proud of. *Guys and Dolls,* they call it, out of one corner of the mouth."

And so on. The accolades flowed. The show was immediately sold out, and it ran for 1,200 performances on Broadway.

In 1950, when *Guys and Dolls* opened, Broadway was in its golden age. The integrated musical—the collaborative, creative interweaving of book, music, and dance pioneered by *Oklahoma!* in 1943—had completely overpowered the musical review, so popular in the 1930s and 1940s. After *Oklahoma!,* Rodgers and Hammerstein gave us *Carousel* (1945) and *South Pacific* (1949). Lerner and Loewe came out with *Brigadoon* in 1947, the same year as Harburg and Lane's *Finian's Rainbow.* All of these shows were not only tremendous successes, they remain famous and popular gems of Broadway. *Guys and Dolls* easily elbowed its way into this illustrious company and sparkled like a diamond among pearls.

Although *Where's Charley?* was well within the definition of an integrated musical, it had an old-fashioned flavor, in part because it adopted Victorian material and broke no new ground. But *Guys and Dolls* was not only contemporary in feeling and collaborative in spirit, the show was a Broadway offering that celebrated Broadway itself. It stood out—and stands out—as a one-of-a-kind triumph. It has played all over the world, in performances ranging from high school productions to two lengthy first-class runs in London. And currently it is playing on Broadway once more, having opened in April 1992 to overwhelmingly enthusiastic reviews, immediately followed by a record-breaking advance sale. People even remotely connected with the show have been hearing from friends they didn't know they had who are looking for tickets. *Guys and Dolls* is once again the Belle of Broadway. The quintessential New York musical is back in town.

This is a strange and lovely experience for me. I did see the original production when I was six years old. I remember only "Take Back Your Mink," the bluish silver furs and footlights, lots of bluish silver legs. (No doubt this was one of the times I was deposited with Nana and the green peppers, rescued every couple of days by my parents, to share some of their adventures.) Over the years I've seen the show many times in various settings, from summer camp to City Center. Seeing it now back on Broadway, as fresh as though it were written yesterday, I can appreciate it as never before. It seems to be a truly timeless show. How ironic, since my father wasn't interested in timelessness. "I don't write for posterity," he used to say. "I write for the here and now. I write entertainment."

Despite the comic flair and the witty cynicism that characterizes most of the *Guys and Dolls* score, my father was, at heart, a romantic. In public he would say, "I'm in the romance business," which seems calculated to give the impression that being romantic was business, pure and simple. But with his friends and colleagues he was more honest. He'd say, "I know I can make you laugh. I want to know what makes you cry." And to Abe he'd say, "Why can't you be romantic?" "I *am* romantic," Abe would reply, "I just think romance is funny."

In *Guys and Dolls* the romance *is* funny. But it is also romantic. The two love stories, for all the laughs they provide, are warm and believable. These wacky people are endearing, and when they overcome the amusing obstacles to happy domesticity the audience is moved and satisfied.

Guys and Dolls has sixteen songs. "Fugue for Tinhorns" sets the mood of the show and employs a classical form to introduce the disreputable characters and their interests. "The Oldest Established," with its humorous and melodic chorale, moves the plot along while it further reveals character. "Bushel and a Peck" and "Take Back Your Mink" are parodies of cheap nightclub acts.

Alvin Colt's costumes for the "Bushel and a Peck" country girls incorporated brassieres that were essentially large daisies. When Michael Kidd saw the sketches he thought it would work well to have the girls pulling out the petals one by one, shrieking, "He loves me, he loves me not." My father agreed and Colt arranged for extra, loose petals to be tucked in under the permanent ones. ("We had bags of those petals! The girls would toss them into the audience.") Since then, daisies have become a sort of trademark for Colt. He always tries to incorporate a daisy into his costume designs.[10]

Years later, Michael Kidd saw a production of *Guys and Dolls* in which the Hot Box girls wore brown sheaths for "Bushel and a Peck." "No daisies, no petals, but they were following the score. And in the middle of nowhere they shrieked, 'He loves me, he loves me not.' It made no sense whatsoever."[11]

Guess what. In the current production there are no daisies, and in the middle of nowhere the girls shriek, "He loves me, he loves me not."

I love you,
A bushel and a peck,
A bushel and a peck
And a hug around the neck,
Hug around the neck
And a barrel and a heap,
Barrel and a heap
And I'm talking in my sleep
About you, about you.
'Cause I love you,
A bushel and a peck,
Ya bet your purty neck I do.

"Take Back Your Mink" was finished very late one night in Philadelphia, orchestrated and choreographed over the next two days, and put into the Wednesday matinee as the second act opener.

He bought me the fur thing five winters ago
And the gown the following fall.
Then the necklace, the bag, the hat, and the shoes—
That was late forty-eight I recall.
Then last night in his apartment
He tried to remove them all,
And I said as I ran down the hall:

Take back your mink,
Take back your pearls,
What made you think
That I was one of those girls.
Take back the gown,
The shoes and the hat,
I may be down,
But I'm not flat as all that.

While my father was struggling with the song, Jule Styne came to Philadelphia to see the show. He called my father from the lobby of the hotel. My father said, "If you don't have any rhymes for 'mink,' don't come up."[12]

"Adelaide's Lament" recounts the trials and tribulations and psychosomatic symptoms of a fourteen-year engagement to a gambler:

The average unmarried female, basically insecure
Due to some long frustration, may react
With psychosomatic symptoms, difficult to endure
Affecting the upper respiratory tract.
In other words, just from waiting around
For that plain little band of gold
A person—can develop a cold.

You can spray her wherever you figure the streptococci lurk.
You can give her a shot for whatever she's got but it just
won't work.
If she's tired of getting the fish-eye from the hotel clerk,
A person—can develop a cold.

"Sue Me" continues this humorous examination of the courtship of Nathan and Adelaide in that pet form of my father's, the contrapuntal duet. Adelaide complains in a shrill litany while Nathan patiently, doggedly asserts his love for her. "Marry the Man Today" is a funny duet for Sarah and Adelaide. "Luck, Be a Lady," Sky Masterson's appeal to the goddess of the crap game, includes a rousing production number—the first and perhaps only production number to be set in a sewer—with unforgettable choreography. Michael Kidd had thought long and hard about staging the crap game as a dance. He met with George Kaufman to present the idea:

> Now George was a very acerbic character. He examined everything with a dry sense of humor. He didn't particularly like musicals. When you did a song he would look at his watch.
>
> He said, "Mike, I don't understand. How are you going to do a dance here? Do you mean to tell me we're going to have a scene where these tough gamblers will be standing around the stage while a bunch of dancers get up and do a dance?" I said, "I'll incorporate all the members of the cast into the crap game. I'll have Nathan taking a cut of every pot, I'll have Big Julie rolling. I'll have all the different characters participate." George said, "Well, I can't see it. It beats me."
>
> So I worked out the dance and came to show it to everybody, knowing that George was dead set against it. We did the number and George sat there with no sign of emotion. When it was over he turned to me and said, "Mike, I hardly have to tell you you've done something very remarkable here. Okay, let's go on." That was the biggest accolade you could get from George.[13]

The title song is another big production number. "Sit Down, You're Rockin' the Boat" is Nicely-Nicely's comic renunciation of sin. "Follow the Fold" is a Salvation Army-type hymn with a little gleam in its eye.

Only five of the sixteen songs are at all romantic, "I'll Know When My Love Comes Along," sung by Sarah and Sky to establish their differences, actually starts their incongruous mutual attraction. "If I Were a Bell" is Sarah's happy discovery that she's smitten. Brother Abernathy sings "More I Cannot Wish You" to Sarah to express his loving wishes for her happiness in love. "I've Never Been in Love Before" is the show's only love duet. It is totally free of cynicism—a purely romantic song.

And then there is one haunting little song, only sixteen bars long, so short it is almost a fragment, a recitative. "My Time of Day" is Sky Masterson's ode to New York, a quiet song with an odd, frequently modulating melody. You don't walk out of the theater humming this one. It has to sink in over several hearings. The lyrics evoke a crystal clear image of New York at night.

> My time of day is the dark time,
> A couple of deals before dawn,
> When the street belongs to the cop,
> And the janitor with his mop,
> And the grocery clerks are all gone.
> When the smell of the rain-washed pavement
> Comes up clean and fresh and cold,
> And the streetlamp light fills the gutter with gold,
> That's my time of day,
> My time of day,
> And you're the only doll I've ever wanted
> To share it with me.

My father always loved this song, and so do I. It's a love song, all right. A love song to my father's city and to the hours that belonged to him, when he would rise at 4:00 A.M. and write, and pace, and smoke, and doodle, and scheme, and contemplate the romance business.

The movie of *Guys and Dolls* was made in 1955. As it happened, Paramount passed on its first-refusal film rights to *Guys and Dolls* because Abe Burrows was on the studio blacklist—one of Hollywood's many not-so-courageous responses to McCarthyism. The Dramatists Guild opened bidding for the property, and other major studios made handsome offers, but Sam Goldwyn won with a record $1 million plus ten percent of the gross.

My father fought hard to control as many aspects of the film as he could, but Goldwyn had strong ideas about the casting, and he owned the studio. The result was the smooth Frank Sinatra playing the rough Nathan Detroit, and Marlon Brando and Jean Simmons—neither of them singers—playing Sky Masterson and Sarah Brown. Several members of the Broadway cast recreated their roles on film, including Vivian Blaine as Adelaide and Stubby Kaye as Nicely-Nicely. Five songs were cut, and my father reluctantly wrote three new ones, "Adelaide," "Woman in Love," and "Pet Me, Poppa." To take advantage of the fact that Sinatra was a singer, Nathan has several songs in the movie.

My father didn't like the new songs much, and he didn't like the loss of control he suffered in the making of the movie. Most especially, he didn't like what Frank Sinatra was doing with Nathan Detroit's numbers. Sinatra apparently felt that Nathan's character should conform to his own well-established crooning style, whereas my father felt that Nathan should remain a brassy Broadway tough who sang with more grits than gravy. Sam Levene, after all, had given his one song such a wonderful Runyonesque flavor that his singing had been easy to forgive—in fact, it had been quite charming in its inepitude.

I am told that my father conducted himself with uncharacteristic restraint for a time, watching Sinatra do his thing—until, finally, he could stand it no longer. After a rehearsal that left his blood boiling, he approached Sinatra with an offer to give him some help with "Sue Me," some tips on what he'd had in mind when he wrote the song, some appreciation for the type of character Nathan is.

"Why don't we meet in my bungalow and rehearse it?" he asked mildly through his clenched teeth.

"If you want to see me," Sinatra said, "you can come to my dressing room."

My father left the set to go outside and jump up and down and scream for a while. When he was calmer, he showed up at Sinatra's dressing room only to find it crowded with hangers-on and noisy with radio music.

"How the hell can we rehearse in this atmosphere?" he said, his blood resuming its full boil.

"We'll do it my way," Sinatra said, "or you can fuck off."

A contrapuntal duet of explosions swiftly followed, culminating in each man's avowal never to work with the other again.

Recently, a different version of this fight between "the terrible-tempered Franks" has come my way. I rather like its imagery: the two of them meeting on a deserted sound stage with only their seconds as witnesses (oh, how *High Noon*!), the air ringing with FUCK YOUs, and the two witnesses, who were acquaintances, quietly and patiently passing the time of day at the other end of the studio. I suspect that the two stories actually represent two of several skirmishes in a lengthy battle between these choleric antagonists. In the end, Sinatra sang the song his way, my father refused to see the movie, and the two men never spoke to each other again.

Both Jean Simmons and Marlon Brando delivered enjoyable performances, Brando being really quite charming and singing very respectably. The movie was a success; most people like it. I don't know if my father ever sneaked a peek at it on television, but *I* do every once in a while. I get a kick out of hearing Frank Sinatra sliding up to the note ("call a lawyer and . . .") in "Sue Me."

My parents always had separate bedrooms—at least as early as I can remember. My mother's room was pearly blue with a huge bed under a satin bedspread. She had a blue brocade armchair and hassock where she drank her (late) morning orange juice and coffee and read the newspaper. A small dressing room led to her elaborately tiled bathroom, which had a fantastic shower with glass doors and spigots on all three walls. I got to shower with my mother sometimes and it was a very special treat.

My father's room down the hall was simpler. He also had a huge bed, and his bedspread, curtains, and armchair (the one with the arms worn down to the stuffing) were all maroon plaid. He had his little electric organ, a gigantic brass spittoon serving as his major ashtray, and an antique barber's chair in which he sat occasionally to have a manicure. His bathroom was plain and white. I often sat on the tub and watched him shave.

Once I realized that their setup was somewhat unconventional, I asked my mother why. She said my father snored so loudly it was impossible to sleep in the same room. He did snore loudly. You could hear him all over the house. But it was more than that. For one thing, he got up before dawn most days, while most days my mother slept until late morning, later when she could. As the years went on their schedules differed more and more. She'd go to bed not long before he'd get up. By the time she was up and about for the day, he'd be taking his afternoon nap. They'd be together in the evenings—party time—and during the hours from sunset to midnight they were perfectly compatible. Except that, on most occasions, my mother was late.

I can see my father in his tuxedo, furiously pacing her bedroom, while she sits at her dressing table, sipping a drink, smoking a cigarette, and polishing her nails.

"We're already late, goddammit—what are you *doing*? Come on, Lynn, let's GO, for chrissake!"

"Just a few more minutes, dear. The polish has to dry properly or it will come off on my dress."

"You've had all fucking day to put nail polish on. Why the hell are you doing it now?" And he storms out of the room, cursing. She continues her slow, languid preparations. He returns, even angrier. Storms out again. Eventually she's ready and they head on out, my father still cursing and my mother still sipping her drink, all the way to the front door.

My mother had always been a procrastinator, it is true—some inborn tendency that she never really tried to conquer. But there was something else going on as well that slowed her down. She had rheumatoid arthritis of the spine. It began when she was in her twenties, but the pain went undiagnosed for a decade. Sometimes she was so crippled she had to rent a hospital bed. Over the years she tried dozens of different treatments and medications, including cobalt X-rays and cortisone, but most of the time, for the day-to-day sub-screaming level of pain she relied on alcohol and Demerol, both in increasing doses as time went on.

It was much more socially acceptable in those days to drink a lot. Even people who didn't drink a lot drank a lot. The entertainment business included alcohol at all events. And if my mother drove to her dressmaker's with her flask by her side, and if she fortified herself for an outing with a couple of vodkas at her dressing table, who would care or comment? Who would even notice?

My mother was wearing several hats in the early fifties: hostess, scout, wife, and mother. In that order. She worked for my father, screening new talent for him to audition, demonstrating his songs, accompanying him to entertainments and ceremonies, dinners and dances, theaters and night clubs. Some of the time left over she gave to me. I occasionally went with her to the beauty parlor (Pagano's), more often to the dressmaker (Carmel Harris), and sometimes to department stores (The May Company, Robinson's). Her one outdoor activity that I remember was sunbathing, which she performed as a kind of meditation. I used to watch her sunning herself in the back yard. She wore a two-piece bathing suit and she would lie face up, quite still, until little perfect beads of sweat had formed a solid mask over her forehead and upper lip. Then she would towel her face, undo her suit top, and turn over. Her patience fascinated me. In fact, everything she did required infinite patience.

Sometimes we would have lunch together. My favorite was cream cheese and green olive sandwiches and Coke in tall frosted glasses with lots of ice. She chopped each green olive with a tiny paring knife and with great care, while the cream cheese softened on the counter.

She taught me to cook, or rather, she let me watch her cook. She had few rules, but they were unbreakable. The flame must always be as low as possible. Everything must be cooked for hours. All cookware had to be cast iron. Margarine was unknown in our house. Most food was improved by adding sugar. Onions were always chopped into fine and uniform cube-lets. Cucumbers were sliced paper thin, salted, and laid out one by one to drain on paper towels. It took my mother a half hour to fry three pieces of bacon. Fried chicken, her pièce de résistance, was done in a deep cast-iron skillet—just chicken breasts and a pound and a half of butter, slow-bubbled on the stove for two or three hours. When my mother cooked dinner we ate at ten. She was, I must add, a wonderful cook. Her meals were well worth the wait, if you hadn't fainted away with hunger in the meantime.

She did cross-stitching. Tiny little stitches exactly covering the purple guidelines on the samplers, and a growing red spot in one corner saved as a blotter for her needle-struck index finger (she couldn't or wouldn't manage a thimble).

Putting on her makeup, she spent twenty minutes on each eye, carefully layering the mascara, pencilling the eyeliner, and applying the eyebrow pencil in perfect feathery strokes to look more realistic.

She was pathologically meticulous. And she was never on time.

The only times I ever saw my parents at odds were when my mother was keeping my father waiting, and it never struck me as anything significant, because my father was such a screamer anyway. But now I see that, no matter how much my mother loved my father and the life they led, she was beginning to undermine her own position, which was more precarious than she realized. Her physical disability and her methods of combatting it mixed potently with her basic langorous disregard for the passing of time and her obsession with detail. And this dangerous brew, cultivated in ignorance of its consequences, had already begun to poison the well.

7

Hans Christian Andersen

By 1951 Sam Goldwyn had wanted to make a musical movie about Hans Christian Andersen for over ten years. He had accumulated some thirty-odd different treatments of the idea, hiring (and firing) some thirty-odd screenwriters over the years. One of them, Samuel Taylor, was a friend of my father, and his suggestions for a Frank Loesser score were rebuffed along with his script. Eventually Goldwyn chose Moss Hart, who based his script on a 1938 treatment by Myles Connolly.

Goldwyn had originally conceived the idea for Gary Cooper. But Moira Shearer's spectacular hit *The Red Shoes* inspired plans to incorporate a bit ballet into the picture, so he cast Shearer and Jimmy Stewart as the leads.

Sylvia Fine, a songwriter as well as the wife of Danny Kaye, suggested to Goldwyn that doing a musical with Jimmy Stewart was an odd idea. "Jimmy's a marvelous actor," she said. "But he's not musical. Why not use Danny? He's very musical, and he wonderful with children." Goldwyn thought it over, cast Danny, and asked Sylvia to write the songs.

> But Moss Hart wanted Frank [Sylvia recalled]. "Loesser is hot," he said. "He just did *Guys and Dolls* and I'm sure he's got another great score coming up." And so it was Sam and Moss who had to talk to me. Strangely enough, I didn't mind very much—some, but not much. And not because Frank and I were close friends—that had nothing to do with it. It was because of the way he wrote.[1]

My father was hired. The contract, signed in 1952, stipulated that for ten percent of the net my father would write eight songs. He wanted to compose the ballet music as well, but instead it was put together from various works of Franz Liszt by the musical director, Walter Scharf. Hart and my father worked closely together to weave the script and the songs into a tight, relatively seamless cloth.

Hans Christian Andersen tells a rather silly and certainly apocryphal story about the Danish writer, making him a cobbler who spends most of his time spinning fairy tales to the village children ("The King's New Clothes," "Inchworm"). The tales delight the children but enrage the schoolmaster, whose classroom is too often empty. Hans is sent packing with his apprentice, Peter, and the pair set off on a journey ("I'm Hans Christian Andersen") to Copenhagen ("Wonderful Copenhagen"). There the first thing that happens is Hans's arrest for showing disrespect to the king's statue. Languishing in his jail cell, he entertains a little girl outside his window ("Thumbelina") while Peter, who has escaped the authorities, discovers that the Royal Danish Ballet needs a cobbler.

Released from jail into the custody of the ballet company, Hans falls in love with Doro, the prima ballerina for whom he makes a pair of shoes in which she can "walk on air." Doro is married to Niels, the hot-tempered ballet master; Hans misinterprets their stormy relationship. Seeing himself as the hero who will rescue Doro from her tyrannical boss, Hans writes her an allegory, "The Little Mermaid," which Doro takes for a ballet idea. Before Hans can declare his love and intentions in person, the company leaves town on its annual tour. While they are away, Hans resumes his vocation of telling stories to schoolchildren ("The Ugly Duckling"), one of whom happens to be the son of the newspaper publisher. Hans's stories are printed in the paper, which tickles him but doesn't keep him from thoughts of Doro as he wistfully cobbles ("Anywhere I Wander").

The ballet company returns, Doro invites Hans to the premiere of "The Little Mermaid," and, in a fantasy sequence, Hans sees himself and Doro getting married ("No Two People"). When Hans arrives at the theater determined to get to Doro, he is intercepted by Niels, locked in a closet, and forgotten. Released the next day by an obviously happily married Niels and Doro, Hans is forced to accept the fact that he can never have her. Off again he wanders with Peter, who reassures him that "You'll go on telling stories. Yes, you will. Because you're

On the set during the filming of *Hans Christian Andersen.* Making sure it was loud and good.

Hans Christian Andersen. You'll tell stories, you'll write stories, you'll even sing stories—over and over and over again."

The film was directed by Charles Vidor, with intensely unnatural sets by Howard Bristol and folksy costumes by Clavé. Hans was played with great charm by Danny Kaye; Farley Granger played the ballet master; and when Moira Shearer got pregnant, she was replaced by Jeanmaire, the lead dancer of Roland Petit's Ballet de Paris. Petit, her husband, became the choreographer and danced with Jeanmaire in "The Little Mermaid" sequence. Joey Walsh played the role of Peter with a slight New York accent.

Kaye's performance was engaging and tuneful. Very tuneful. He sang every song in the score, occasionally supplemented by a chorus and joined only once by Jeanmaire. Originally, Farley Granger and Jeanmaire were to sing "No Two People" as evidence that they were indeed a happy couple, but even that duet was reassigned to Kaye and incorporated into Hans's fantasy sequence. This was just one more disappointment for Granger, who liked almost nothing about the film except working with Jeanmaire. She spoke no English when she was signed but worked hard with Granger and Hart to learn her part. Granger found her to be "wonderful—a joy to work with."[2] Of the movie itself, he said, "Look at the plot: Boy meets girl, boy loses girl, boy gets boy."[3]

Well, yes. But the songs in *Hans Christian Andersen* are delightful. For the most part, they seem simple, well suited to children's stories, with easily remembered tunes and clear, interesting lyrics. But they are also very clever and musically more sophisticated than they seem on first hearing.

"I'm Hans Christian Andersen," which introduces the character, is a fast-paced ramble. "The King's New Clothes" sets to music the fable of the emperor swindled into thinking he has been sold a magic suit of clothes that only very wise and intelligent people can see. The king and queen sing, "Isn't it great? Isn't it rich? Look at the charm of every stitch! The suit of clothes is altogether, but altogether, it's altogether the most remarkable suit of clothes that I have ever seen!" When the king dons his magic suit for the parade, the crowds all cheer—except for "one little boy, who for some reason hadn't heard about the magic suit, and didn't know what he was supposed to see." He cries out, "Look at the king! Look at the king! Look at the king, the king, the king! The king is in the altogether, but altogether, the altogether. He's altogether as naked as the day that he was born! The king is in the altogether, but altogether, it's altogether the very least the king has ever worn!"

"Wonderful Copenhagen," the best known song in the *Hans Christian Andersen* score, is a cheerful waltz, delighting in the lovely city my father had not yet seen. The Danes adopted the song as their own, and when its composer visited Copenhagen a few years later, he was welcomed as if he were a national hero.

Wonderful, wonderful Copenhagen,
Friendly old girl of a town.
'Neath her tavern light,
On this merry night,
Let us clink and drink one down
To wonderful, wonderful Copenhagen,
Salty old queen of the sea.
Once I sailed away,
But I'm home today,
Singing Copenhagen, wonderful, wonderful,
Copenhagen for me.

My father referred to "Thumbelina" as an insignificant little ditty, not a real song. Whenever he wanted to make a point about a cheap song, his own or someone else's, he would mention "Thumbelina." He never gave himself credit for writing exactly what the scene required: a charming "little ditty" meant to entertain a small child.

Though you're no bigger than my thumb,
Than my thumb, than my thumb,
Sweet Thumbelina, don't be glum.
Now, now, now! Ah, ah, ah! Come, come, come!
Thumbelina, Thumbelina, tiny little thing,
Thumbelina, dance, Thumbelina, sing!
Oh, Thumbelina, what's the difference if you're very small?
When your heart is full of love, you're nine feet tall!

It certainly entertained me. I was seven when he first performed it for me, and I was enthralled. When he said, "I could write that junk any day of the week," I was stunned.

"Thumbelina" was nominated for an Academy Award but lost out to the title song from *High Noon*.

Andersen's tale of The Ugly Duckling is one of his best. And my father's song, I think, tells it with appreciation, warmth, and wit:

> (Spoken) There was once a farm near a deep lake. In a clump of flowering brushes near the water's edge a lady duck sat on her nest. All her eggs had hatched except for one very large egg. Friends said she should abandon the egg—that a turkey had somehow got into her nest and laid the big egg. She should be out on the water, they said, teaching her ducklings to swim. She was about to agree when all at once she heard
> a tap . . .
> and a tap-tap . . .
> and a *c-r-a-c-k!*
>
> (Sung) And out came an ugly duckling
> With feathers all stubby and brown
> And the other birds
> In so many words said QUACK get out of town.
> QUACK get out, QUACK, QUACK get out
> QUACK, QUACK get out of town.
> And he went with a quack and a waddle and a quack
> In a flurry of eiderdown.
>
> That poor little ugly duckling
> Went wandering far and near,
> But at ev'ry place
> They said to his face
> QUACK get out of here
> QUACK get out, QUACK, QUACK get out,
> QUACK, QUACK get out of here.
> And he went with a quack and a waddle and a quack
> And a very unhappy tear.
>
> All through the wintertime, he hid himself away—
> Ashamed to show his face, afraid of what others might say.
> All through the winter, in his lonely clump of weed
> 'Till a flock of swans spied him there
> And very soon agreed, "You're a very fine swan indeed!"

(Spoken) "Swan? Me a swan? Aw—go on!" "Take a look at
yourself in the lake and you'll see." And he looked and he
saw, and he said, "Why, it's me! I *am* a swan.
Wh-e-e!!!"

(Sung) I'm not such an ugly duckling,
No feathers all stubby and brown.
For, in fact, these birds, in so many words
Said "TCHK! The best in town.
TCHK! the best. TCHK, TCHK, the best!
TCHK, TCHK the best in town!"

Not a quack, not a quack, not a waddle or a quack,
But a glide and a whistle and a snowy white back
And a head so noble and high!
Say, who's an ugly duckling?
Not I.

There is a commercial recording of my father performing this song (as well as "The King's New Clothes"), his QUACKS and TCHKS and his Broadway accent simply perfect.

"Anywhere I Wander" is a simple, pretty ballad; "No Two People" a happy little duet in which the overlapping patter plays with rhymes:

No two people have ever mooned such a moon,
Juned such a June
Spooned such a spoon.
No two people have ever been so in tune
As my macaroon and I.

"Inchworm" is a two-part invention, another example of the interwoven, contrapuntal duet that my father enjoyed writing so much. (While one part repeats, "Two and two are four, four and four are eight," etc., the second part sings, "Inchworm, inchworm, measuring the marigold, you and your arithmetic, you'll probably go far . . . Seems to me you'd stop and see how beautiful they are.") It was his favorite song in the movie, and so, in June 1953, he was delighted to receive a letter, dated "Now," with no return address, and handwritten in a peculiar, curvy, loopy, caterpillian script:

> Dear Loesser your song Inchworm makes me very happy; not only from an inchwormitarian point of view (I know you must realize that people will not be so repelled by us after this) but from the aspect of downright beauty. It is conceivable that if Robert Burns and the god Pan, and Antoine de St. Exupery, and Euclid had gotten together for three days and three nights they might have been able to write almost equally good words, but as I see it no group of musicians nor any other one musician could have written the beautiful music. It is simple, yet it is so intricate, the harmony is perfect and the counterpoint—well it just gives me a headache when I think of what it would be like to try to write it tho I suppose for you it was easy.
>
> I'd like to send you a leaf or something in appreciation of the delight your song has given me, but since that probably wouldn't be the correct thing to do, I'll close by promising you that after this I'll try to admire the marigolds. Respectfully, a Kansas inchworm. (Please excuse the writing. It is not a customary practice, and besides, my back has been aching a little today. Have been following my hunches a little too often lately.)[4]

My father noted that the letter was postmarked Lawrence, Kansas. He had his secretary find the local newspaper with the biggest readership, then placed a five-inch-square ad in the *Daily Journal World:*

I N C H W O R M

F. L. SAYS
THANKS FOR
THE LETTER

Happily, the inchworm could read as well as write. It telegraphed "GRATITUDE GRATEFULLY AND HAPPILY RECEIVED" and wrote to explain that its name was Emily Preyer, a kindergarden teacher and the daughter of a piano teacher. "I have always made up stories for the children, so when I knew I had to write you about "Inchworm" I just made up a story for you. Your 'thanks' in our paper was one of the nicest things that ever happened to me."

Just before the picture was finished, Sylvia Kaye suggested that Goldwyn arrange for a recording of the "remarkable score" of *Hans Christian Andersen* to be sold in theater lobbies:

> I said to Sam, "When people come out of a musical, that's when they want to buy the record." Sam thought it was a good idea.
>
> Then Frank called me when the album was made. He was at the top of his temper. He yelled, "Listen! I'm not in the Danny Kaye business! I'm in the Frank Loesser business. I'm not interested in Danny's record being *the* record. I want everybody who sings to record these songs." I said I still thought it was a good idea, that it would be good for his business and good for everybody. It wasn't going to stop other people from making records.[5]

Hans Christian Andersen was released in November 1952 to reviews that generally panned the screenplay but celebrated the score and Danny Kaye. The film turned out to be a box-office winner, earning more than $6 million. The album—sold by the thousands in theater lobbies—was a smash.

I remember my father working on the score of *Hans Christian Andersen.* Not that it appeared to be work as he performed "The Ugly Duckling" and "Thumbelina" over and over again to my delight. He and my mother worked on "Inchworm" frequently in my presence, my mother singing the meticulous measuring part, of course. They sang "Wonderful Copenhagen" in beautiful harmony and "No Two People" with happy confidence. I relished the times I watched them singing together, and I relished the other times they shared with me, the times I'd be allowed to eat dinner with them in the dining room, or when we'd all go to a movie—Disney, naturally—where my father almost always fell asleep and snored until we jostled him, shushing and giggling. My father escorted me to my first dance—a fancy affair sponsored by my fancy school—at which we shared a table with Fred Astaire and his daughter. Toward the end of

My father, Johnny, and me. My father is taking me to my first dance.

the evening, when our fathers graciously asked us for a dance, we little girls exchanged long-suffering looks, and she said, "Stuck again."

We got our first television sometime around then. My father told me something very special was about to be delivered and took me out to the street to wait for the truck. This was going to be a wonderful surprise, he told me. I began to imagine all sorts of wonders: a two-wheel bike, a jungle gym, a Ferris wheel. . . And when the truck came and the men unloaded what looked like a very large radio, I couldn't hide my disappointment. "We already have radios," I said, pouting.

"Now don't you be so hasty. This is no ordinary radio. Wait and see. We're going right inside and hook it up and you will be thrilled."

The machine was lugged into the playroom and plugged in and fiddled with and behold: the twelve-inch square on the front suddenly glowed, and Buffalo Bob came to life, introducing Howdy and Clarabell and the gang. I stood there watching it for a few minutes, impressed by the magic, but bored by the contents. "I'm going upstairs to read," I announced, providing my parents with a little story to tell about their rather bookish young daughter for many years thereafter.

I loved to read. But more than that, I loved to be read to. My father never read to me. My mother did on rare occasions. I don't think Ida was literate enough to read anything beyond elementary children's books aloud. The task fell to my mother's mother, Gran.

Gran hadn't lived with us since I was an infant in the Navarro Hotel in New York, but she had moved with us to California and lived a few blocks away in one of those entities rare in California in those days, an apartment. She came over to our house several times a week and spent time with her grandchildren. She did our shopping for us at the Farmers' Market, and I often went with her.

I'm sure the Farmers' Market has shrunk like everything else in my childhood, but at that time it was a veritable state fair to my eyes. We would go from the butcher to the vegetable man to the chocolate lady in the window who was covered up to her elbows in liquid fudge as she hand-dipped coconut drops and caramel creams. We would stop first at the newsstand where I was allowed to buy two comic books and one piece of bubble gum. At the end of our shopping sprees we'd refresh ourselves at the doughnut place. Gran would dip hers in her coffee, I'd eat mine with a glass of milk. On the way home we would usually stop at her favorite book store, and I remember her excitement when a book she had been waiting for had come in.

Gran was a skinny, sickly, complaining woman with a hooked nose and dyed and curled bright red hair. She bore an unsettling resemblance to the Wicked Witch of the West, but, in fact, she was very affectionate with us, in a kind of sour way. She used to read me wonderful stories about explorers and adventurers in Africa and Asia and other exotic places. Man-eating-tigers on the loose. Elephants charging. Living in tents in the jungle, with snakes and hyenas and giraffes. Safaris. Mountain treks. South Seas islands. She left me her wonderful old collection of travels and adventures, and they are now in my library—beloved reminders of the woman who introduced

Gran.

me to the beauty, the power, and the great pleasure of the well-written book.

My father, who supported her, tolerated Gran with some irritation and some affection but never had any intense reactions to her one way or the other. My mother, on the other hand, hated her. It was as though she never forgave some long ago transgression, some deep disappointment or betrayal. Gran certainly was difficult. Always unwell in some way, and always discussing it at length; always anxious about something one of us was doing ("Susan! You mustn't eat that banana—it's almost green! It will give you a stomach ache and we'll have to call the doctor and you'll be sick for a week—"); always nagging my mother about something. My mother was outwardly kind to her, giving her a role in our household and occasionally including her in their social activities, but she argued with her over almost anything she said, made fun of her behind her back, undermining any authority she might have had over Johnny and me, and on occasion would chew her out and send her away in tears.

As a kid I tended to take on my mother's grown-up opinions. But although I criticized Gran, she was almost as important to me as Ida. I knew that if she thwarted me I could go to my mother and have Gran's decision overturned in a flash. I joined my mother in mocking her concerns. I was impatient with her aches and pains. But I did love that bony old lady, and we had some wonderful times together.

My parents weren't only traveling from coast to coast in the fifties. They made several trips to Europe as well as local excursions to San Francisco, Tijuana, and Las Vegas.

My father loved Las Vegas. He wasn't a big gambler, but he loved the atmosphere and what he considered to be the egalitarian nature of the place. He said it was the only place in the world where you could find truckdrivers and cleaning ladies rubbing shoulders with lawyers and doctors at the roulette tables. No dress codes, no closing time. Anyone over twenty-one could lose any amount of money, any time.

I didn't see the insides of the casinos. I spent most of my time at the pool when they took me to Las Vegas. At the pool, my mother would cultivate her perfect little beads of sweat, and my father would, as they say now, schmooze.

I watch him from my lounge chair as he dives in and swims out and back across the pool at the Desert Inn. Dragging himself out of the water and over to his cigarettes, he mutters unhappily about being "winded." I am ten, he is forty-four, and I know he has just experienced something negative, irritating. I'm not sure if I'm supposed to know something or do something about it. But very soon he's once more in animated conversation with his cronies, and we can both forget it.

It stays with me, though. The image of my father striking out across the pool—beginning strong and fast and coming up gasping and disappointed. It didn't have to be that way, I tell him. You could have stopped smoking, worked on your body, stayed healthy. I could be talking to you right now if you had taken care of yourself.

But I know what his answer is. He always has an answer (It's my house and I'm bigger). "It was my body and my right to abuse it. Okay, okay—I lived a relatively short life. But I put more into my lifetime than you can dream of. And—just a goddamned minute! Who the fuck told you you could write a book about me anyway? You know how I feel about crap like that."

John and Gwyn Steinbeck had divorced in 1948, and in 1949 John met Elaine Scott, whom he married the next year and spent the rest of his life with. Elaine met my parents soon after she met John, and even though my mother remained close friends with Gwyn, the four of them spent many happy times together. Both the Steinbecks and the Loessers traveled to Europe with some frequency in the fifties, mixing business and pleasure, and, as often as they could, they enjoyed Paris together. (During one of these trips my father sent his sister a postcard from "Le Tour F.L.")

In Paris they always stayed at the Hotel Lancaster, a small, elegant establishment with a garden where John and my father liked to sit and scheme together. Most evenings they would all go out, and as Elaine told me, they rarely had a dull moment:

> Once the four of us got all dressed up to go to a Russian restaurant called the Karnilov. It wasn't very far from the hotel, but since we were dressed up we hailed a taxi. As we started to get in, Frank said to the driver, "Restaurant Karnilov," and gave the address. The driver said, "It's too near to drive you. You must walk." And of course that was like waving a red flag in front of a bull. Frank said, "We don't want to walk. The ladies have on high heels, we're all dressed up, so we're going to ride in your taxi." The driver said, "I refuse to take you. It is economically unsound." Well, this made Frank furious. He shepherded us into the cab, and once we were in, the driver had to take us by law. Frank said in English to John, "I'm going to show this son of a bitch a thing or two. He can't lord it over me like that." And John said, "How?" "I think I'll overtip him." John thought it an odd way to humiliate a Parisian taxi driver, but Frank wanted to be grand, he was so angry. We got to the restaurant and Frank overtipped the driver. As we got out, the driver turned and yelled, "Bon appetit, monsieur." And Frank yelled back, "Oh, bon fuck yourself!"[6]

God knows how many ideas got kicked around in the garden of the Hotel Lancaster or in John's New York townhouse or in my parents' Beverly Hills playroom. One was a musical version of John's *The Pearl.* Another was an idea for Fred Allen, who would play a traveling magician in an unwritten musical they called *The Wizard of Maine.* All that exists of that project is a file folder of correspondence. Still another unhatched scheme remains a tantalizing mystery.

> Dear Frankobitch [John wrote to my father in 1958], I have a great idea. I am setting down to write it up. It will be a short novel. It will do all right for itself, I hope. Only this idea is also a natural for a show with music. No one can write this book but me, and I don't think anyone could handle it musically but you.
>
> I'm not kidding, Frank. I don't fool around about such things. And I need a show like holes in both of my heads. Only this idea cries out for that treatment after I have it written, but if your mean little profit taking soul together with your god damned stinking talent is intrigued, I am prepared to tell you about it. I'm going to do the book anyway and will probably make a pretty penny out of it, so I am not throwing myself on your mercy. But if in the purple future you might want to play around with something that is old and most new, sharp and mean, timely and timeless, slapstick and with great dignity, a comedy with its feet in sorrow (and I dare you to beat the sales talk), then I will talk to you about it.
>
> And if you aren't interested, screw you! And I will still like you, I think. (Apart from that I would like to see you. I haven't watched you twist up a telephone cord for a long time.)[7]

Certainly none of their ideas bore fruit in the early fifties, because neither of them took the time away from major individual projects. John was working on *East of Eden,* among other things, and my father, even while writing the *Hans Christian Andersen* score, was working intensely on the most ambitious project of his career.

8

The Most Happy Fella

Sidney Howard referred to his 1924 play *They Knew What They Wanted* as a comedy. But it is not exactly funny. I would call it an old-fashioned melodrama with a happy ending. An aging, wealthy Napa Valley wine grower named Tony—a simple, good-natured, functionally illiterate Italian-American—falls in love at first sight with a young San Francisco waitress. Too shy even to speak to her, he gets her name—Amy—from her boss, comes home, and has his foreman, Joe, write her a letter for him "in good English" proposing marriage. Joe is young and handsome and restless, a traveling ladies' man and union organizer whose strongest feelings, like most of his lines, have to do with the Wobblies (the I. W. W.—International Workers of the World). When the play opens, Joe has been ghostwriting love letters from Tony to Amy for several months. Amy, having accepted Tony's marriage proposal, is on her way to meet her groom.

Tony dreads their upcoming meeting, and with good reason. His insecurity about the difference in their ages inspired him, when he and Amy exchanged photographs, to substitute a picture of Joe. Now he drowns his anxiety in wine and has a serious accident on his way to meet Amy's train, breaking both legs. While he lies in a ditch awaiting rescue, the postman discovers Amy waiting forlornly at the station and delivers her to Tony's house, where the first person she encounters is, of course, Joe. Tony is brought home on a stretcher. Amy, by the end of a confused confrontation with Joe, realizes who is who and what has happened.

Finding herself with no job, no home, and about to be married to a much older—and now disabled—man who speaks broken English, Amy is understandably distraught. She agrees to go through with the wedding (which, on Tony's insistence, takes place immediately, even before his bones are set) because she feels she doesn't have a better alternative. At least she will be provided for. But following the festivities, after Tony is carried off to be mended, a hurt and needy Amy ends up in Joe's arms and, briefly, in his bed.

A couple of months pass, and Tony and Amy are doing surprisingly well together. He's still pretty much laid up, but she enjoys nursing him through his slow recovery. They develop a loving companionship for which they are both grateful and through which they both blossom. Joe, who agreed to stay until Tony was on his feet again, is about to leave. He and Amy maintain a polite, distant relationship, their one-night stand all but forgotten. All is well, except for one little thing. Amy is pregnant.

"Amy came to see me last week," the doctor tells Joe. "I didn't tell her what the trouble was, I didn't have the heart. I put her off. Oh, it's easy to fool a woman. But you can't fool a doctor, Joe." Joe then tells Amy. (The play also has lines like "Tony's a white guy even if he *is* a wop.")

Amy decides she must confess her night of craziness to Tony and then go away with Joe, who feels he must do the right thing by her, even though they are not in love. Tony—by turns enraged and wounded, unable to believe that Amy is not in love with Joe—by and by becomes more concerned about Amy and the baby. "How you goin' mak' money for keep him? . . . Pretty soon Joe is leavin you desert, and den w'at is goin' happen? . . . No! No! NO!! Ees no good! My Amy havin' baby in da street! Ees no good." Tony decides—and Amy gratefully agrees—that she will stay with him, they will bring up the baby together, and "people will say 'Tony is so goddam young an' strong he's break both his legs an' havin' baby just da same!'" Joe is free to return to his wanderings and his Wobblies, and the curtain comes down on Tony and Amy with their arms around each other.

In 1924 the play was considered both shocking and daring. As Elliot Norton wrote in the *Boston Post* some twenty years later, "It dealt with unfaithfulness, and although that has not been an uncommon theatrical theme, it was generally believed that this sin could not be forgiven on the stage. In *They Knew What They Wanted,* it is."[1] The opening night reviews were, without exception, good ones, and the play won the Pulitzer Prize. Revived on Broadway in both 1939 and 1949, it didn't fare as well. *Time* magazine provided the epitaph:

> When it won the Pulitzer Prize in the mid 1920s [it] had a fresh slant and a fine cast. Revived without lustre in 1939, it seemed sadly dated. Dumped down on Broadway last week, it seemed all but dead.[2]

In 1951 my father, still basking in the glow of *Guys and Dolls* and in the midst of writing *Hans Christian Andersen,* was nonetheless looking for ideas for a new musical. His friend Samuel Taylor, the playwright who had worked on a treatment of *Hans Christian Andersen* and was an early champion of my father's for that project, put him on to *They Knew What They Wanted.*

> Our idea was that I was going to write the book and he was going to write the score. But after working for a week, I realized that this wasn't going to be feasible, because I just couldn't live his kind of life. We were very good friends, but we were quite different. I couldn't stand those parties that went way on into the night, with all those characters, all trying to be "on" all the time. And Frank's work hours were a little bit strange.
>
> So after a week, I said to him, "I'm not going to do this." He was quite stricken. He said, "What will I do? Who will I get?" And I said, "Don't get anybody. Do it yourself."[3]

When my father expressed his insecurity about writing dialogue, Taylor said, "Any time you have doubts about what you're doing, write a song." And he did. As the show evolved, it quite surprised him: in the beginning he had thought of it as a simple play, in which he would place his songs. But then Taylor pointed out something that changed his course.

> I said, "You have to realize that this is the Tristan and Isolde story. Sidney Howard told me he had based it on *Tristan*. If you analyze it, it's there." That stirred Frank up. And he thought, "If that's what it is, I can do what Wagner did."[4]

Well, what Frank Loesser wrote wasn't exactly Wagnerian. But he did expand the play considerably, adding scenes and characters and writing a deluge of music for the show he called Project Three that would become *The Most Happy Fella.*

The new characters include Amy's waitress friend Cleo, originally from Dallas, whom Tony invites to the vineyard to provide company for Amy and who falls for Herman, a field hand, also from "Big D." Tony now has a sister, Marie, who has looked after him all her life and is desperately jealous of Amy. Amy herself has become Rosabella—because Tony, not knowing her name when he falls in love with her, makes one up. (She is called Rosabella up until the very last scene, when Tony says, "Now, tonight, we start all over. I sit in da ristorante. You wait on me. Omma no scared. Omma say, 'Young lady, what's-a you name?'" Rosabella meekly says, "Amy.") There are Pasquale, Giuseppe, and Ciccio, three chefs who sing lusty trios in mock Italian opera style; and there are other, smaller speaking roles that embellish the story.

My father made other changes as well. Joe no longer talks about the Wobblies (this Joe probably never heard of them). The doctor tells Rosabella herself she is pregnant (apparently it was no longer that easy to fool a woman). Rosabella does not plan to go off with Joe, although it momentarily seems that way to Tony, which fuels his pre-reconciliation pain and rage.

My father worked on the show for five years. He used classical forms, molding them to his dramatic aims. He wrote arias, recitatives, duets, trios, two-part inventions, choral numbers, purely orchestral sections—and scattered pop tunes among them like candy flowers on the cake.

The show became huge. There were twenty speaking roles, a twenty-four-member chorus, twelve dancers. He insisted on enlarging the usual twenty-six-piece orchestra to thirty-six to achieve a rich, full, serious sound. In fact, the orchestra pit at the Imperial Theatre had to be enlarged before the New York opening to accommodate the extra musicians.

He steadfastly refused to call *The Most Happy Fella* an opera. In fact, any such reference annoyed him. It was "a musical—with *lots* of music." Period. And, really, he was right. But he used operatic devices as well as other classical forms deliberately, to achieve the desired effects. He knew what he wanted.

Part of what he wanted, I will always believe, was to impress Arthur and Julia, to show them how he could create popular entertainment with the classical forms and themes they so cherished. As Bill Schuman said of my father, despite his anti-intellectual stance he was most definitely an intellectual. Familiarized from birth with "good" music and "good" literature, he was hardly a stranger to classical themes and sounds and structures. Insatiably curious, always learning, he dove into Project Three with passion, incorporating recognizable aspects of opera and symphony, fugue and invention, using a classical vocabulary in a Broadway syntax. He was breaking new ground while being true to his craft, and he wanted Julia and Arthur to take note and acknowledge his achievement.

My father had by then established his own publishing company to maintain as much control over his work as possible—control and autonomy being of major importance to him after his years of indenture to Paramount. Finding himself in the three-way role of composer, lyricist, and librettist, he opted to keep the producing end of the show in the family as well. My mother had been working for Frank Music Corp. since its inception as a talent scout and song plugger. It was she who discovered "Unchained Melody," the company's first big hit by songwriters other than my father (Alex North and Hy Zaret), and it was she who first saw the potential in the nascent *Kismet* score when Robert Wright and George Forrest played it for her. She took on this new challenge with enthusiasm and formed a partnership with Kermit Bloomgarden to co-produce *The Most Happy Fella.* Kermit had recently produced Lillian Hellman's adaptation of Anouilh's *The Lark* and Hackett and Goodrich's *The Diary of Anne Frank.* He was in demand.

Although my father had the last word, my mother did most of the casting and all of the talent scouting for *The Most Happy Fella.* She auditioned over 2,000 people, sitting through weeks of Metropolitan Opera performances in search of the operatic voices my father wanted. She traveled to Italy in search of Tony, and she thought she had found the perfect one in Tito Gobbi, one of Italy's greatest opera stars. In Rome she prevailed on friends to introduce her to Gobbi, who apparently found her as charming as she found him and was at least mildly interested in playing the role. But in the end he decided that doing a Broadway show would jeopardize his operatic career.

Eventually my mother found her Tony. After she heard Robert Weede at the San Francisco Opera, she took my father (and me!) to San Francisco to see Weede in *Macbeth.* It was an adventure I'll never forget. For one thing, it was enormously exciting to take an airplane up to an exotic, beautiful city, go out to dinner with my parents, go to the opera, stay up way past my bedtime, then take another plane home. For another, my father was wearing a new suit, and when he took his seat at the opera, the chewing gum someone had thoughtfully left on it became embedded in his trousers. Not two minutes after we sat down, just as the lights dimmed—I heard him hiss to my mother, "Goddammit, I've sat in a fucking wad of chewing gum!"

He was livid, but you don't jump up and down or scream at the opera, so all he could do was sit there squirming (making matters stickier) all through the first act. He spent the second act in the men's room waiting for the housekeeper to apply whatever cleaning solvent she had on hand to his suit bottom;

during the third act he was engulfed in fumes, his own and the solvent's. He was neither amused—we, of course, were—nor particularly attentive to the opera. By the time he cooled down, Weede's performance was nearly over, but my father didn't need to hear much of that voice to know that, no matter what had happened to his suit, Tony had been found.

My father for years told a story about running into an old friend one day early in 1955. "Hey, Frankie," the friend said, "nice to see you again. What's new?"

"I'm writing a new musical," my father said. "It's almost finished now. I'm writing the music, and the lyrics, and this time I'm writing the book as well."

"That's terrific! Who's producing it?"

"Well, actually, my wife is producing it with Kermit Bloomgarden."

"No kidding. Who's the director?"

"I haven't decided yet—I might try to direct it myself."

"Fantastic, Frankie! You've written the whole thing, your wife is producing it, you might direct it yourself—so tell me, who gets the girl?"

My mother's arthritis was no better these days, and she was drinking more and more. Although she rarely appeared downright drunk, she was often boisterous, her loud laugh at the theater, for instance, announcing her presence in the audience to the cast. At intermission, just as the curtain began its descent, she would grab her coat and make her way as fast as she could up the aisle to get a seat at the nearest bar. Likewise at the end of the show. It used to make me angry and embarrassed, and I would stay in my seat, meeting her over at the bar only after the curtain calls. She and my father were spending most of their time apart, and she was feeling bad, and behaving badly.

I didn't know she was feeling bad, but I knew my mother was different. By late 1955, my brother and I stayed in Beverly Hills most of the time, while our parents worked in New York, visiting us (separately) a couple of weekends a month. Since they had always had separate bedrooms, their separate visits didn't send off any alarms in me, and neither did their separate New York apartments. I just went on assuming that whatever they did was normal and acceptable. But there was something about my mother. She would call frequently, sounding busy and distracted, with a forced, mean-spirited cheerfulness.

"I was watching Ed Sullivan the other night," she said to me on one such call. "He had Elvis Presley on and he actually called him 'Pelvis Eserly.'" She laughed.

"Who?" I said.

"Elvis Presley—you know, the one with the sexy pelvis. That's the point."

"Elvis Who?"

"You mean you really don't know who Elvis Presley is? Don't you watch TV? Don't you know anything? What's the matter with you?" What was the matter with me, indeed.

Each time I saw my mother I noticed harder edges and louder laughter. My father didn't seem to be changing at all. I saw him less, but we still had fun together and he had the same energy and the same temper. In hindsight I can see that he was taking off personally and professionally, leaving my mother in a defensive position in the dust. He wasn't concerned about her health, made few allowances for her pain, and was increasingly irritated with her behavior. He wanted her there, with him, supporting him. He wanted her skills to cast the show, to raise the money, to bounce creative ideas off of. He was working on the show of his life, and he had no time for the time she squandered. His short fuse and demanding high standards only made my mother later, louder, less and less dependable. Not that she was a completely innocent victim. She had options, and she chose poorly, picking a role for herself that became as unattractive as it was unsuccessful. She almost seemed to be in competition with him.

It was at this point that my mother sent Jo Sullivan to sing for my father. Her judgment in casting the show had been excellent. Having found almost all of the principals, she outdid and undid herself when it came to Rosabella. Much later, she said, "When I heard Jo sing, I recognized a quality that I was sure Frank would love. I thought I understood exactly what he wanted. And, oh boy, was I right."

Jo Sullivan was from Mound City, Illinois (population 2,500), on the banks of the Mississippi, where Illinois, Kentucky, and Missouri all come together. When she was very young, Jo wanted to become an air hostess, the most glamorous job she could imagine. But by the time she was thirteen, her mother had convinced her that what she really wanted was to be an opera singer.

After two years of lessons with a local teacher, Jo moved on to Mrs. Frederick Nussbaum in St. Louis. Once a week she would get up before dawn, ride the train for four hours, take a singing lesson and a piano lesson, then get back on the train. Later she spent a year of high school in St. Louis, boarding with an aunt and intensifying her studies. During this time she entered and won the St. Louis Symphony contest. The prize, which she shared with another girl, was to give a concert with the orchestra.

After high school she returned once more to St. Louis, her aunt's house, and her musical studies. But the next year her aunt moved away, and Jo came to New York to try for a Juilliard scholarship. Her piano playing wasn't skillful enough to win her a scholarship, but she managed to find a singing teacher named Brown whose wife happened to be president of Lord and Taylor. Jo worked as a file clerk at the department store, studied theory and composition at Columbia University, and took singing lessons from Mr. Brown.

Some two years later, she got on the "Arthur Godfrey Talent Scouts" radio show:

> I didn't win, because it was fixed. Two harmonica players called The Polka Dots beat me. Sometimes the Godfrey people would get you jobs, and they got me a job singing at the Sawdust Trail, a saloon on West 44th Street. There were lots of sailors, and the bartender would tell them to behave and all that. Three of us were singing there. One of the others was Teresa Brewer, and she didn't do too badly herself.[5]

Jo's first job on Broadway was in the chorus of *Oklahoma!* Following another couple of chorus jobs, she created a nightclub act for herself and traveled around the country, teaming up with various performers—comedians, magicians, Shandra Kali and his oriental dancers, George Gobel.

In 1950 she got a part in Benjamin Britten's *Let's Make an Opera,* an eccentric two-part theater piece. The first act is a play about a group of people who decide to write an opera and the problems they have with it. The second act is the opera itself, in which the audience participates. When *Let's Make an Opera* opened, Howard Barnes wrote, "Let's not." The show ran for five days. Marc Blitzstein had directed, and when his English translation of Kurt Weill's *Threepenny Opera* came to the Theatre de Lys in Greenwich Village, Jo was in a good position to audition for the show. She won the role of Polly Peachum in this celebrated first American production, starring Lotte Lenya as Jenny, Scott Merrill as MacHeath, Charlotte Rae as Mrs. Peachum, and Beatrice Arthur as Lucy Brown.

> We opened in the spring [Jo recalled], got bad reviews, and closed in a month. Brooks Atkinson was the only critic who liked it, and at the bottom of every review he published after that, he'd write, "Bring back *Threepenny Opera.*" So we opened again the next year, with exactly the same show and exactly the same cast. The only difference was that I had one more song. Now that didn't make the show, believe me. But suddenly the show got great reviews and it ran for five years. I can never figure these things out.[6]

Jo was working in *Threepenny* when auditions for *The Most Happy Fella* began. When my mother sent her to audition for my father, he was so impressed with the loudness of her singing that he sprang to his feet and, laughing, closed all the windows. Then he went downtown to see her in *Threepenny,* which he hated, not liking Kurt Weill's style. Jo, he liked. He had her audition again several times (testing her range with "Happy Birthday" in ascending keys) before he gave her the role.

My mother soon found herself in an excruciating position. As co-producer she was inextricably involved with the show, which she had a deep and proprietary love for. She had lived with it for five years. It was a part of her, and she could not, would not, abandon it. But day by day, as she watched *The Most Happy Fella* blossom into life, she also watched the blossoming of my father's love affair with Jo.

She would walk into a restaurant and they would be there at a table for two. She would try to reach him about a problem or a decision and he would be "unavailable." Everybody could see what was happening, and everybody was talking about it. But not with a whole lot of sympathy. After all, they said to each other, Lynn was almost asking for it, the way she acted, the way she drank.

I'm looking at some old pictures of my mother. Here she is at eight—a pretty little girl, seated on a pony. She has ear-length blond hair, topped by a beret. Soft hazel eyes with a dreamy expression. A full mouth and a full face.

Now she's a teenager, standing on a beach in a one-piece black bathing suit. Her hair is to her shoulders, parted on the side, hanging in her face a little. She is lovely in this picture—long and lanky, full of promise. She stands there on the beach, swimming cap in hand, looking just a little impatient with the photographer, as if she's itching to be off into the water or flirting with the boys but willing to be nice and pose for a couple of minutes.

A little later, probably around the time she met my father, she's standing in front of a house, dressed in a coat with a fur collar that she is clearly very proud of. Her hair is ear-length again, curled now, and her eyes are still soft and dreamy. She's going to New York to seek her fortune, and the world is hers.

Later still—in the 1940s, around the time I was born—it's shoulder-length hair. Shoulder pads. A big smile, and one hand held over her stomach. Is she pregnant?

It's *1948*. She and my father are at the piano, performing "Baby, It's Cold Outside" for a series of promotional photographs. He's looking at her—his eyes supplicating, twinkling—

while she coyly looks away. Next, they look at each other mischievously. Then they touch noses in loving conspiracy, singing the final phrase. Her hair is very short and very blond and very curly, and she wears more makeup now.

And *1956*. She is in the process of divorce. Her hair is short and curly on top with the rest pulled back taut against her head. She is wearing her Broadway producer's gray tweed suit and the severe black-framed eyeglasses she has come to consider her trademark. The eyes behind them are not dreamy. This woman means business.

But the photograph only shows her veneer, not the pain behind it. For a long time I believed that veneer, believed my mother was one strong cookie—a hard drinking, tough talking, independent woman. When, one day during that time, I discovered her crying and asked her what was wrong, she said, "I'm only human." I was terrified, sure that she was telling me she had a fatal disease and was dying. I couldn't imagine that she was hurting emotionally enough to cry.

At forty, my mother had lost her man, her lifestyle, and her status. She hadn't seen it coming and so she took no steps to stop it. She didn't see, as even I can see from this distance and with indirect evidence, that before my father ever met Jo Sullivan he had grown intolerant of what my mother was becoming. She must have felt so safe in her role, so secure in her position, so sure that she was the only woman my father could ever love, that she let herself lurch down that vodka trail without a thought for the consequences.

My father was far too self-absorbed, far too busy with his flourishing career, to help my mother overcome difficulties that she herself didn't recognize. By the time *The Most Happy Fella* opened, he had had enough. He was more than ready for a new life, and he left.

She was only forty. I can't get over that. Forty seems so young to me now. I met my second husband when I was thirty-seven. Surely she could have met someone else, begun a new life. She did meet an occasional man, and she even had a boy-

My mother.

friend for a while after the divorce. But no one ever really stole her heart. It had been claimed twenty years before and was no longer available.

She always used to say that my father fired her. A clever way of putting it and with a kernel of truth, considering how long and loyally she worked for him. But her unemployment broke her heart, and no matter what clever things she would say about it, she never recovered.

But the show must go on. Once Robert Weede and Jo Sullivan were signed, there were still three additional major roles to fill. In the role of Tony's jealous sister Marie my mother cast Mona Paulee, a brilliant Metropolitan Opera mezzo-soprano. Originally Marie had a lot to sing, but much of her music was cut on the road—one of the many sacrifices made in the general pruning the show so clearly needed. As originally conceived, Marie was a relatively sympathetic character: you could empathize with her jealousy because she so movingly conveyed her deep caring love for Tony. With most of her loving, moving songs cut, she became simply a heavy—a selfish, short-sighted, frustrated old maid. But the show was shorter.

Susan Johnson played Cleo. On the day she auditioned, she had a terrible cold:

> I heard they were looking for a cross between Shirley Booth, Patsy Kelly, and Eve Arden. I went to sing and told the accompanist to skip the verse. This little man ran up, "What verse—what verse?" I said, "Someone to Watch over Me." He said, "Sing the verse." I sang it and then I sang "I've Got the World on a String." I could hardly talk in between—I coughed in between. I had to sing the verse to the second song too. And then he had me sing scales. I went directly from the audition to the drugstore for cough medicine. Frank followed me in, grabbed my hand, and took me to his office to teach me some music from the show. He told me later that I impressed him because I didn't apologize for my cold. I just sang over it.[7]

Susan has a strong mezzo voice and a stage personality not unlike a blend of Shirley Booth, Patsy Kelly, and Eve Arden.

Shorty Long, a country-western singer who led a group called Shorty Long's Santa Fe Rangers, had met my father back in 1949, when Frank Music published a song he recorded. He also made records of "Have I Stayed Away Too Long" and "Rodger Young." My father remembered his voice very well and called him to audition for the role of Herman, which fit him like a glove.

Morley Meredith, a Metropolitan Opera baritone, was originally cast as Joe. His big voice was magnificent, but he just wasn't right for the part dramatically. As my mother put it,

> His voice was pure gold, no rough edges. But he was too neat. His bottom didn't belong in blue jeans. There was no way to make his hair stay ruffled up—it always fell back into place. His open shirts buttoned themselves back up. He was just not believable as a macho itinerant farm worker.[8]

On the road in Boston he was replaced by Art Lund, who had been a vocalist in the Benny Goodman band and had sung for my mother at the auditions.

> He had been a jazz singer and certainly his range did not approach Meredith's. But I remember being astonished when he stepped out on a bare cold stage without benefit of microphone and belted out some extraordinarily strong, beautiful tones in a couple of ballads. There was something so gutsy and so masculine about Art's singing that it stayed in my mind. So I sent for him in Boston. Overnight, our rehearsal pianists taught him "Joey," and he auditioned it and just absolutely slayed everybody. He stepped into the part two nights later.[9]

Lee Cass filled the minor role of the Postman (and also the Cashier). When he auditioned, my father had him sing "The Dodger Song" from Aaron Copland's *Old American Songs (Newly Arranged)* (1950):

> Yes—the candidate's a dodger
> Yes a well-known dodger
> Yes the candidate's a dodger
> Yes and I'm a dodger too.

* * *

Lee had to sing the song first as a thirty-year-old, then a forty-year-old, and so on until my father allowed him to retire at seventy-five.

Once the principals were cast, it became apparent that there was far too much music to learn in the four to five weeks of rehearsal time Equity rules allowed. The cast agreed to bend the rules and learn the whole show before the first rehearsal so they could use those weeks to develop the direction and staging. Each performer learned only his or her own material; no one heard the whole score put together except Herb Greene, the musical director, and his assistant, Abba Bogin, who had been copying and splicing little bits of tape for weeks. The whole cast, including the chorus, convened on the first day of formal rehearsals to "sing down" the show at the Schumer Warehouse on West 53rd Street. Everyone was excited to be putting the show together.

> We all sat there [Abba recalled] and the music just rolled over us. There were tears in our eyes. By lunchtime everybody knew we were walking into something very special. This was not just another show. What we didn't know was that down the block there was a show that had done the same thing a couple of weeks before called *My Fair Lady.*[10]

My Fair Lady did steal some thunder from *The Most Happy Fella,* opening a few weeks earlier to unqualified raves, winning the Tony, and running for over six years. Some people wonder if *The Most Happy Fella* would have run longer than its 676 performances had it opened first.

Abba Bogin, who met my father when he was recruited by Herb Greene for *The Most Happy Fella,* worked on three of the last four Frank Loesser shows, in capacities ranging from musical secretary to musical director. Over the years he taught my father a great deal about how to achieve the musical effects he wanted.

> Frank had a very slow, labored way of writing. Self-taught. Very often his spelling was wrong—for instance, he'd write F-sharp when he should have written G-flat, or he'd tie two quarter-notes together when he could have written a half-note. By the time he'd put a piece of music in front of me it

> usually made sense, except for that kind of thing. And I'd play it and he might say, "Wait! What are you playing there? Is that A-flat in the bass? Naw, I don't want A-flat. Try D-flat. That's the sound I want."
>
> Frank would be at every orchestra rehearsal, whether in the pit, in a hotel room, or in a rehearsal hall. He'd sit and listen, then stop the music and say, "Wait a minute—I don't like that. Play that for me again." And he'd turn to the orchestrator or the conductor and say, "That's on the back beat, and I want it on the downbeat," or whatever, and the changes would be made until it came in the way he wanted it. It got changed and changed again, a fifth and a ninth and a twelfth time, if necessary.[11]

My father did not do his own orchestrations. Undoubtedly he could have learned how, but almost no Broadway composer does—there just isn't enough time when you're putting on a show. As Abba points out,

> The pressures are so great—there's so much to do in so little time. Somebody comes up with a new idea on a Monday. They think about it on Tuesday. They freeze what they want with a piano rehearsal on Wednesday, and they'd like to get it in the show by Friday. This means that while the new material is being set with the cast in the afternoons, the orchestrator has to work it out. Meanwhile the composer is writing something else. He has no time to orchestrate.

My father would give the conductor a melody line and perhaps some incomplete counterlines. The conductor would work out a piano arrangement, which my father would edit verbally. Then it was orchestrated. And at that point, continues Abba,

> what became important was the color. For instance, a flute, a violin, and an oboe can all play the same thing, each with its own distinctive sound. As the orchestrator proceeds he comes up with more ideas and he writes them in. Because you can always thin the score. But if you underwrite and it's too thin, you've got to stop, think of something, put it in under pressure. If you have a counterline that sits in a certain range and could be played by the cellos, the bassoon, or the trombone, write it on all three lines. When you realize in the first rehearsal that it's going to be too loud, you can say, well,

> I really like the trombone. Let me take the cello and the bassoon out. Then you might say, nah, I don't like that. I'd rather have a silkier sound. You tell the trombone not to play and the cellos to restore what they just took out. Eventually you get the sound you want.[12]

Every musical assistant who worked for Frank Loesser was required to sign an agreement specifying that—for the fee of one dollar—anything they wrote, fixed, or changed became Frank Loesser's (or his heirs' or assignees') property. He had heard a story about some songwriter way back in the early part of the century who had an assistant write a small passage in a song for him. Years later, after both the songwriter and his assistant were long dead, the family of the assistant sued the family of the songwriter, wasting much time and money in litigation. And so my father had these one-dollar agreements and one-dollar checks drawn up by his equally crafty lawyer, Harold Orenstein, who did not rest until each and every check had cleared. You never know.

Jo Mielziner was chosen once again to design the sets and lighting; Motley was hired to design the costumes; but no director was sought until the show was cast, even though directors usually like to have a hand in the casting. Kermit Bloomgarden asked Lillian Hellman to suggest someone, and she recommended Joseph Anthony. Although Anthony had been a dancer—indeed, he had been Agnes DeMille's dancing partner for two years—he had no experience directing musical theater. But when Lynn and Frank and Kermit approached him, he was willing. And I'm sure he had no idea at the time of what he was getting himself into:

> Well, you have to know that Frank was an egomaniac [he said ten years later]. It's part of his talent, probably. He saw the show so clearly, heard it so absolutely, had it so powerfully in mind that it was very hard for him to see it otherwise. He talked generously about the contributions of others but, in fact, one of the reasons he didn't like to work with too powerful pros, names, stars, was because he couldn't coach them. They'd say, "Listen, I have my own way." He'd rather have somebody he could take over to his house and coach . . . He

> worked on all these people, coaching them like mad, and yes, his imprint was powerfully on every scene, every song, every performer . . .
>
> He just loved to come in and entertain the cast for a half-hour. He had the talent and was a highly entertaining man, but it invariably wasted time. I think he would have fired me if Kermit had permitted it. Because I finally said the cast was beginning to get confused between what Frank was doing with them privately, behind my back, and what I was trying to accomplish with the show. And I think at that point he would have happily gotten rid of me and gotten somebody he could have manipulated with greater ease . . .[13]

Susan Johnson told me that once while Anthony was working with her, my father walked up on the stage, interrupted, and said "something offensive":

> I just left the stage. You simply don't walk up there when the director is working. I got a dozen roses the next day and a card that said, "I apologize profusely for my actions yesterday, and I realize that you're entitled to three 'Go fuck yourselves.' But from the look you gave me as you left the stage, you've already used one of them."[14]

Dania Krupska, who was hired at the last minute to choreograph, got along very well with both my parents, and, in fact, was one of the few people who remained friends with both of them after the divorce. My father actually felt she should be directing the show and he continued to undermine Anthony's work by having private conferences with her, running staging ideas by her, and treating her as if she actually were the director (she did direct a later City Center revival at his behest). During rehearsals he sent her a steady stream of clever notes and poems. Most of them were jibes at Joe Anthony, but one of them, at least, was simply an expression of his affection for Dania:

Waltz

There's nothing I've seen
On Balanchine
That does such good things for my soul
There's no special dimple or mole

On Loring or Kidd or Cole
There's nothing so warm
In Robbins' form
That brings tender thoughts to my mind
Like my choreographer's
Very adorable
Tear-drop
Behind.

It was during this show that my father started referring to himself as God. He would send notes to people signed "God," post notices from "God," even wore a sweatshirt with "God" emblazoned on it. His "Loud Is Good" sign was prominently displayed at rehearsals, and he dominated the production with a mixture of humor, fury, and generally outrageous behavior. The "God" business continued beyond the show. It shows up in memos, notes, and letters throughout the rest of his life. I never thought they were funny, except for this one (not sent):

> Dear Mr. Berlin,
> Thank you for your request. The fact that *you* love it does appeal to me. But calling on me to bless the whole place is stretching things a little. This blessing would have to include Philadelphia, Rock Hudson, and some other items I am too scrupulous to include. Incidentally, the ocean is never white with foam, except around Atlantic City at high tide. But "foam" is indeed a good rhyme for "home," and I congratulate you on your craftmanship. But please, no commercial endorsements.—God.

He was stretched taut—in the midst of a divorce, an affair, and the most ambitious show of his life. And his vision of the show prevailed, and his colleagues did forgive him his behavior. Most of them—amazingly enough—found him wonderful to work with.

When the show went into rehearsal in January 1956, it was almost four hours long, with ninety percent of the dialogue sung. Much of the recitative was soon cut in favor of straight dialogue, which takes less time. The first music to go was most of Marie's part, followed by much of Rosabella's early recitative and a couple of songs—including "House and Garden," a loss still mourned by both Jo and Abba.

So home I go to my cheap little furnished room
With my copy of *House and Garden.* House and garden—
Now those are two very faraway, safe and sound, ladylike words.
You know, mine's American colonial,
With a brass-plated knocker
And a chintz-covered rocker,
And there's a view of a pretty green maple tree busy with birds.
And there I sit in the middle of it all,
A-rocking in the rocker,
Crocheting on a shawl,
And the ladies and gentlemen who come to call
Say "please," and "I beg your pardon."
Ah but it's just in my dear old, dog-eared, year-old
Copy of *House and Garden.*

After five weeks of rehearsal in New York, the show went on the road, first to Boston, then Philadelphia. In Boston they opened to raves, and the next morning there was a long line at the box office. There was also a long low line of clouds in the sky, and by noon the first of five consecutive blizzards had begun. The snow was so frequent and so deep during their Boston run that most of the time they played to audiences of ten or twenty people.

One of "God's" least funny, most offensive proclamations was inspired by the weather:

> There is a puerile tale circulating among earth children that snow is my dandruff or some such unappetizing allusion.
>
> Snow is snow.
>
> Christ knows where it comes from: Boston. And he's my kid, and don't know from shit.
>
> There will be no further nonsense about rain being angels' tears. The few angels here are busy laughing at Mary Martin in that harness.

In Philadelphia the weather was better, the reviews just as favorable, and the houses full. My father was still editing right up to the New York opening on May 3, 1956, at the Imperial

Jo during rehearsals for *The Most Happy Fella*.

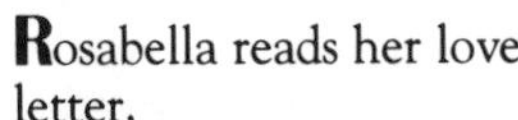

Rosabella reads her love letter.

Theatre with its modified pit. The show now ran just under three hours. Originally the Playbill did not list individual songs, because it was so difficult to separate one musical number from another.

The music is richly—almost wildly—varied. Tony's role is the most operatic, with the most recitative. But he rhymes, too. One of his songs, "Rosabella," describes his feelings as he decides to send Rosabella Joe's "pitch":

She t'ink maybe omma young man
Wit' a handsome-a kinda face.
'At's-a why omma gotta do what omma do.
She t'ink maybe omma young man
Wit' a handsome-a kinda face.
An' me, I don't wanna show her what's true.
Oh my beautiful Rosabella
Sweet like a flower,
Rosabella, look! My heart he's in you power.
Rosabella, young like a baby,
Rosabella, say some day you love me, maybe.

Tony and Rosabella's duets are intense, repetitive, Verdiesque—except for the charming "Happy to Make Your Acquaintance":

Rosabella: Happy to make your acquaintance.
Tony: 'Appy to make you acquainatance.
Rosabella: Thank you so much, I feel fine.
Tony: T'ank you so much, omma feel fine.
Rosabella: Happy to make your acquaintance.
Tony: Acquainatance.
Rosabella: And let me say the pleasure—
Tony: Da pleasure—
Rosabella: Is mine.
Tony: Da pleasure's-a mine.
Rosabella: How do you do? Pleased to know you.
Tony: 'Ow do you do? Pleased to know you.
Rosabella: And though my English is poor—
Tony: My English is-a goddamn poor!
Both: Happy to make your acquaintance.
Rosabella: Now won't you please say, likewise.
Tony: Look-a-wise.

Rosabella: No, Likewise.
Tony: Like-a-ways.
Rosabella: No. Likewise.
Tony: Oh, Like-a-wise.
Both: I'm sure.

Rosabella has the second largest singing part, with several aria-like solos. For instance, "Somebody, Somewhere":

Somebody, somewhere wants me and needs me,
That's very wonderful to know.
Somebody lonely wants me to care,
Wants me of all people to notice him there.
Well, I want to be wanted,
Need to be needed,
And I'll admit I'm all aglow,
'Cause somebody, somewhere wants me and needs me,
Wants lonely me to smile and say hello.
Somebody, somewhere wants me and needs me
And that's very wonderful to know.

Joey sings a couple of straight-out ballads, of which "Joey" is the best known:

Like a perfumed woman,
The wind blows in the bunk-house—
Like a perfumed woman,
Smellin' of where she's been.
Smellin' of Oregon cherries
Or maybe Texas avocado
Or maybe Arizona sugar beet.
The wind blows in
And she sings to me,
'Cause I'm one of her ramblin' kin.
She sings—
Joey, Joey Joey,
Joey, Joey, Joe
You've been too long in one place,
And it's time to go, time to go!

Cleo and Herman, together and separately, sing the comedy numbers and the two songs aimed at a larger popular audience,

"Big D" and "Standing on the Corner." Cleo's leitmotif is "Ooh My Feet," originally written for the cop in *Guys and Dolls* but saved in the trunk for a better opportunity:

> Ooh my feet! My poor, poor feet!
> Betcha your life a waitress earns her pay.
> I've been on my feet, my poor, poor feet
> All day long today.
>
> Ooh my toes! My poor, poor toes!
> How can I give the service with a smile
> When I'm on my toes, my poor, poor toes
> Mile after mile after mile after mile after mile.
>
> This little piggy's only broken,
> This little piggy's on the bum.
> This little piggy's in the middle,
> Consequently, absolutely numb.
> This little piggy feels the weight of the plate
> Though the freight's just an order of melba toast,
> And this little piggy is the littlest little piggy,
> But the big son-of-a-bitch hurts the most!
>
> Ooh my feet, my poor, poor feet!
> Betcha your life a waitress earns her pay.
> I've been on my feet, my poor, poor feet
> All day long today,
> Doing my blue plate special ballet!

The three chefs sing two comic opera trios—caricatures, really—which were written to show off Arthur Rubin's incredibly high sustained tenor notes. Artie, who was in the chorus of *Silk Stockings* when he auditioned for *The Most Happy Fella,* had gone to my father's office and sung "Softly, As in a Morning Sunrise," which ends on a high B-natural. My father hired him on the spot and proceeded to invent the trio and write "Abbondanza" around him. Always a businessman as well as a singer, Artie was known to drive a hard bargain. (He became executive vice president of the Nederlander Organization, one of the two giant theater management companies in New York.) He met his match in Frank Loesser.

"The Ed Sullivan Show" was in its heyday at the time,

and my father had booked what had become known as the Abbondanza Trio to sing their other big number, "Bien Venuto," on Sullivan's show. ("Abbondanza" itself was never performed outside of the show—one of my father's dictums.) He booked the act himself, agreed that the trio would be paid a total of $900, called Artie and said, "I've just booked the trio on Ed Sullivan. You're each getting three hundred dollars." To which Artie replied, "Why did you book me for three hundred? You know I make more money now than the other two guys. I want six." My father refused to renegotiate the deal. Artie refused to perform. Stalemate.

Two weeks went by, and the TV date was imminent. My father approached Artie once more, demanding that he perform for $300. Artie again refused. Eventually my father gave in and paid him the extra $300 out of his own pocket. The trio performed "Bien Venuto," all went well, and the issue appeared closed. A couple of months later my father called Artie and said, "I'm going to make the Abbondanza Trio formal. I'm going to hire you and the other two guys; we'll sign an exclusive contract."

"Sounds terrific," Artie said. Contracts were drawn up and signed, and the trio waited for its gigs. And waited. After months had passed, Artie finally said, "Frank, what happened to the Abbondanza Trio?"

"Well, you signed, didn't you?"

"Yeah, but when are we going to work?"

"Never. That's why I signed you to a contract. Nobody can ever use the trio but me. And I'm not planning to use it."[15]

At the New York opening, the critics—most of them—were enthusiastic. John Chapman *(Daily News)*: "A superb musical show. . . As distinguished as it is delightful. . . Loesser's musical inventiveness seems without limit." Robert Coleman *(Daily Mirror)*: "A work that will be revived again and again, for it is a masterpiece of our era . . . one of the most gorgeous scores we have ever heard on the stage." John McClain *(Journal American)*: "A great tribute to the talents of Frank Loesser . . . a brilliant and ambitious solo effort." Richard Watts *(Post)*: "An expressive score, a sound dramatic book, excellent singing and acting, and a forthright style."

Some of them had reservations. Walter Kerr *(Herald Tribune)*: "[Loesser] has made the most of his contrasting veins—the free emotional outpourings that opera allows, the tempo and blare that belong to musical comedy—all night long . . . *The Most Happy Fella* is something to be seen. I could wish that it were something to be more deeply felt; an excess of very rich seasoning has obscured the simple, central flavor of a touching tale." Brooks Atkinson *(New York Times)*: "[Loesser's] music drama is not as single-minded in its devotion to a theme as . . . *Carousel.* Nor has it the artistic integrity of *Porgy and Bess.* But it goes so much deeper into the souls of its leading characters than most Broadway shows and it has such an abundant and virtuoso score that it has to be taken on the level of theatre art."

Some were turned off. Wolcott Gibbs *(The New Yorker)*: "It is possible, unfortunately, to appreciate all or most of the merits of a work of art without deriving much entertainment from it . . . the evening somehow lacked any particular magic for me. . . Altogether, it is an admirable production. I wish I could report that I enjoyed it more." Henry Hewes *(Saturday Review)*: "When a musical-comedy composer turns to opera he is apt to seem a child on a man's errand. So it is with Frank Loesser, whose *The Most Happy Fella* is a dull, poorly blended mixture of musical trifles." Leonard Hoffman *(Hollywood Reporter)*: "One slice might have been enjoyable, but having eaten the whole cake, with its gaudy mélange of dramatic and musical dressing, only resulted for me in a case of severe indigestion . . . there is far too much of everything except the main ingredient which got lost in this rococo recipe, namely, the story."

There was one review that had special significance for my father. His brother Arthur wrote in *The Cleveland Press:*

> I have just seen my brother Frank Loesser's new show, *The Most Happy Fella,* in New York. It was very impressive and the music is the great focus of attraction. It is understandable

that some of the reviewers who mixed reservation with their approval were straight drama fans who did not care too ardently for music. I am glad to say the public does not agree with them.

The music is practically continuous; there is very little spoken dialogue. The singing is of a high order of merit, beginning with opera star Robert Weede.

In fact, hardly any Broadway musical yet has had such a fine array of vocal skill. The three men who do the rousing "Abbondanza" trio fill the theater with wonderful, powerful, ringing tones. Moreover, there is a large orchestra which produces many varied effects of tone color. It is led by Herbert Greene, an excellent musician who knows the score by heart.

Naturally the show is full of the pop tunes and patter songs at which Frank has been so successful: the wolf-pack quartet, "Standing on the Corner Watching All the Girls"; the English and etiquette lesson, "Happy to Make Your Acquaintance"; the noisy dance extravaganza, "Big D." These are the "hits," that is to say the ones with which you will be brainwashed if you persist in leaving your radio faucet open.

But the music offers other interesting dramatic points. In the first act, when the waitress expands about her pained feet, the slightly dissonant, obstinate orchestral bass figure gives a good picture of her monotonous, achy job. In Act II the hero, "Tony," who has been injured, walks with a cane for the first time after leaving his wheelchair, and the music goes into a 5/4 rhythm to accompany his limping. Later on, when he walks, silent with jealosy and rage, the music expresses his thoughts in reminiscent fragments of past melodies. . . .

I'll admit it's a special kind of show that may be important in the emerging development of the American musical theater. Anyway, you don't really know or care whether a show is "good." All you care is whether it is successful.

Well, I can encourage you. The advance sale for*The Most Happy Fella* is reported as on the order of $400,000, and the weekly take is something like 50 G's.[16]

Conspicuously absent here is any aesthetic judgment on the music itself. Much is made of the talented interpreters of the music, and it is noted that the music is almost continuous and serves to illuminate the feelings of the characters. But does the reviewer like it? Does he think it is good? He implies, really, that he doesn't, but why should Little Frankie care? All he wants is to make lots of money from it.

What could my father have thought about this review? Since he never once spoke harshly of Arthur, I can never know, but I imagine that it hurt deeply. There goes Little Frankie making lots and lots of money, still writing the kind of garbage that washes over us daily. Certainly don't credit Little Frankie with a musical intellect, or a serious musical thought. Just point out that he continues to appeal to the grungy masses and thus wins for himself yet another commercial (read: low-class) success.

Julia, although she didn't put it in writing, had no more respect for her son's musical ability than Arthur did, and *The Most Happy Fella* did not change her mind. To her he remained a crass anomaly in an otherwise intellectual family. He was an embarrassment, with his expensive clothes, his town house, his chauffeured limosine. A show-off, a prankster. He was never able to elevate her opinion of him, try as he might.

At the same time, he couldn't resist behaving exactly the way she expected him to behave. Mama needs a TV? Okay—here, Mama, the biggest console in the store. Let's take Mama out to dinner—we'll go to the Oak Room and I'll wear my Let's Go-Mets illuminated bow tie. Mama could use a new winter coat—call the furrier.

My cousin Ted Drachman remembers a scene at Nana's apartment in the late fifties. My father was on the phone with a business associate, obviously frustrated about something.

"What's the matter?" she asked.

"I need some money."

"Well, how much do you need, Frank?" she asked, as though she could supply it.

He looked at her for a slow beat and said, "Half a million dollars." Ted recalls that she reacted "with a certain amount of slightly disapproving astonishment."

She detested his excesses, and he was excessive and flamboyant and "Broadway" and "Jewish" in great part because all of it rankled her. But *The Most Happy Fella* was a serious work, intended to be taken as such. She saw it as another gaudy bauble.

There are people who find *The Most Happy Fella* pretentious, its reach exceeding its grasp. William Schuman felt that *Guys and Dolls* is a much better piece of writing—more cohesive, more consistent, its genius lying in its Broadway style and its Broadway limits. I can see what he meant, but I cannot be objective about *The Most Happy Fella.* I know that it was my father's most earnest creative effort, the one that means the most to him. Whether it is completely successful as a musical work, whether it is in fact pretentious, whether it will be studied or forgotten in years to come are all questions best argued by other, more knowledgeable people.

For me, it is part of my own personal history. During the creation and the run of *The Most Happy Fella,* life as we all knew it changed irrevocably. My brother and I were torn from our comfortable, provincial, indulged life in Beverly Hills and moved to New York. New schools, a new, ultra-urban environment, and new relationships with our separated parents—whom, we discovered, we had hardly known. We didn't do well.

9

Divorce

My father told me about the divorce. That year my parents, who were working furiously on *The Most Happy Fella* in New York, took turns coming home for weekends.

"Tomorrow let's go to Griffith Park," he said. "We'll take a walk, have a talk."

"Goody! Can I bring Laurie?" or Debbie, or Gail.

"No, we can't bring anyone else. I want to talk to you about something."

Only a few days before, my friend Laurie had said to me, "We have to be extra nice to Phyllis. Her parents are getting divorced." Laurie and I felt great eleven-year-old pity for Phyllis. Having your parents get divorced was as shameful as Susan Ackerman getting left behind in the fifth grade. We felt sorry for Phyllis, and we felt superior and condescending toward her. Divorce was something that automatically put you in a lower class of people.

Looking back, it surprises me that this was so. Surely many many people in the L.A. show business community were divorced. I did have a few friends whose parents had split, but they weren't among my school chums, the kids I spent my day-to-day life with. Amazing but true, the great majority of my classmates had stable families.

So when my father reminded me that he and my mother

were living apart and told me they were probably going to get divorced, all I could think at first was how could I admit this shameful circumstance to Laurie and the rest. My status with my friends was going to change, and I was about to be the object of scathing pity. I might be ostracized. I was terrified.

"Of course we know you'll want to live with your mother," he said.

"What if I want to live with you?" I asked, suddenly brought back to the fundamentals, and taking a stab at some input of my own.

"That wouldn't work very well. I wouldn't be able to be around very much. We think you and Johnny will be much happier with your mother."

I hadn't spent much time with either of my parents. I had no idea what it would be like living with my mother, except that instead of seeing both of them on special occasions it would now be only my mother who would decorate a day with her appearance. I was trying to measure the damage, if any, this might cause my life at home (in contrast to the devastation at school) when he tossed off the bombshell.

"We're all going to be moving to New York next month."

Moving? Permanently? But what about our house? My friends? What about bike riding and badminton and roller-skating? Would we take Ida? How could I get on without her? Where would I go to school? Who would take care of the cats? This was beyond terror. This was looking into the void.

My mother was given the house in the divorce settlement, which she sold. We gave away the cats, we let our maid go, we packed our clothes and put the furniture in storage, and Johnny and I and Ida (thank God) moved to New York in the late spring of 1956, right after the opening of *The Most Happy Fella.* My father took a furnished sublet apartment on Fifth Avenue, and the rest of us moved in with "Auntie Gwyn" Steinbeck, also divorced, also the one who got the house, which she had held onto.

We lived with Gwyn for a couple of months, and Thom and Johnny Steinbeck and I spent many evenings in huddled, preteen, suggestive games ("I'm going to hypnotize you, now," says Thom. "You will be under my power, but you won't do anything you wouldn't really want to do if you were awake. Take your nightgown off."), while our mothers tied one on in the kitchen and Ida and my brother went wherever it was they lived in the big, dark brownstone on East 89th Street. Johnny Steinbeck became my closest friend and remained so for a long time. We shared the special loneliness of uprooted, confused children whose scattered and celebrated parents had their own, more complicated troubles.

My mother thought she was doing me a wonderful favor by enrolling me in a coed progressive school, where I spent the seventh grade in a fog, learning next to nothing and spending all my free time (which was a lot) necking. Coming from a very prissy all-girls school in California, I went wild in New York. Instantly boy crazy, I gave up the security of Ida's care for the romantic promise of eternal love. By the time I was thirteen I had gone through several boyfriends and acquired a reputation. My mother saw some of the light finally and put me into a private girls school in the eighth grade, where I was forced to study and reintroduced to a much needed structure, but it was too late for me to revert to a pre-boy state. I was hooked on them. They already provided excitement, and I knew that one of them, one day, would provide blissful security. Anyone whose focus in life was non-boy threatened my fragile world, and I became the angry young woman who was oh so much more sophisticated than her classmates.

At home, my relationship with Ida deteriorated—she was all Johnny's now—and I was forging a new bond with my mother, who was also going wild in New York. She acquired a very handsome, younger, hard-drinking, big spending (of her money) boyfriend. She was trying hard to be happy and be loved, sort of like me. And she began to confide in me, and tell me I was her best friend. For a while I ate it up, flattered and proud that my mother and I were so close. While my young brother could do nothing right, I could do nothing wrong. My mother fostered what we both thought of as my superior intellect and maturity, and she fostered my life with boys. She wanted to know *everything.* And I pretty much told her everything, for a while.

I had no cause for rebellion at home, but I was considered a rebel at school. I was an obnoxious, loud-mouthed little citizen of the world, spouting strong opinions without any real introspection but with great false confidence. I wore lots of makeup and swore with gusto. My mother thought I was perfect.

My father, when I saw him, seemed less sure of my behavior. It was different with him. His approval was much harder to come by, and I struggled for it. His personality was so dominant and raucous that my strident little know-it-all voice often went unheard at his house. When he did hear me, and when he disagreed with me, he would point out flaws in my argument, or suggest a better approach or solution to a problem, or give me a little lecture on the topic, laced with wit and carrying a sting.

I was stung easily. I saw my father in two lights only. He either approved or he disapproved. If he approved my whole life was validated; if he disapproved, I was reduced to a speck of dust. I am quite sure that he was unaware of his omnipotence in my world. He was simply trying to guide me the way any parent might, only he didn't have the time or interest or patience to walk me through the hard parts. He was so grand a presence and our time together so limited, I would savor his sentiments like riddles from an oracle.

I am sad to say that our relationship never fully transcended this state. The older I got the more I slowly grew and changed and understood, and the more we could share together. But always, inside, I worked for his approval. When I didn't get it, it was hard to see anything else. As a young teenager I was so attached to this view of him I hadn't any idea who he really was. I didn't care who he was. Had I recognized a human being in there, it would have diminished his great power. I loved that power. I loved my father—loved him madly—and I didn't know him for shit.

My father and Jo moved in together in 1957, renting an

apartment on the Upper East Side. Jo was everything my mother was not. Young, healthy, on time, not exactly soft-spoken, but compared to my mother, downright demure. She was even shorter than my father. Tiny, in fact.

I visited them often, and I had a mad crush on Jo. I thought she was the most sophisticated, most beautiful, most wonderful woman I had ever met. She taught me how to wax my legs. She took me to the theater and didn't embarrass me. She said cute, semi-Southern things, like "What a hoot!"

My mother was outwardly very accepting of Jo and of Jo and my father together. She used to say she had a "very Noël Coward relationship" with them. She never said anything against Jo to me. But once, in the fitting room at Best & Co., where we had made our fall pilgrimage for my winter wardrobe, she let me know she wasn't oblivious. I was trying on dresses.

"That one is just lovely on you, Susan."

"I hate it. I don't want it."

"What's the matter with it? It fits you perfectly."

"I just hate it. It's ugly."

"If Jo Sullivan had a dress like that, you'd love it," she finally snapped. I remember that I was ashamed, because it was true, although I hadn't thought about it in those terms, and I realized at the same time that my mother saw, and was hurt by, my adoration of Jo. I felt awful. I denied that Jo had any influence on me. We continued to fight about the dress, but I gave in.

My mother was striking out on her own as a producer. We had moved into a large duplex apartment on the Upper West Side, and she started to give parties again. For several years our apartment was buzzing with activity, as each project was discovered, developed, and tried out. Every one of them failed.

Her boyfriend started getting mean when he was drunk, and one night he tried to strangle her on the kitchen table. She said goodbye to him and to their joint theatrical ventures, and continued to search for a hit. Her parties were well attended those first few years, but slowly, surely, people backed off, recognizing a loser when they saw one, not wanting to risk the taint of association with her. People who had been my parents' friends—the Feuers, the Burrowses, the Bloomgardens, the Steinbecks—all gravitated to my father.

When I was fourteen and Johnny eight, my mother let Ida go. I think she actually believed she could take care of us herself. She had never felt much of a kinship with Ida, and now that our lives were changing so much, why not make one more alteration. Johnny and I came home from summer camp to find Ida gone. This was much more of a blow to my brother than to me. But for both of us it was as though a door had slammed shut, locking our childhood away forever. Ida returned to California, where she worked once more as a baby nurse, never staying in a job beyond six months so as not to become too attached. Johnny and I heard from her regularly, but we were soon too busy with our new and scary lives to write back very often. My mother, feeling guilty, kept in touch.

As it turned out, I was just old enough to manage, after a fashion, but Johnny was surely too young to get himself up and fed and off to school while our mother slept. Recently my brother and I tried to recall who did take care of him during those first few years after Ida's departure. We knew it wasn't me. We decided it must have been one of the live-in maids we had, one after another, although neither of us can remember clearly.

My brother did poorly at school (small wonder) and he had a series of tutors, including my father, who failed utterly to instill intellectual curiosity in his young and floundering son. Terribly impatient with him, scathingly critical, and unable to understand just what was going wrong between Johnny and the textbook, my father only frightened him and made things worse. "I remember how he glared at me," Johnny recalls. "Those furious eyes—that terrible stare."

Oh yes. I remember that look. That was the look that said, "Beware, you little speck of shit. I am omnipotent, and I disapprove of your entire existence." That was the look to avoid, to head off before it happened. The idea was to get a laugh, a hug, an endorsement.

When I was four or five I went to my father and asked, "Poppy, are you proud of me?"

"Of course I am," he said. "I'm very proud of you. As proud as proud can be."

"Poppy, what's proud?" I asked.

10

Greenwillow

In 1957 my father was working on a project with Garson Kanin, an original idea about two people who, never having met, imagine each other in elaborate and delicious daydreams while living their mundane lives until they actually come face to face one day and really fall in love. The project, variously called *The Purple People, The Dream People,* and plain old *Project Four,* never got off the ground. While he was still grappling with it, my father was approached by Robert Willey, a general manager and actor, about a rather different sort of property: a short novel by B. J. (Joy) Chute called *Greenwillow.* Willey wanted to make a musical out of it.

Greenwillow, a whimsical, near-fairytale of a novel, is the story of an imaginary village peopled by quaint-spoken characters in a faraway time. Evocative of the past (there are no machines at all, people wear cloaks and carry lanterns) but of no *particular* past, the village sits contentedly on the banks of the Meander river, whose source and destination lie somewhere in the outside world, a world that excites no interest in the denizens of Greenwillow.

With one significant exception. Amos Briggs, husband of Martha and father of six, is a wandering man and the son of a wandering man. Cursed with the call that took his father, he is destined to spend his life traveling the world, visiting his family only occasionally, "planting" a new child each time.

His oldest son, Gideon, has always known that he too will be called to wander. So he has vowed never to marry—never to have a wife and children to abandon—and thereby to end the curse.

In the village there is a church with two doors for its two ministers: Reverend Lapp, a tall, thin, dour man who spends his time meanly wrestling with the devil; and Reverend Birdsong, who simply appeared one day with a wicker suitcase, an umbrella full of hawthorn blossoms, and a heart full of good cheer. Lapp grudgingly accepted Birdsong as a colleague and now the two reverends conduct consecutive services every Sunday, each dispensing his distinct views on life, each involved in his own way in the doings of the villagers. And the villagers, who have suffered at length under the stern and bleak guidance of the Reverend Lapp, are delighted with the Reverend Birdsong.

Dorrie is a young woman who long ago fled an orphanage and was taken in and raised by the two cheerful old maids, Miss Emma and Miss Maidy. Dorrie bakes. And bakes. And bakes. Gooseberry tarts, ginger cakes, bilberry cakes, cherry pies, and citron buns pour out of her oven. She also cleans house like an angel, even dusting the firewood. She is just grown, just ready for love, and she is smitten with Gideon Briggs.

At the traditional Christmas "candlewalk"—where only those candles that stay lit as they are carried around the church represent wishes that come true—Dorrie wishes for the call not to come to Gideon. Her candle is blown out, but she loves Gideon so much that she swears she won't mind being the wife of a wandering man. The townspeople too are rooting for Gideon and Dorrie to marry, but Gideon is deaf to all pleas. He loves his home and he loves his village and he loves Dorrie, too. He hates the thought of wandering but is determined to end the curse of the wandering Briggses. He will never marry.

Meanwhile, the Briggs family has been loaned a cow by the village skinflint, Thomas Clegg, over whose soul the Reverend Lapp has been struggling with the devil, unsuccessfully, for many years. The cow is sickly and pregnant; the Briggses have agreed to care for her over the winter, give half her milk to Clegg, and return her and her calf come spring. An unfair arrangement perhaps, but the Briggses are good-hearted folks and don't complain. Then Gramma Briggs, the lusty, crusty matriarch of the family who sits in her rocker gumming turnips, visits her one-time suitor, Thomas Clegg, on what turns out to be his deathbed, to elicit the outright gift of the cow. When he dies without giving in, Gramma—the only witness—reports that Clegg had a last-minute change of heart. The news that old Thomas Clegg has repented of his sins, rejected the devil, and given up the cow makes Reverend Lapp almost as smug as Gramma.

Spring comes, fulfilling many promises. The cow calves in May, and in June Martha Briggs has her seventh child, the one Amos planted when he was last home for two nights and a day. The birth is a difficult one. The two reverends pray with the family in the yard while Dorrie and the midwife attend Martha. At this moment Gramma's deception is revealed ("Thomas Clegg died ornery, mean as pizen water"), and Reverend Lapp, aghast to learn that he has not beat the devil after all, kneels to pray with the rest at Reverend Birdsong's gentle urging. "He put his hands up together, making a church of them, and he leaned his head so that it touched the tips of his prayerful fingers. 'Dear Father,' he said with awful difficulty, 'dear Father, bless this house.'" Whereupon the cry of the newborn is heard, and Dorrie emerges from the house to say that all is well.

But now Gideon hears his call, as he knew he would. He wanders off through the meadow, into the woods, following the voice calling his name. To his surprise he is led back to the meadow—he is being called to his own land. "'I'm to stay,' he whispered. 'My call's come at last, and it's cried me home.'"

Home he stays and marries Dorrie. The day before the wedding, the Reverend Birdsong calls upon the newly softened Reverend Lapp, umbrella and wicker case in hand. Birdsong is leaving Greenwillow, his work accomplished, moving on to bring his saintliness to another place. But we know that Greenwillow will be safe and content with the Reverend Lapp.

Greenwillow is a charming little book, filled with magic and moral lessons. But it has no real drama, very little conflict, and no villain. (The mean Mr. Lapp sometimes comes close, but he is really more misguided than villainous). Despite these drawbacks to successful dramatization, Bob Willey was intent upon bringing *Greenwillow* to the stage. He felt strongly (and still feels) that the simple good feelings and gentle love embodied in the story should carry an audience easily into Greenwillow's timeless world. He knew this wouldn't be easy, but he had great faith. He also felt from the beginning that if anyone could bring the book to life on stage, it was Frank Loesser:

> For a long time I had been impressed with Frank's absolutely marvelous heart. He seemed to have more human feeling than any of the people I had known or whose work I had seen. And that was what *Greenwillow* required. Frank didn't know me from Adam, but I sent him the book cold. And the next thing I knew he wanted to meet with me and talk about it.[1]

My father agreed to write music, lyrics, and book to the delight of Joy Chute, who sent him the following letter:

> Dear Frank Loesser,
>
> I have been sitting here, with typewriter poised, trying to think of some way of expressing the great pleasure I feel in knowing *Greenwillow* is to have your very special gifts in its translation from book to stage.
>
> I have an awed appreciation of what is required to put a musical production on Broadway in terms of energy, imagination, talent, courage, wilfulness and possibly a touch of moon-madness, and I find myself extremely fortunate in being associated with you and Bob Willey.
>
> I hope you will have great satisfaction in the production in the most professional and profound sense of the satisfaction of the craftsman. In the words of a well-known songwriter, "More I cannot wish you."[2]

On the envelope, in orange pencil, my father wrote, "File affectionately."

My father's business interest now included a small producing company—Frank Productions, headed by Allen Whitehead—

which became co-producer so my father could oversee all aspects of the production. The contract, drawn up in the summer of 1957 among Robert Willey, Frank Productions, and Frank Loesser, stipulated that the songwriter/author had complete artistic control over "the Manager's selection of performing artists, stage directors, dance directors, conductors, and/or their substitutes." The number of pit musicians was also up to my father, although he agreed not to exceed thirty-six and, in fact, used the standard twenty-six. Naturally, the one-dollar agreements were in effect.

When my father started writing the show, he immediately encountered difficulties. The main problems lay in the descriptive nature of the novel, which didn't easily lend itself to dialogue, and the need for a good deal of preliminary exposition that was difficult to make lively. There was also the whimsical, imaginary character of the story and setting, not to mention the whimsical, imaginary characters themselves. Everything about the novel was wistful, and nothing about it was dramatic.

The earliest draft I have seen was written in December 1957. It consists of a sheaf of handwritten dialogue on yellow legal pad paper, with a boldly printed cover note to my father's secretary clipped to the front: "MARGIE—MAY GOD HAVE MERCY ON YOU! (I DON'T)—F." A second draft is dated May 20, 1958. Both drafts are of an extended first scene. Birdsong opens the show by talking with the birds, and Gideon ends the scene by discovering his father has left home again and vowing his celibacy. I don't know if my father went further than this on his own, but I do know that by the summer of 1958 he was having so much trouble with the book that he began to solicit help.

In August he sent the novel to Paul Osborn, whose plays include *On Borrowed Time* and *The World of Suzie Wong*, and whose movie scripts range from *The Yearling* through *East of Eden* to *South Pacific*. Osborn replied that it wasn't for him. "It's not one of those where it's obvious where to grab hold of it, or where to go after you have."[3]

In December he sent the book to Albert Hackett and Frances Goodrich, who had adapted Dashiell Hammett's "Thin

Man" stories for film in 1937, and who most recently had been acclaimed for their play, *The Diary of Anne Frank.* The Hacketts, too, felt that *Greenwillow* wasn't for them:

> We thought the book beautifully written, the story and characters enchanting. There is a gentleness, a fairy-tale quality that makes for the loveliest reading—we could smell the meadow flowers, taste the sugar cakes hot from the oven. But we don't know how to translate that into theatre.[4]

Eventually he found Lesser Samuels, a Hollywood screenwriter whose work included *The Earl of Chicago, No Way Out,* and *The Silver Chalice* (Paul Newman's debut). In January 1959 Frank Loesser and Lesser Samuels signed an agreement that Samuels would co-author the book.

Loesser and Lesser worked well together, tossing ideas and trial dialogue at each other, and the book finally began to take shape. But the original problems remained, even after the reinforcements were called in. Now there were two book writers struggling mightily to dramatize the undramatic.

They made a few changes in the story. In order to make Lapp more of a villain, they have him convince Dorrie to wish "Gideon be gone from my heart" at the candlewalk ceremony. The wish appears to come true when she becomes interested in another young man, Andrew. In the end, Gideon hears his call, but the voices of the villagers are stronger as they rise in concert to call him home. And Dorrie's wish, as explained by the Reverend Birdsong, was really the Reverend Lapp's wish, and therefore not valid. Andrew be gone. Gideon and Dorrie are happily united.

Probably because of the spiritual, unworldly nature of the Greenwillowians, the authors had enormous difficulty in making them seem real on stage. Although supplied with virtues and vices, cuteness and eccentricity, they remained phantoms of the imagination, unwilling to plant their feet on solid ground. At this point my father asked a psychologist he knew, Dr. Milton Saperstein, to provide psychological biographies of the characters. Dr. Saperstein described the family history, personal tastes, breakfast habits, and medical and psychological quirks of each person in the town, but still they didn't come to life.

Probably there *was* no way to bring this literary fantasy to the stage successfully. As Abba Bogin, the musical director for the show, put it:

> I think that both Frank and Lesser really didn't know what kind of identity to give the show. Were they writing about a Tennessee village? A little old English town? Someplace on the banks of the Danube? It had no identity, this town of Greenwillow. I mean, even Brigadoon, which only appears once every hundred years, is still part of Scotland, and everybody there is Scottish. Nobody knew what dialect to play *Greenwillow* in.[5]

At one point, when they were considering using a Tennessee Hills approach, the creative people all took a trip to the Grand Ole Opry in Nashville for possible casting. The Opry people, delighted to have Frank Loesser as their guest, lined up all sorts of performers for him, director George Roy Hill, Allen Whitehead, and Abba Bogin. One major country-western star after another performed for the Loesser party, but, in Abba's words:

> We spent two or three days in Nashville and found nothing. These people were so stylized that you couldn't get them into the kind of nonentity style that *Greenwillow* needed. Finally we all agreed that we were better off with trained professional actors you can give an attitude and a style to.[6]

My father didn't have these kinds of problems with the music. Most of the songs were written early on, many of them in mixed meter, some with time signatures that are unusual in popular music. All of them are melodic. "The Music of Home" celebrates the sounds of tea kettles and robins and crickets "and the old oak meadowgate swinging on her hinges—in tune with the crackle of the hearth, aflicker and aflame." The tempo slows and quickens alternately. "Summertime Love" also changes tempo several times.

My father used to say that songs should be written for those moments when the emotion is too strong for ordinary speech.

"Gideon Briggs, I Love You" is a good example, beginning with a spoken, "It makes me want to shout!" and continuing in song:

And to sing it out
And to leave you no doubt when I say
Dorrie I dearly love you, love you
There it is plain as daylight.
Dorrie I dearly love you, love you
Love you with all my heart.

"Walking Away Whistling" has a haunting melody that evokes wistfulness, sadness, and magic. "Greenwillow Christmas" is a short, happy carol that sounds downright traditional.

"The Sermon" is a gem of a contrapuntal duet on the subject of the coming of winter, sung by the two ministers in overlapping and interweaving lines. In his deep growling bass, Lapp sings, "The coming of winter, the coming of wretched cold, cold winter, is a warning, a warning to repent! Give heed, lest wild storms kill your trees. For your sins, God will punish you. Your trees will die. Branches fall. Let sinners all beware. You should know, from Genesis six: five: God saw that the wickedness of man was great." And Birdsong, in a cheerful tippy-toe tenor, sings, "The coming of winter, blessed old winter. Nights of long deep featherbed sleep, and a hot plum porridge in the morning. Rejoice! The merry white snowdrifts, nippy breeze calling: dance, dance, dance, there's wind in the sky. Branches fall, so there's good, good firewood for all. Be glad! Of course you know, from Genesis one: thirty-one: God saw everything that he had made, and behold, it was very good."

Comedy numbers include "Could Have Been a Ring," sung by Gramma Briggs and old man Clegg about their early romance ("Could have been a hurry-up saying of the vows, building of the crib, raising of the brows . . . Could have been a writing down on the Bible page, telling 'bout his name, lying 'bout his age"), and "Clang Dang the Bell," on the baptism of a calf.

"He Died Good" lays to rest mean old man Clegg:

He died good. He died good.
Come his dying moment

He died good.
How nice for the widow
In her widowhood . . .
Spiteful, hateful,
Hog mean, pinchpenny,
Blasphemous,
Poisontongue,
Flinthearted,
Evil-eyed . . .
A lifetime of living
As no human should.
And wonder of wonders:
He died good.

"Never Will I Marry," a passionate, despairing ballad, sung by Gideon, with a strong, driving melody and a time signature of 6/4, is the only song from the show that has survived outside of the production. Barbra Streisand, for one, recorded it, and it is still around.

"Faraway Boy," Dorrie's wistful imagining of what she might say to a future lover, was written in three hours one fruitful evening:

Oh Sir, tis not a new thing
This feeling of joy
Well Sir, 'tis all because of
Some faraway boy.

Some faraway boy
With a name past recall
And a face I'd not likely
Remember at all.

Some faraway boy
Who first wakened my heart
If there's love there for you, Sir,
He made it all start.

"What a Blessing," originally called "Birdsong's Waltz," is a charming soliloquy on the devil in all of us:

Oh I know it's the devil who tempts me to crime
And to sin and corruption, and worse,

But I find in resisting him time after time
That I can't quite believe he's a curse.
For in fact, I believe—The reverse.

What a blessing to know there's a devil
And that I'm but a pawn in his game,
That my impulse to sin
Doesn't come from within
And so I'm not exactly to blame.
What a blessing to know there's a devil
Ever leading me into some vice,
And though easily led
I can hold up my head
Knowing I'm fundamentally nice.

What relief, oh what blessed relief
That a thief is by nature no thief
And a liar is merely the innocent buyer
Of lies from the liar-in-chief.
So of course, the remorse may be brief.

Tucked away in an old folder are dozens of pages ripped from my father's trusty yellow legal pads, scrawled with trial lyrics and ideas for this song:

How secure
(Oh) how ______ly secure
Is my/the feeling of knowing I'm pure

What a joy to redeem
Our divine self-esteem

WABTKTAD [What a Blessing to Know There's a Devil]
Who incites me to riot and brawl
When I'm caught in the act
It's a comforting fact
That I'm not really bad after all
rotten at all

WABTKTAD
When I've heard myself telling a fib
What a refuge/haven/comfort I find
In recalling to mind
I was never that clever or glib

What a handy relief from my shame—
Very nicely relieving my shame—
Who deliberately led you to shame—

Viciously
Ambitiously
Repetitiously (gas)
Meretriciously
Perniciously
Maliciously

Satanic smile
Hellish temper
Impish delight
Demon rum
Infernal nuisance
Hell of a fix
Fiendish delight (glee)

The one major problem he had with the songs was finding an opening number. After discarding Birdsong's conversation with the birds, he tried having the voices that called away Amos Briggs echo throughout the theater. Allen Whitehead remembers why this particular approach was scrapped:

> We spent hours at a studio one Sunday with all kinds of crude electronics—the best they had at that time. There must have been four or five tracks. And then *The Sound of Music* opened out of town and used the same technique, so that was that.[7]

Then there was "Riddleweed," which, Abba says,

> was absolutely dreadful. Everybody hated it. Nobody thought the number would work except Frank. He liked the tune, and he liked the idea of a sort of mystic weed that foretells a visitor, to try to get an atmosphere going. But the number wasn't good, and we orchestrated it and choreographed it and cut it and rewrote it, and nothing seemed to work. So finally, after the first week in Philadelphia, he decided he'd have to do something about it, so he came in with a new song called "My Round-bellied Beauty."[8]

"My Beauty" had the same tune as "Riddleweed," but it was a love song for Gideon to sing to his pregnant cow. My father proudly performed his new opening number for the musical director, orchestrator, rehearsal pianists, stage manager, company manager, and producers—who met it with embarrassed silence.

"Well, if you don't like it, say so!" he said. "Tell me you hate the fucking thing! I'll throw it out the window. Tell me *something.* Don't just sit there!" Pause. "Goddammit."[9] And back he went to work. This was now the second week in Philadelphia. Everyone was staying at the same hotel. Around 4:00 A.M. Abba's phone rang.

> In a fog, I say "hello." This wide-awake voice says, "You sleeping or fucking? . . . In that case, get your ass down here. I've got something to show you. And what do you want for breakfast? We're just ordering." So I get dressed and go to his room. Jimmy Leon, the rehearsal pianist, is there. So Jimmy plays an introduction and Frank starts to sing "A Day Borrowed from Heaven." It's sensational.
>
> "Is that the new opening number?" I ask. "It is if everybody likes it," he says. "I think it's wonderful," I say. "Really? Good," he says and goes to the phone and calls Don Walker [the orchestrator]. "You sleeping or fucking?"[10]

They put "A Day Borrowed from Heaven," another song with an odd rhythm (7/4), in the show two days later.

Don Walker was the orchestrator, Abba Bogin the musical director. Set design was by Peter Larkin, and Alvin Colt, who had designed the marvelous, now legendary costumes for *Guys and Dolls,* created the cloaks and britches.

They had Anthony Perkins in mind for Gideon from the beginning. Perkins had recently been praised for his performance in *Look Homeward, Angel,* directed by George Roy Hill, and he was filming *Psycho* at the time. Although he had no experience in musical theater and was certainly not known as a singer, Perkins actually did like to sing and had even made an album, which must be quite a collector's item now. He projected an innocent, rather fey quality, this tall, gangly male ingenue, and also a sense of moral integrity, all of which strongly suggested Gideon to the authors.

But could he sing well enough to carry the role? They decided to take a chance on him, and my father spent many hours coaching Perkins through his songs, telling him when and how much to tilt his head, move his hands, take a breath. He introduced him to the Loud Is Good school of musical theater and made sure he pronounced every Loesser lyric so that it was clear to the back of the house. This did not endear him to the actor.

With Perkins came George Roy Hill, who had no experience with musicals either but was very well known and worked well with Perkins.

> Tony wanted me to direct, but I wasn't sure I wanted to. I think Tony was afraid to tackle a big singing role, and he wanted me there very much, so I went against my better judgment. I had been warned about Frank, and I had no desire to get into it, but I loved the material.
>
> Curiously, it wasn't as bad an experience as it sounds from the telling of it. I became very fond of Frank, which is odd, because we fought every inch of the way. He could see the funny side of everything, so he would be hollering and I would be hollering and suddenly one of us would break into laughter. There was no meanness in the fighting.[11]

The problems my father had with the writing were compounded by his and Hill's conflicting visions of the show. While Hill tended toward a light opera approach, he felt that my father waffled between that and a standard Broadway vision; and when he got nervous about how the show was playing, he'd lean heavily toward the straight, out-front, gag-laden Broadway style.

> It was a style that suited *Guys and Dolls,* but I wanted to do more of the style of *The Most Happy Fella.* When Frank had confidence in the material it was alright to stage it that way. But when something didn't go well he would get very upset and say, "You've got to punch it in, punch it in. You've got to get down there and let them see their faces. You've got to go right out to the audience." Now this was one way of staging it, certainly, but it wasn't the way I wanted to stage it.[12]

More problems: originally the choreographer was to have been Jack Cole, signed in September only to announce in November that he was about to do a movie and would be able to work with the show only on weekends, commuting from the coast.

"I'll sue the shit out of him," my father said. Lesser Samuels looked calmly at my father and said, "You can't mount a lawsuit on the stage. It doesn't play well. We've got a show to get on. Let's get a choreographer."[13]

So Cole's contract was canceled in formal arbitration and they signed Joe Layton. To everyone's relief he worked out beautifully, creating lively dances, including a Halloween ballet that even the critics who panned the show liked very much.

In those days, dance music in Broadway musicals was usually written by someone other than the major composer and credited separately, an arrangement my father never liked. Instead he would hire a composer, hand him some "yard goods," and tell him to use those melodies to create the music for the choreographer, subject to my father's approval. The composer, of course, would be asked to sign the one-dollar agreement making his work the property of Frank Loesser.

For *Greenwillow* the dance music was originally assigned to a young up-and-coming composer named Charles (Buddy) Strouse. He was delighted to get the job but warned the group from the beginning that a show he had written with Lee Adams might find a producer at any moment, in which case he would have to leave *Greenwillow.* The same week that Jack Cole accepted his job in Hollywood, Strouse announced that *Bye Bye Birdie* was going into production. (In fact, it followed *Greenwillow* into the Shubert Theater in Philadelphia.)

Two with one blow—no choreographer, no dance music to choreograph. In this case the void was filled by Billy Goldenberg, who turned up at so many auditions as an accompanist—and was such a good one—that he captured my father's attention. He too went on to bigger things in Hollywood, where he has written the music for many films, TV movies, and TV series.

Originally a young singer named Zemi North, who looked perfect for the part of an innocent seventeen-year-old girl, was cast in the key role of Dorrie. But her acting wasn't strong enough—her innocence and inexperience proved to be quite sincere—and in Philadelphia she was replaced by Ellen McCown.

McCown was playing Polly in *The Boy Friend* when my father was writing *Greenwillow.* She and my father and Jo were friends, and he would call her from time to time and say, "Ellen, I'm working on a tune—could you come over and sing it for me?"

She worked for him informally in this way for about a year, and she was very interested in playing Dorrie. But Dorrie is supposed to be seventeen, Ellen was thirty, and my father was concerned about the discrepancy. Ellen knew she'd have a hard time getting the part, but she auditioned for it and was put on hold.

> One day he called me early in the morning. He said, "Can you get over here in twenty minutes? I'm getting all the dancers lined up and I want to see how old you look next to them." I said, "Frank, I look hideous. There's no way I'm going to stand up next to all those gorgeous little dancers and be judged. At least give me until later this afternoon." He said, "You have to be here in twenty minutes. Take a cab." I got very flustered and tearful. He said, "Well, don't commit suicide," and hung up on me.
>
> I didn't hear another word for ages. I wanted to know what was going on with the show but didn't dare ask anybody. Then the news began to filter back from Philadelphia that they were having a lot trouble and that Zemi wasn't working out very well. But I thought my friends were telling me these things to make me feel better. I was going to a shrink at the time, and he said, "Why don't you just go down to Philadelphia and see the show?" Well, I did. Got on a train, went to Philadelphia; walked into the matinee. Not a soul knew I was coming. All the management people were backstage, and each of them thought that one of the others had called me.[14]

They were, in fact, delighted to see her. At Allen Whitehead's suggestion Ellen called my father, who was in his hotel room—he hadn't been to the theater since the opening. She gave him some encouraging words about the show, then returned to New York. The next morning my father called her, told her to come back to Philadelphia, hole up in a hotel room, and learn the script. Within a few days she went on. Ellen was reliable, attractive, a strong actress, and a lovely singer. She and Perkins got along splendidly, and everyone was happy with her, despite the fact that she wasn't seventeen.

Cecil Kellaway, a short, round, cheerful, older actor, was cast as Birdsong. The role was delicious, and Kellaway was perfect in it—the stage came wonderfully to life whenever Birdsong was on. William Chapman, a tall, thin, handsome man with a glorious voice who had originally auditioned for Joey in *The Most Happy Fella,* was cast in the role of Lapp. Thomas Clegg was played by Lee Cass, who had sung the Postman and the Cashier in *The Most Happy Fella.* Pert Kelton—the original Alice in "The Honeymooners," and Mrs. Paroo in *The Music Man*—was Gramma Briggs.

They were supposed to go into rehearsal at the end of December, just after Christmas. On December 24, George Roy Hill lost heart and quit.

> It was just before we went into rehearsal [Hill recalled], but the battle lines were very clearly drawn from the start. Joy Chute called me and begged me to stay. I said, "It's going to be no good. Frank and I don't see eye to eye on this." But she talked me into coming back.[15]

The problems with the show never let up. Perkins was both insecure about his singing and critical of his material. Unhappy and demanding, he did not take kindly to my father's constant coaching. Hill and my father continued to fight over their respective concepts, at one point physically. "I once made a lunge for him and had him up against the wall with my hands around his throat," Hill told me. "He kept saying, 'Watch your hands, watch your hands, watch your hands.'"[16]

My father understood quite well what wasn't working in the show and had good ideas about how to fix it, but in his concern for the integrity of his art he stepped on nearly everybody's toes.

An author who only half jokingly refers to himself as God, hands out edicts in rapid-fire succession, and constantly needles his performers will not necessarily help a struggling company, even when he is right. The personality conflicts cast an even greater shadow on a show already in trouble over fundamental problems with the writing. The wonderful spirit of collaboration, so important to the success of *Guys and Dolls,* was not to be found in this production. Nor was the excitement of being involved in a major creative breakthrough that had buoyed people through the difficult times with *The Most Happy Fella.* People were working very hard, but often at cross purposes, and by the time *Greenwillow* went on the road to Philadelphia early in the spring of 1960, no one had much confidence in any aspect of the production.

During a dress rehearsal in Philadelphia, the cow—a brown and white guernsey named Buttercup Hyacinth Bertram III—shat on the stage. Morale was so low at that point that no one laughed. The Philadelphia reviews, to no one's surprise, were not good. My father would have closed the show then and there, but he felt committed to it and responsible to all of the people involved. To give the show every chance to make it, he decided, despite his reservations, to take it to New York.

Opening night in New York, March 8, 1960, my father was pacing, irritable and unapproachable, in the back of the theater. I was simply excited—I was sixteen, and this was the first time I'd attended the opening of one of my father's shows. And after all, my father was an unstoppable success—what could go wrong? Yet as the overture ended and the curtain went up, I could feel waves of tension and anxiety coming from him, reaching me in my seat toward the back of the orchestra. When the tracked scenery hit a snag during the first set change, I glanced behind me and saw my father taking off, out the door. During intermission we found him quietly getting drunk at Jilly's, the bar next door. He didn't go back for the second act. He didn't go to Sardi's to wait for the reviews. Jo took him home. Lesser Samuels had left town on a cruise that day. Bob Willey, Allen Whitehead, George Roy Hill, and Joy Chute saw it through.

The New York reviews were mixed, although mostly bad. John Chapman *(Daily News)*: "*Greenwillow* . . . is filled with songs, robust, lilting or charming; its company is one of the best . . . But I'll be blessed if I can tell you just what it's about." Richard Watts *(Post)*: "gravely disappointing." Walter Kerr *(Herald Tribune)*: "The new musical at the Alvin is do-it-yourself folklore, which means that it is spun right out of somebody's head instead of out of somebody else's past, and folklore may just be the one dish in the world that can't be cooked to order." Robert Coleman *(Mirror)*: "Having scored a triumph with the semi-operatic *Most Happy Fella,* Frank Loesser has now tackled folk opera in *Greenwillow.* Ambitious though his latest venture be, we must report regretfully that it doesn't quite come off." Kenneth Tynan *(The New Yorker)* was perhaps the cruelest and certainly the most amusing:

> You may get some notion of the rarefied atmosphere of the place when I tell you that it makes Glocca Morra look like a teeming slum. To put it another way, Brigadoon could be the Latin Quarter of Greenwillow. Fancifully, I picture the village cutups trooping into the corner apothecary's, where they linger disconsolately over their sugar muffins and dock-leaf cordials. Evening service is over, and there is nothing to do until milking time except sing madrigals. "'Tis a handy-dandy night, and the moon rides high," says one of them in the local patois. "Let's go over to Brigadoon and pick up some broads." Unfortunately, no such scamps as these are on view at the Alvin. All the same, I don't want you to go away with the idea that everyone in Greenwillow is a model of virtue; no, by Jimmy-go-jerkins and rum-tickle-ree—to coin an oath that the townsfolk themselves might have coined if any of them had ever got around to using foul language . . . On the whole it is barely credible that this simple-minded extravaganza is the work of the man who created *Guys and Dolls.* In the last ten years, Mr. Loesser has traveled from urban ingenuity to grass-roots ingenuousness; with *Greenwillow* he has reached the end of the line and we must all wish him a rapid recovery, followed by a speedy return to the asphalt jungle.[17]

Brooks Atkinson *(New York Times),* on the other hand, loved the show. "Mr. Loesser and Mr. Samuels have collaborated on an ideal libretto set somewhere between here and far away. Out of his bountiful music box Mr. Loesser has provided a warm and varied score that captures the simple moods of the story . . . a musical play that brings distinction to the stage and pleasure to the people out front." And John McClain *(Journal American)* liked it, noting that "it is loaded with the sort of homespun pathos and humor which should keep it running until the scenery quietly comes apart." Long before that—on May 28, after ninety-five performances—*Greenwillow* folded.

A cast recording of the show was made around the time of the opening. (It is now a collector's item). Someone posted the "Loud Is Good" sign at Webster Hall, and the cast and musicians gathered at the appointed time. It was raining. My father was late leaving his office. Standing in the downpour on 57th Street he watched with growing irritation as cab after cab went by full. Finally he saw what he took to be an empty one. As the taxi crawled by in the traffic my father charged it, yanked open the door, and saw the tiny old lady crouched in the corner of the back seat. "Stand up, you cocksucker!" he bellowed and slammed the door shut.

My father and Jo were married April 29, 1959, in the middle of the *Greenwillow* tribulations. They were both uneasy about their decision, and it took them some time to settle in comfortably together. "We didn't get along the first year at all," Jo told me. "I think we both worried that we had made a terrible mistake. He was writing *Greenwillow,* and I would spend hours at the movies just to get out, because he was such a pain in the ass."[18] I wanted to live with them, but they had other ideas, other visions of their life together. Wary and bickering, they had no interest in making a cosy place for me. And I, who saw nothing amiss with The Perfect Couple, felt rejected and relegated to West 81st Street, where my mother slept until mid-afternoon, had a vodka and Coke for breakfast, and was just hitting her stride at my bedtime, when she wanted to "dish." I remained a guest at my father's house—a frequent guest, but never really at home there.

My father and Jo's only wedding picture.

My brother and me, on friendlier terms.

Although he was depressed over it, my father was not devastated by *Greenwillow*'s failure. Once it opened, he was able to let it go, regretfully, and allow it to live its short life on its own while he and Jo took an extended trip to Europe. They were gone for six months, visiting London, Paris, Rome, Marrakech, and Copenhagen (where they were pursued by "Wonderful, Wonderful Copenhagen" to the point that they dreaded entering any restaurant with a band). I got postcards ("X marks the spot where our room is") and letters ("Hello, Little Cutie, from London, where the fountain pens in hotel rooms are no safer than ours"). And a poem:

WELCOME TO CLARIDGE'S

Whose clam-gray upstairs halls,
Lined with quite sensible
Shoes
Quite sensibly set out for a polish
In the customary quiet of
Ten in the evening—
Quite properly separated
(The gentlemen's from the ladies')
All of it benignly watched over
At proper intervals
From the high, very clean ceiling
By fifteen sensible watts worth
of amber approval,
Give
Some sort of goodnight blessing
To the whole idea
Of sensible
Permanent
Fat-headed
Maridge's

On closing night, the *Greenwillow* company received a cable: "Oops, sorry."

11

How to Succeed in Business Without Really Trying

There once was a self-made Madison Avenue mogul named Shepherd Mead who wrote a satiric little handbook about rising to the top of a business organization by devious, humorous, and cynical means. The book, *How to Succeed in Business Without Really Trying,* became a bestseller in 1952, and Mead became altogether too rich and successful to feel comfortable in the workaday world. He retired at the ripe old age of forty-one and moved to the English countryside to write additional handbooks, such as *How to Succeed with Women Without Really Trying* and *How to Live Like a Lord Without Really Trying.*

In 1955, Willie Gilbert, a playwright, and Jack Weinstock, a neurosurgeon who wrote plays in his spare time, adapted the book for the stage. In 1960, that indefatigable agent Abe Newborn came to Feuer and Martin with the play, which had never been produced. Apparently it wasn't very good, but it had certain elements that Cy and Ernie liked: a story line and a couple of likeable major characters (who remained and were developed in the show). Cy was soon convinced that the property could be made into a musical.

They approached Abe Burrows and my father, neither of whom was interested. The story line was weak, they said, plus there was little drama, and no romance. (No romance!!!) But Cy and Ernie were not to be discouraged by such trifles. They knew Frank and Abe could bring it off. They pushed. Abe gave in first, agreeing to write and direct, and then joined forces with Cy and Ernie to work on my father.

It was September 1960. *Greenwillow* had closed in May. My father and Jo had just returned from several months in Europe, and Jo was looking at townhouses. My father was kicking around several creative ideas, including musical versions of Anouilh's *Time Remembered* and Steinbeck's *The Pearl.* He was eager to get back to work, but this property was not at all appealing to him. Nor was he particularly keen on working with Feuer and Martin again, despite their track record together. *Guys and Dolls* was ten years behind them, after all. He didn't want to revisit the past or give up the control he had exercised in his last two shows. At the same time, here was a constellation of theater people that almost guaranteed a big hit. And that was tempting. It had been ten years since he had worked with Abe, but they were still good friends. Abe needed him, and my father had very strong feelings about the obligations of friendship. Cy and Ernie needed him too. And, after *Greenwillow,* he needed a hit. In the end, he couldn't resist.

He began writing the score in late September and completed the bulk of it by the end of January 1961, probably working faster than at any other time in his career. But Abe was a little slower getting the book down on paper. Abe worked in longhand, and he worked best when someone was there to laugh at his jokes. So Cy sat with him—as he had before and would again—sometimes typing the lines for him, and often providing the laughter that would inspire Abe to write more. And as the book evolved, new opportunities arose for the songs, which my father would amend, append, revise.

The show, as it eventually took shape, actually had plot, drama, and romance, although it had even more comedy, satire, and social commentary. J. Pierrepont Finch, a window washer, has come into possession of Mead's book, from which he reads as he rides the scaffold, cleaning the windows of the World Wide Wicket Company:

> BOOK VOICE: Dear Reader: This little book is designed to tell you everything you need to know about the science of getting ahead. (FINCH *turns front toward the audience, and turns page in book.*) Now let us assume you are young, healthy, clear-eyed and eager, anxious to rise quickly to the top of the business world. You can!
>
> FINCH: *(Looking up)* I can!

And so our hero begins his climb. World Wide Wicket is the perfect company—"big enough so that nobody knows what anybody else is doing." Having fortuitously collided with J.B. Biggley, the company president, Finch proceeds to the head of personnel ("I was just speaking to Mr. Biggley") and lands a job in the mailroom. From there his rise is meteoric and his story full of jokes and jibes at the business world.

Rosemary, a secretary, provides the love interest; the boss's nephew, Bud Frump, is the comic heavy; and Hedy La Rue, J.B. Biggley's bimbo girlfriend, assures dramatic complications.

With the book and the songs well under way, Cy and Ernie began to fill in the blanks—costumes, sets, choreography. While looking for a choreographer, Cy saw an industrial show with a terrific number choreographed by a young man named Hugh Lambert, who had done a little television work. Cy went to Ernie and Frank and Abe: "There's a kid who's really hot. I've seen this number of his and it's fresh and it has drive and a lot of energy." They hired Hugh Lambert on the strength of that number, which went into the show as the "Pirate Dance," a spoof on a television giveaway show. But, as Cy told me,

> Then Lambert went on to do the rest of the show, and we found out that the *only* thing he could do was that number. He was a one-shot guy. I went to Bob Fosse, ready to fire Lambert and hire Fosse as choreographer. Fosse read the book and heard the score. He said, "Look, I don't want to hurt this kid. He's just starting out. Don't fire him." So we kept Lambert as choreographer and hired Bobby for "Musical Staging." Lambert never did another thing on the show. He stayed around, polishing his Pirate Dance, and got his billing. Fosse choreographed everything else.[1]

Costumes were by Robert Fletcher, who costumed several other Broadway shows, the *Star Trek* movies, and the gigantic TV series "The Winds of War." Scenery and lighting were by Robert Randolph, who also designed *Sweet Charity, Funny Girl, Little Me,* and *Bye Bye Birdie.*

Elliot Lawrence was the musical director. His first show was the recent hit *Bye Bye Birdie,* which made him rather new to Broadway, although as a musician he was well known and well respected. My father chose Elliot, and then he asked him for a favor.

> He said to me, "Cy Feuer has this uncle who's a musician. He's played in all Cy's shows. I'd like you to go to Cy and say, 'Cy, under no condition can I have your uncle play saxophone in this show.' It doesn't matter what Cy says—I have final okay. Just know that behind you, you have me."
>
> Well, I didn't know Cy Feuer. I trudged obediently over to Feuer and Martin's office. Cy was very nice to me, sat me down, we talked about the show—how great the songs were—very friendly. Then he said, "Okay, so what can I do for you?" I said, "Cy, I can't have your uncle in the saxophone section on this show." Well, he started screaming at me, circling around me as I sat in the chair—a fury of a man. He went on and on. I was terrified.
>
> In the end, the uncle didn't play, but they paid him to be around. He didn't talk to me.[2]

The first person cast was Robert Morse as Finch. Morse, who had appeared in Abe's recent *Say, Darling,* was the quintessential brash but adorable young man. For the role of Bud Frump, Morse in turn suggested his friend Charles Nelson Reilly, who at that time had a small part in *Bye Bye Birdie.* Cy and Ernie didn't know Reilly's work and were looking for a singer-dancer, which he wasn't, so it was quite a while before they auditioned him. But finally, in Reilly's words,

> I got to audition at the Lunt-Fontanne Theatre, where *The Sound of Music* was endlessly playing. I mean, the walls were *permeated* with the songs from that show. This was after they'd seen anybody between twenty-five and thirty-five who could walk. I'm not a dancer, but I knew the dance sequence to "Put On a Happy Face," which was a real number—a lot of tapping. It had taken me months to learn it. So I thought I'd audition with that. I tried to get the two girls who I danced with in *Birdie* to come with me, but at the last minute they were unavailable. So I did the number alone, explaining what they were supposed to be doing while I was doing what I was doing—and every time I got near the walls I burst into something from *The Sound of Music.* I was petrified—and I was crazed.[3]

And they loved him.

Bonnie Scott, a complete unknown, was cast as Rosemary. She left the show very early in the run to return to obscurity and was replaced by the stronger Michele Lee, who also did the movie. Virginia Martin played the colorful part of Hedy La Rue, and Claudette Sutherland was Rosemary's friend Smitty.

For J.B. Biggley, the pompous, silly president of World Wide Wicket, Abe Newborn came up with another of his novel casting ideas. He came to Cy and said, "Rudy Vallee." Cy said, "Rudy *Vallee*? Jesus Christ, what does he even look like these days? I haven't seen him in twenty years!" And so Cy found himself on his way to Canada:

> Abe Newborn and I flew to London, Ontario, to go to this little vinyl nightclub where Vallee was appearing. We had to charter a bush pilot to get there. We met Rudy. He was a dirty old man, doing a dirty old act in this cockamamie club in the middle of nowhere. He even had a screen that he projected bits from his old movies on. It was terrible. He still talked like he was the biggest star you've ever seen. He was very condescending to us. Getting back on the plane, New-

> born said, "Well, what do you think?" And I said, "I think he's perfect. What an idea!" When we got back I told the guys about Rudy, and everybody approved him on my say-so. And when he came down everyone was delighted—until they had to start working with him.[4]

Although he was indeed perfect in the role, Vallee was impossible offstage. His rehearsal salary was too low. His car fare wasn't reimbursed. His dressing room was too small. Abe didn't give him any direction. And as to Frank Loesser—well, I think I'll let Mr. Vallee speak for himself:

> I had Frank Loesser problems from the outset. A few days before the New York rehearsals began he phoned me to drop by his office to go over the tunes. His half-humorous parting words were, "I am going to put you on the rack."
>
> This annoyed me faintly and I immediately called Abe Burrows, whom I felt I knew well enough to use as a confidant. "Now look here, Abe," I said. "If I am going to have a lot of headaches with Loesser about my singing, I'd rather bow out right now. Who needs that crap? I'd much prefer to get the hell back to California."
>
> "Now, now, Rudy," Abe replied. "Just calm down. Don't worry about it. It'll be all right."
>
> That first day Loesser's office became a conservatory of music with him acting as voice professor.
>
> "Rudy, you're singing incorrectly," he said. "You're closing on your consonants."
>
> "Maybe you're right, Frank," I said. "Fortunately I've managed to squeak by with this handicap for about thirty-three years. I guess it's a little late in life to acquire a new technique." I had been wined and dined by composers as great or greater than Loesser to persuade me to introduce their tunes.
>
> . . . As we discussed the rendition of the numbers I began to realize that Loesser regarded them as true works of art and, as befits masterpieces, proper performances could only come from considerable rehearsal on my part. If there is one thing that heats up my blood, it is when someone tries to make a big thing out of nothing. And here is where the composer's feathers got ruffled.
>
> "Frank, don't you realize that these are extremely simple

songs?" I said politely and candidly. "I can do them about as well the first time as I can the thousandth."[5]

One of the songs that Vallee wanted to make nothing out of was "A Secretary Is Not a Toy." Originally written as a waltz in which Vallee admonishes his staff to treat their secretaries with the proper respect, the song wasn't working. For one thing, Vallee refused to do it the way my father wanted it done. He refused to stick to the rhythm, he crooned, he added and subtracted notes. At the top of an early manuscript of this song, my father wrote, "Freely, but without unnecessary whimsy as to freedom!" No doubt this instruction was in response to hearing Vallee have his way with it.

Rehearsals had begun August 3, 1961. On August 9, my father went to Cy in high dudgeon. "That son of a bitch won't take my tempo," he said. "I want the song done the way I wrote it. You're the producer—do something!" So Cy took my father and Vallee into the little office at the rehearsal hall and said, "Rudy, Frank has an objection to the way you're doing this song."

Vallee said, "Look, boys, do you know how many hit songs I've made in my time? It was due to my performing these songs—and changing the tempos—that they became the massive hits they were. You've got to admit that, being in this business as long as I have, I have a nose for these things, and my interpretation is usually what sells the material."

"Well now, Rudy," Cy said, "I don't really care about that. In this case we are doing a show. Frank wrote the songs. He wrote this particular song in a particular way, and he wants it sung in that way. And I want you to do it that way."

Rudy said, "You're making a big sacrifice."

Frank said, "GODDAMMIT, YOU SON OF A BITCH—"

Cy (restraining Frank): "Rudy, I'm telling you, the song has got to be done Frank's way, and that's all there is to it. Let's cut this crap and get on with it."

Vallee, mumbling something about doing them all a big favor, left, whereupon my father turned on Cy and said, "You

At work on *How to Succeed.*

miserable shit, you didn't hit him! Why didn't you hit him?" And he walked off the show. Took his music and quit. Went home and sent a telegram of resignation and took no calls, not even the message from Cy that, if he wanted, Cy would hit Rudy in the morning.[6]

Now my father, although explosive, was not prone to make career decisions like that on a whim or to punctuate a tirade. He had been stewing over his arguments with Vallee for some time. On top of this, he felt that Cy and Ernie had set him up to be the heavy, keeping Vallee in line without getting involved themselves. I'm sure that he also felt hobbled to be once again a member of a team—a team of high-powered people, each with his own strong opinions, each with his own clout. None of them—not Feuer and Martin, not Abe Burrows, and not Bob Fosse—was about to let Frank Loesser run the show. And the show was coming together, with everyone participating in every aspect of it. That wonderful collaborative spirit was back and working. But there was a price, and my father found it hard to pay. I think it all came down around him in that little room at the rehearsal hall. He didn't simply walk off the show in a Rumpelstiltskinian rage. He was really hurting.

Unable to reach my father any other way, Cy finally sat down and wrote a 500-word telegram imploring him to come back. Three days later, responding both to Cy's entreaties and his own sense of responsibility and commitment, he did. From then on Cy made a point of impressing his own criticisms on Vallee, but Vallee continued to sing "A Secretary Is Not a Toy" his own way, and it continued not to work.

They went to Philadelphia in September, and the song was cut. But no one wanted to let it go. Cy, Abe, Bob, and my father had a meeting: What to do with the number, which was basically so good. They met until 4:00 A.M., until they couldn't see straight. At some point during the marathon session, Bob Fosse said, "You know, I see a kind of giant soft-shoe." The comment was swallowed up in the conversation, but Cy remembered it later and asked him what he had meant.

"Well, I've got an idea for it. Can you give me a rehearsal hall for a few days and send one of the piano players over with me and Gwen [Verdon]?"

Cy rented the Masonic Temple across the street from the Shubert Theatre where they were playing, and he told Bob to keep his work a secret from my father until it was ready.

> On the third night Fosse showed it to me [Cy recalled], and it was just sensational. Instead of a waltz, he had changed the tempo to a big jazzy number that would use most of the company. Forty people would come on stage in small groups, all doing these soft-shoe steps and each singing a fragment of the lyric. So the following night after the show I brought Frank over. We sat and watched the number. At the end Frank got up. "Jesus Christ!" he said. "This is brilliant! But how the hell can you use the lyric that way? I'll have to write you a whole new lyric!" And he did.[7]

> A secretary is not a toy,
> No, my boy; not a toy
> To fondle and dandle
> And playfully handle

In search of some puerile joy.
No, a secretary is not,
Definitely not, a toy.

. . . .

And when you put her to use;
Observe, when you put her to use,
That you don't find the name "Lionel" on her caboose.

. . . .

A secretary is not a thing
Wound by key, pulled by string.
Her pad is to write in
And not spend the night in—
If that's what you plan to enjoy.
No!
The secretary you've got
Is definitely not
Employed to do a gavotte—
Or you know what.
Before you jump for joy,
Remember this, my boy,
A secretary is not
A tinker toy!

In my father's file on this song are many many trial lyrics and lists of rhyming words. Despite all the fuss—and thanks to Bob Fosse's magnificent save—he seems to have really enjoyed playing with the verse:

A secretary is not a small
Version of
Volley ball.
If you're feeling eager,
Run down to Davega
And there you can grab
The McCoy—
No!
A secretary is not,
Definitely not
A toy.

Savoy	Helen of Troy
goy	Iroquois
hoi polloi	soy

annoy	Myrna Loy
avoirdupois	enjoy
	Matsu-Quemoy
	hobbledehoy

The score is so completely integrated with the book that it really doesn't stand alone. Only one song, "I Believe in You," became a popular hit, and even then it had to be removed from its original context. In the show our hero sings it to himself in the mirror, to the accompaniment of five or six kazoos in the pit, impersonating electric razors, while a chorus of fellow employees chants, "Gotta stop that man" in the background.

Now there you are,
Yes, there's that face;
That face that somehow I trust.
It may embarrass you to hear me say it,
But say it I must, say it I must!
You have the cool, clear eyes of a
Seeker of wisdom and truth;
Yet there's that upturned chin, and the
Grin of impetuous youth.
Oh, I believe in you, I believe in you.

As Cy Feuer points out, everyone is a monster in the show. Even the long-suffering Rosemary is a rather brittle parody of the corporate wife:

I'll be so happy to keep his dinner warm
While he goes onward, and upward.
Happy to keep his dinner warm
'Till he comes wearily home from downtown.
I'll be there waiting until his mind is clear,
While he looks through me, right through me,
Waiting to say: "Good evening, dear,
I'm pregnant; what's new with you from downtown?"

Several songs lampoon various aspects of the corporate life. Besides "A Secretary Is Not a Toy" there is "Company Way" ("I play it the company way, wherever the company puts me, there I'll stay"), and "Coffee Break," sung to an "ominous cha cha rhythm" ("If I can't make three daily trips where shining shrine benignly drips, and taste cardboard between my lips, something within me dies").

Gwen Verdon always worked with Bob Fosse on his shows, whether officially or not. In this case their collaboration was unofficial, although, as she recalled, she was assigned one specific job:

> Bob had this idea for "Coffee Break," and he felt that if he could just get a little piece of it on the stage so Frank could see the style, he might like it. So my job was: Take Frank in the dressing room and discuss anything you want, but keep him away from the stage for about an hour and a half. Well, we had the best time—talking about shows I had done way back in 1947, and so forth. And then there was a knock on the door and they said, "Come on out, Frank, Bob wants to show you something." "Tell Bob I'm busy," Frank said, and we spent the rest of the day talking away. He saw "Coffee Break" after dinner that evening, and of course he loved it.[8]

It was Fosse's idea to have everyone so addicted to coffee that they went crazy when deprived. They screamed and fainted; one dancer even staggered into the pit in his agony.

"Been a Long Day" is a trio for a "mezzo, pezzo & futz," according to the manuscript. The first version is sung by Smitty, Rosemary, and Finch, followed by new lyrics for Bud, Biggley, and Hedy. In each instance the song actually functions as script, furthering the plot. This song was sketched out in December 1960, the earliest manuscript labeled the "'Find-a-Key' version."

"Grand Old Ivy" is a take-off on a school song, sung enthusiastically in march tempo by Biggley and Finch. At one point there were plans to dissolve into a big parade, hence the manuscript note: "Lead to tutti frutti noisi crashi."

Toward the end of Act One, the show needed a production number. The plot required an office party at that point, and Cy and Abe were trying to come up with an ingredient that would transcend the usual office-party cliches. So they went to my father for some input.

He thought about it overnight, then asked Abe to give him a scene "down-in-one" before the party, in which Rosemary crosses the stage with a box, saying that she's going to sweep Finch off his feet with the "Paris Original" she's just bought. She sings:

I slipped out this afternoon
And bought some love insurance,
A most exclusive dress from gay Paree.
It's sleek and chic and magnifique,
With sex beyond endurance.
It's me!
It's me!
It's absolutely me.
. . . . . .
This irresistible Paris original,
I'm wearing tonight;
I'm wearing tonight
'Specially for him.

And then the scene changes to the party. Rosemary enters in her clingy new dress, still singing:

For him—
For him—
This irresistible Paris original
I'm wearing tonight—
(FIRST GIRL *enters R. wearing same dress.*)
She's wearing tonight,
And I could spit!
Some irresponsible dress manufacturer
Just didn't play fair.
I'm one of a pair
And I could—
(MISS KRUMHOLTZ *enters L. wearing same dress.*)

And so it goes—all the women are wearing the same dress, and the song becomes a big number featuring twenty identically dressed indignant women.

In "Cinderella, Darling," the other secretaries beg Rosemary not to give up on Finch ("Don't, Cinderella, darling, don't turn down the prince! Don't rewrite your story; you're the legend, the folklore, the working girl's dream of glory").

"Love from a Heart of Gold" is an exaggeratedly schmaltzy waltz for Biggley and Hedy, and there was no way Vallee could have ruined it. He was perfect for it. My father's manuscript denotes the style to be "quasi-barbershop" and, after adding the second verse, he pens, "New verse—crappy enough?"

"The Brotherhood of Man" finale (a "moralist handclapper," the vocal to be in the style of "Dixie ostinato") is another satire—this one in the shape of a revival hymn, sung after all is lost and found again.

Several additional songs were written for the show but didn't make it to Broadway, including "Business Man's Shuffle":

> When a busy executive invites you to dance
> Don't be fooled into thinking that his mind's on romance.
> Don't expect to be thrilled by some technique fresh and new
> 'Cause there's only one step he's ever learned how to do.
> Only one step
> The poor schlepp
> Can do.
> It's called the—
>
> Business Man's shuffle
> The Business Man's shuffle
> He hates to dance
> But it's his chance
> To walk around and think.
> To think about business
> And while he thinks business
> The girl supplies
> The excercise
> To keep him in the pink.

All the songs are satire, the music as satirical and joke-filled as the lyrics. Even the one romantic ballad, "Rosemary," is broken up with a musical joke. Finch sings, "Just imagine, if we kissed—what a *crescendo*—" (whereupon the orchestra plays nine bars of Grieg's piano concerto while Finch stands transfixed by the idea) "not to be missed."

There is nothing really serious in *How to Succeed.* It is a romp from beginning to end, and the music is never out of character and never stands out.

The show went to Philadelphia and opened at the Shubert, to disappointing business. Noël Coward's *Sail Away* was packing them in at the Forrest, and *How to Succeed* was getting the leftovers. But the audiences slowly increased—from a quarter of a house the first week to three quarters the sixth week—and the feeling was good.

It opened in New York at the Forty-sixth Street Theater on October 14, 1961 to virtually unanimous raves. Walter Kerr of the *Herald Tribune* found it "Crafty, conniving, sneaky, cynical, irreverant, impertinent, sly, malicious, and lovely, just lovely." Taubman of the *New York Times* wrote that it "belongs to the blue chips among modern musicals."

As to the score, most reviews were along the lines of Richard Watts's in the *Post:* "It is possible that Frank Loesser's score lacks any outstanding hit song, but it is invariably gay, charming, and tuneful, and it has the enormous virtue of fitting in perfectly with the spirit and style of the book's satire."

The only flat-out pan came from the *Village Voice.* The unbylined review called it

> tolerable. Perhaps a bit more. In the end it lets you down, betraying its own soft satire in the yet softer mush of total sentimental identification with the target of its satire—the mores, ethics, absurdities of the typical American business office . . . There isn't a note of music to speak of, though Mr. Loesser's lyrics have good sardonic velocity.[9]

I think, truly, that my father wasn't very proud of this score. He had sacrificed his creativity for the good of the show as a whole, and, as Jo says,

> It was not the great personal triumph for Frank that it was for Abe. He didn't think the score was a challenge to him. He had let it be secondary to the book. It's a brilliant score in that it does what it does very effectively, and nobody else could have written it, but it wasn't what he wanted to do at the time.[10]

How to Succeed ran for over three years (1,417 performances), the fifth longest running musical in Broadway history at the time. My father watched over it protectively, giving the actors and musicians his notes from time to time. Some of them are preserved. To Charles Nelson Reilly: "Prepare for vocal delivery of 'Coffee Break.' I know some of the notes are low for you and you have to arrange your gut to negotiate them. Tough titty." To Bonnie Scott: "'What female kind of trap can I spurring' cannot be understood and is not attractive. 'Spring' is one syllable. And the way your face looks right before you sing this line is one of the most important things to remember." To Claudette Sutherland:

> Could I see some dark to light transition between "land of carbon paper" and "land of flowered chintz"? The first is, "oh this old every-day shit-house at peon's wages," and the second visualizes vast and comfortable suburban glory. That was the purpose for my putting the word "this" in front of "land of carbon paper"—so you could kind of disdain it.

And to Bobby Morse:

> We NEED you to sing out loud with the girls at the end of "Long Day." You have already played "helplessly trapped" when the girls grabbed you by the armpits, and by the time you are called on to sing, you should be resigned to the idea of going to a nice dinner with this tomato. Whether or not you should continue to play "helplessly trapped" is possibly a matter of your own instinct, but if you don't sing, and sing the right notes, and sing them loud, I'm bringing you up on charges. I have a Diners Club card, and can charge anything.[11]

All members of the cast had signed a waiver giving up any royalties from the cast album. This is a common but not universal practice in Broadway productions, the rationale being that unless a performer is a superstar indispensable to the songs' success, he or she is not due any fees beyond those stipulated in the original contract.

Rudy Vallee was among the signatories, but a few days before the first of two Sunday recording dates, Vallee's lawyer called

Allen Arrow, one of my father's attorneys, to say that Mr. Vallee felt he was entitled to a royalty of five cents per album.

"No, he's not," Allen said. "He signed the waiver like everybody else."

"Mr. Loesser can certainly afford the five cents."

"Maybe he can, but it's not fair to give Mr. Vallee a royalty and not any of the other principals."

"Well, I'll have to call you back."

And he did, saying that unless Vallee got his five cents per album, he was going to have laryngitis that Sunday. Allen reported this glitch to my father, who said, "Tell that son of a bitch that I don't need him. The show's a hit, and I don't care whether it's Rudy Vallee or Eddie Cantor in the part. Tell him that if he's got laryngitis on Sunday, he can have it for the rest of his life—he's out of the show." So Allen called Vallee's lawyer back,

> and I told him that if Rudy was going to have laryngitis that Sunday, he should stay home for the rest of his life. I thought I was throwing him out of the show. But Frank knew better than I did. A few days later Vallee said he would take some cough medicine.[12]

The show closed in March 1965, having won various awards, including the 1962 Pulitzer Prize, which my father and Abe shared ($250 apiece). Abe was excited about the prize, but my father referred to it as his "Putziller" and refused to take it seriously.

While he was in Philadelphia with the show, Jo quietly moved into the townhouse on East 70th Street she had finally convinced him to buy. The beautiful five-story house became a great source of pride for him and Jo, lovingly decorated over the years with an eclectic mix of antiques, artwork, knicknacks, and gadgets. My father was particularly fond of the gadgets. He was always adding a new one—a bank with a mechanical hand that would pop out and snatch the coin placed on top, a wind-up Frankenstein doll that lost his trousers and turned red, antique mechanical toys. He had one of the earliest telephone

With Abe Burrows, happy recipients of the "Putziller."

answering machines, on which the very first message he got was an anonymous one: "Hey Frank, I've got a great idea about how to make money, how to make money, how to make money . . ." repeated until the tape shut off.

The basement was divided into two rooms. One was his workshop, from which issued many pieces of serious furniture as well as more light-hearted creations: a wooden aquarium (complete with painted wooden fish), a bookcase in the shape of a piano (to house his *Oxford English Dictionary*), lathed pedestals (in the form of buxom women).

In the other room he recreated one of his favorite amusements, a penny arcade. He had a pinball machine, a "Skil-ball" machine, a cotton candy machine, and three old-time hand-cranked movies. Each game worked for a penny, hundreds of which were at hand in a large jar. In the middle of the room was a bumper pool table. At lunchtime, my friend June and I often snuck over from our school across the street to play pinball and bumper pool and smoke cigarettes with my father, who—with his witticisms and funny doodles and ideas to keep us from getting caught—was even more entertaining than the games.

A couple of the German language jibes were retrieved from the trash during one of those lunch hours:

> Please call me dew
> And never mind the zee—
> No German custom ever could be sillier.
> (After all, we've been sneaking into motels for seven
> years together)
> And YOUR form is already quite familiar.

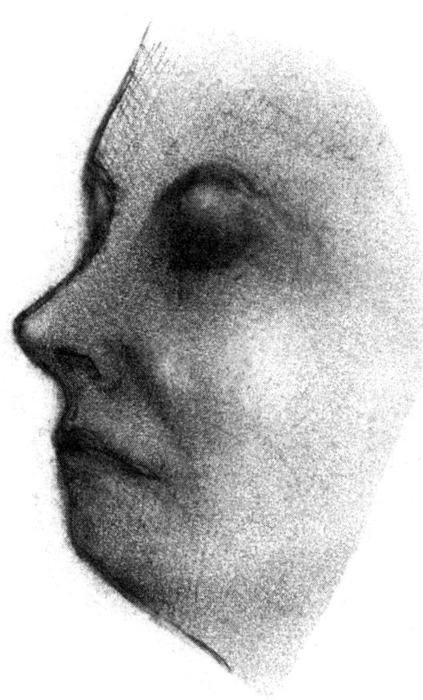

One of my father's pencil sketches of Jo.

FROM THE GERMAN PRIMER FOR CHICKEN CHILDREN

The moment the fireworks popped,
Ich hobba gehopped.

It was wonderful for me to have my father living across the street from my school. Because he had no regular schedule he was very often home during the day, and visiting with him was always an adventure. He never talked about his work with me, and he always seemed to have time to be entertaining and amusing.

If I was upset and angry about my horrid headmistress's latest cruelty, he would develop clever, sophisticated, fantastic schemes to thwart her—schemes that would have required far more patience and careful planning than I could have managed (which he counted on), but schemes that got me to laugh and feel better because he was on my side.

I was at the age of the endless teenage telephone call, and I was always on a diet of one kind or another. I kept a series of drawings and notes he passed to me one evening as I gabbed away with June on the phone:

A picture of a person made up of ragged-edged squares entitled "Young Lady Made Entirely of Ry-Krisp."

A drawing of a supine figure (you can see the soles of her feet and her nostrils) who is saying, "Paul, I am too weak from starvation to kiss you goodnight. Would you mind lifting my adorable slim figure to walking home position?"

A bunch of little floating circles: "We are calories. We have come all the way from Southern California to FATTEN YOU!"

A pair of worried eyes: "I just drank a glass of water! Do you think there's anything in it?"

And so forth, until finally, a note in large bold capital letters: "IF YOU HAVE THE STRENGTH ON YOUR DIET, <u>HANG UP SOON!!!</u>

Giggle heaven.

My father and Jo entertained frequently, and occasionally Arthur and Jean would fly in from Cleveland for a party. My father always looked forward to Arthur's visits, and when his brother was a guest, he was the guest of honor and the star of the evening. Without much coaxing, Arthur would usually give an impromptu after-dinner concert, and he was always magnificent. One night he was giving his all to some unpublished Gershwin on the grand piano in the living room with its windows wide open to the night air. The doorbell rang and a policeman came stomping into the room. "Knock it off, buddy. People are trying to sleep," he said.[13]

In October 1962, their first child, Hannah (my father always called her Hannah Banana), was born.

> The baby is wonderful and fat [my father wrote]. She greeted the Steinbecks yesterday all dressed up in a pink thing with real booties and stared them down like good babies do. Today Jo and I are going to wheel her in a carriage briefly and be very proud.[14]

Somewhat later:

> Hannah is great! I think I'll ask her to study orchestration so when she grows up I can say SO HELP ME HANNAH![15]

Jo had put her career on hold to be a mother. She told me she knew that one of the things my father had objected to about my mother was that she was not a homebody, and Jo was determined to be just that. They had a couple of maids and a butler, and a limousine and a townhouse and lots and lots of money. But they didn't have a nurse for either of their children. Jo was a hands-on mom, and I didn't really recognize it then, but I'm sure I was jealous. I was eighteen and in my freshman year at Bennington College, and so I didn't spend as much time with them. But when I did, I was so glad to be there. When I came down from Vermont for a weekend or a vacation, I would always go over to my father's house at least once to have dinner and spend the evening with them. It was very different from being in my mother's house. Jo didn't drink much and dinner was at a reasonable hour and the rest of the evening was better than a party.

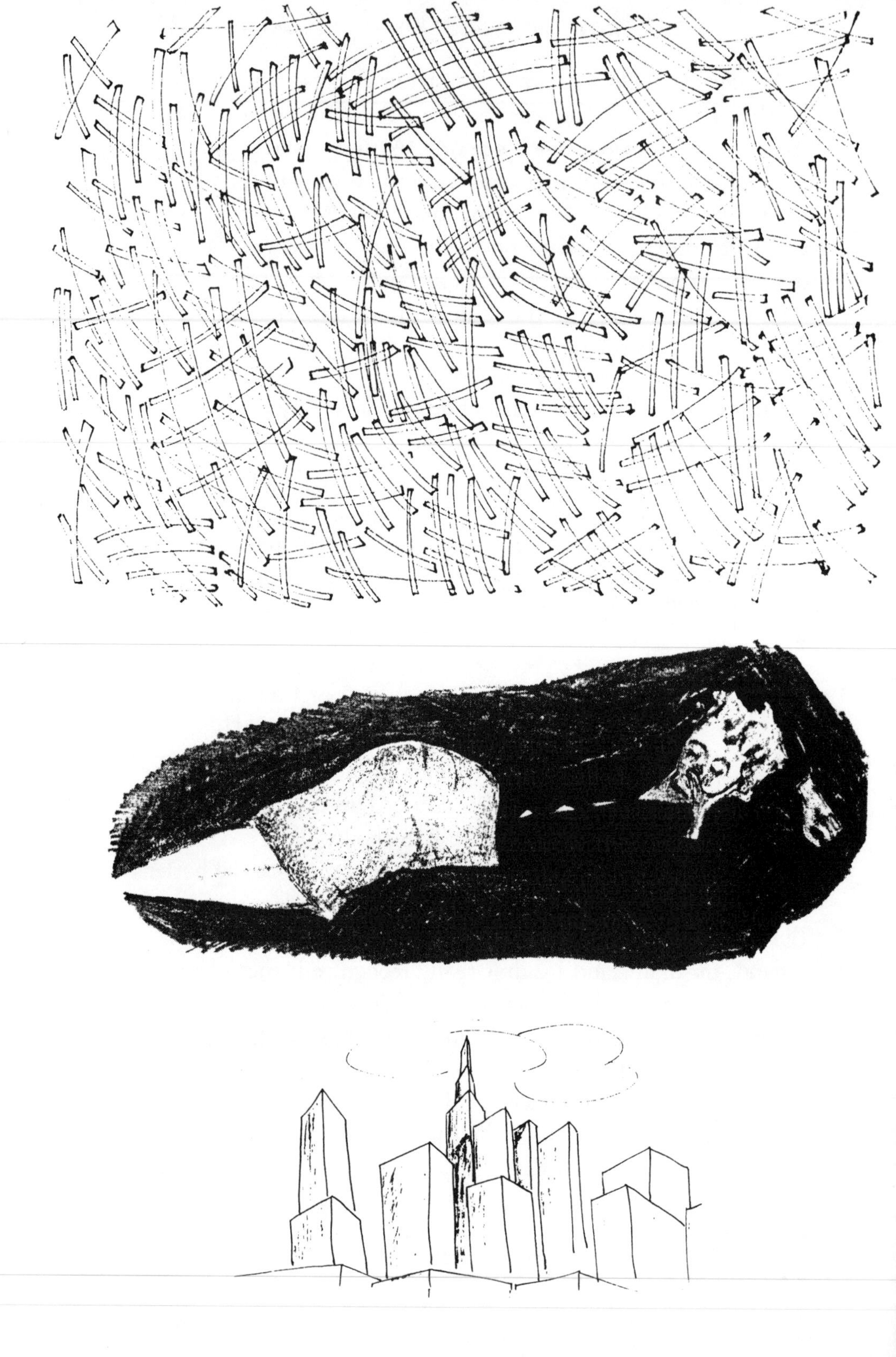

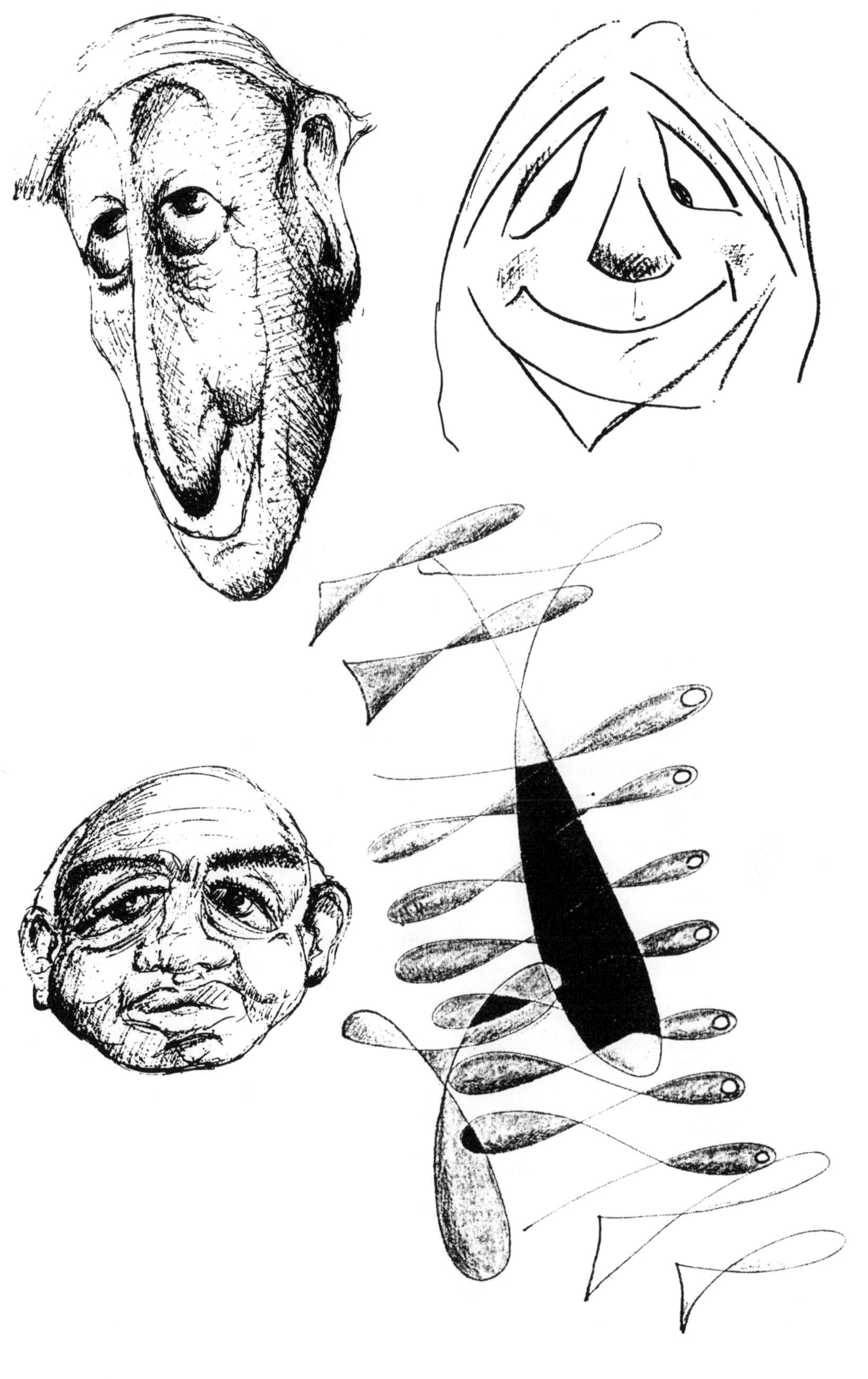

I can still feel the cool maroon leather armchair next to his desk where I used to curl up while we watched television. Actually, he watched the television, which served as fodder for his comments and poems and doodles. We watched him. This poem was in response to *The Silver Chalice:*

> Paul Newman is too curly,
> Too pearly and too early.
> He really will not flip you till the early sixties, girlie.

On *Bill of Divorcement,* starring John Barrymore:

> So long, oh recollected kicks
> You dig your graves in dug-up flicks
> Oh treacherous performing art
> Your document preserves your part
> The horse was great, but dig the cart—
> Oh Barrymore, you spastic fart!

And almost any entertainer (I don't know which one) could have inspired the following:

> SOME SINGERS propose to be conductors by making little jerky rhythmic motions invented too long ago by their betters, for better reasons.
>
> SOME SINGERS recompose and arrange all musical literature in their respective repertoires because they know better how it should have been written in the first place.
>
> SOME SINGERS whisper for a living while microphone salesmen are without honor.
>
> SOME SINGERS—Oh well, fortunately, MOST SINGERS ARE SEWING MACHINES.

I don't suppose the following lines were penned in response to the television. Perhaps we were discussing poetry:

> Hooray, Hooray, Hooray, Hooray, Hoorah!
> Oh note, the joy, the verve, the lah, de dah!
> For I, recall, tonight, iam, bic verse
> (which in my extreme youth I employed
> in reciting Gray's Elegy)

With which, I used, to charm, the Po, lish nurse.
Hoorah, hoorah, hoorah, hoorah, hooray!
A bum, like me, can limp, as slick, as Gray
(the Polish nurse exited real pregnant,
but right after we got a Spanish one
who dug—)
Olé, Olé, Olé, Olé, Olé!

He loved to watch the Mets. The original Mets who fumbled and tumbled and lost ninety-nine percent of their games. He watched them loyally and knew all their names and all their foibles. He yearned for them to win a game, but he happily forgave them their ineptitude because they were so wonderfully entertaining.

Although he enjoyed his TV, his gadgets and his games, and entertained and delighted us with his wit, my father's imagination was most profoundly captivated by the world of business. He had a talent for it and a leaning toward it that were probably partly responsible for the authentic ring of his *How to Succeed* lyrics. When he started his own company back in the forties, he cultivated it like a garden, tending it carefully through the years, watching it grow and thrive. *How to Succeed* may not have been his favorite project,, but its subject matter was both near and dear to him as the exuberant owner of three interconnected businesses himself. Business was my father's second professional love, and he was very, very good at it.

12

The Businessman

In 1948, having watched Irving Berlin retain control of his work and thrive by publishing his own songs, my father decided to follow suit. He began by forming Susan Publications, Inc. (that's me!) with Edwin H. (Buddy) Morris. "Susan" was a paper company only. Morris did the nitty-gritty work as "sole selling agent" while my father, with the legitimacy and clout of a company name behind him, began to acquire properties. He started with the score of *Where's Charley?*, some not-yet-published songs, and a few movie songs he was able to wrest from the studios. The catalogue steadily fattened, and in 1950 the Frank Music Corp. was born, its first solid meal being the Susan/Morris company. By January 1952, Frank Music had added the scores of *Guys and Dolls* and *Hans Christian Andersen*, occupied fully staffed offices in New York and Los Angeles, and was beginning to acquire other songwriters.

My father was always interested in other writers—interested in nurturing them, developing them, and making money from them. In the fifties the music publishing business was very different from today. Herb Eiseman, who ran Frank Music for several years, recalls that in those days

> Writers would write songs and shop them around to various companies, and the company would say, "Yeah. I like that

> song. I think we could possibly get a recording contract." And the song pluggers would take the songs around to the A & R men [artists and repertoire] at the record companies. And they in turn would say, "I have a young singer—Andy Williams, for instance—this song would be good for." So they'd show the song to the artist. If the artist liked it, he would record it. As soon as the Andy Williams record would come out on the market, you'd try to get other people to come out with their versions. For some songs we'd get seven or eight recordings out within a matter of months of each other, all being played on the radio. No one would ask for an exclusive.
>
> Later the A & R people started saying they didn't want any other record out before sixty or ninety days. They'd imply that otherwise you'd never get a song recorded with them again. Things started changing with the advent of the Beatles and people like that who were writing their own material. Now it's a whole different business—songwriters perform their own songs and aren't about to give their publishing over to someone else. They start their own publishing companies. They've become a self-contained act.[1]

The first big hit for Frank Music Corp. by someone other than my father was "Unchained Melody" (Alex North and Hy Zaret), followed by "Cry Me a River" (Arthur Hamilton). Then there was Ross Bagdasarian, who created The Chipmunks, and Josef Marais and Miranda, a folk duo specializing in South African music, who had a hit with "Marching to Pretoria." At least it was a hit at our house; I can still hear it.

One day in 1952 my mother got a call from her friend Annie Lederer (the former child star Anne Shirley and the wife of screenwriter Charles Lederer) about two young songwriters—Robert Wright and George (Chet) Forrest—who had been writing for the movies since they were practically infants. In addition to their considerable movie credits, they had adapted Grieg's "Peer Gynt Suite" for their show *Song of Norway* (1944) and the music of Villa-Lobos for *Magdalena* (1948). (They haven't stopped yet. Their most recent show was 1989's *Grand Hotel.*) On that day in 1952 Bob and Chet played a couple of songs for my mother from a new show they were writing, *Kismet.*

(Most of the music in *Kismet* is adapted from Borodin, but some of it is pure Wright and Forrest). My mother loved their stuff and introduced them to my father, and so began a long and happy association with "the boys," who recall their first meeting fondly:

> Frank came into the room and said, "Don't think I don't know who you are. I kept track of you all the time I was at Paramount. You wrote . . ." and he quoted one of our most complicated and unsuccessful lyrics, the whole thing, even sang it for us. We were bowled over.
>
> Before that afternoon came to an end, Frank said, "I'd like to publish your score." I don't think we gave it a second thought. We had had a contract with Chappell, but they had shown a distinct lack of interest and had let it lapse. So we were free.
>
> Frank was very close to the show—brought everybody to hear it. And Lynn and Dick Gray plugged the score. Nothing was ever exploited like that score was. I think there were something like thirty-six different records made before the show ever left its California tryout for Broadway.[2]

Frank Music published everything that Wright and Forrest wrote until my father's death in 1969.

In 1951, Richard Adler and Jerry Ross played my father a song they had written called "Strange Little Girl." In Richard's words:

> He liked it immensely. He said, "I'll give you a five hundred dollar advance on it," which was a huge amount in those days. He was very tough, very critical, but very good with us, very encouraging. A year after we met he introduced us to George Abbott. We played our stuff for Abbott, who said, "Very good. You're not ready." He said the same thing the next year. Then in 1953 we had "Rags to Riches." That year when we played for Abbott, he said, "I've got something you might be interested in. It's called *Seven and a Half Cents.*" Everybody else had turned it down, including Frank. But I really loved it, and Jerry did too. And that's how *The Pajama Game* came about.[3]

Adler and Ross stayed with Frank Music through *Damn Yankees,* then decided to go it alone—by this time their exclusive deal seemed too constricting. As Richard says, "Perhaps it was a bit ungrateful, as I look back on it, but he had us for both shows, so he got the cream. And I think he would have done the same. After all, he couldn't wait to get away from Paramount."

Richard will never forget a song he had written called "Pretty Bird."

> Frank said, "I'm going to take this song and get it into a picture." He took it, and two or three months went by without a word. We called him up. "Oh yeah," he said, "I'm showing it around. Haven't gotten much yet." I said he had good connections at Paramount, what about them? He said, "Oh, them. They only offered me twenty-five hundred." "Twenty-five hundred dollars! What did you do?" He said, "I turned it down." Now, we were broke at that time, dead broke. We were getting fifty dollars a week as an advance. Twenty-five hundred dollars in those days was like twenty thousand now. I was depressed and furious. But Frank was a very principled and tough man. He thought the song was worth more.

Did he get more for it?

> It STILL hasn't been published. I own it now. It has never been recorded.[4]

In 1955 Meredith Willson came to Frank Music with *The Music Man*, a show my father had suggested to him after hearing his reminiscences about his Iowa childhood. My father put him in touch with Feuer and Martin, who, although they liked the show, had some reservations about the book and eventually turned him down. Several revisions later, Willson went to Kermit Bloomgarden; *The Music Man* was produced in 1957 and ran for 1,375 performances. Frank Music, of course, published the score, as well as everything else Willson wrote after that.

The composer Mark Bucci (*Sweet Betsy from Pike, The Thirteen Clocks, Tale for a Deaf Ear*) was a protégé of my father's for a time, under contract to Frank Music from 1957 to 1960.

> I had heard he was fond of developing writers, so I just called him up. I used to meet with him at his apartment. My music was always too science-fictiony, too fancy, I think, for Broad-

way. But I wanted to write a commercial musical. And Frank, having done *The Most Happy Fella,* wanted to write an "important" opera. Every time I'd come up with something, he'd say, "Write more down to earth. Write another 'California, Here I Come.'" Eventually I broke our contract through a legal technicality. He was a little possessive, wanted to hold on to me, but I sensed it was time to move on. And when we parted, he used that "California, Here I Come" line on me again, once too often. I said, "And you go write another *La Boheme.*"[5]

Some of the many writers my father took an interest in have had very successful careers, although not always as songwriters. One of them is Alfred Uhry. In 1958, long before he wrote *Driving Miss Daisy,* Uhry was writing songs in partnership with a friend from Brown University, Bob Waldman. The two of them came to New York in search of their fortune and got an appointment with my father.

We got a call the next week [Uhry recalled], and they told us they wanted to sign us to a contract for fifty dollars a week. This was 1958. You could almost live on that. So for more than three years I worked at Frank Music. Sometimes we'd do commercials—I wrote the theme song for "Hootenanny Saturday Night," and it was on television every week. Mostly, though, we'd write theater songs, and Frank would criticize them. We'd write a song and go to his office, and he would devote a big chunk of time to teach the two of us how to write better. It was really a remarkable thing. This was a busy man, and he clearly was working with us because he loved it and really felt we would get somewhere.

He used to say, "If you're sitting in the theater and you hear the song once, it's like a freight train. You see the cars go by. You see the coal car, the caboose, you don't see all the details, and it only goes by once. So keep it simple."

What I owe him most is this: Every Word Counts. I didn't know that before I knew Frank. He was talking about lyrics, not dialogue, but he taught me that even "the" counts. Of course I applied his teaching to lyrics then, but now that I write plays, I find it invaluable.[6]

When you're a big shot in the theater, everybody sends you material to evaluate—whether you ask for it or not. My father was no exception. All kinds of people found him and submitted raw ideas, lyrics, tunes, outlines, scripts. Occasionally, as with *Greenwillow,* he would be delighted. Much more often, he wasn't. As he put it to me in a letter once:

> I've been reading—reading an enormous assortment of crap, mostly plays, for people who want composers, want investors, want producers, want compliments—none of whom, even for a moment, admit the desperate *want* of a playwright.
>
> In the last week an old friend (a director) has sent me a sheaf of lyrics written by himself—his purpose being to find out if he is *any good at it.* I'm supposed to read them and make a noise like an oracle. The same day Tony Quinn, not satisfied with being the world's most somethingest actor, rushes me to read a whole novel (which, like a fathead, I did) to say if it will make a musical for him to produce. Also in the last week I've read a new musical adaptation of *Cyrano de Bergerac* (there are maybe a dozen on the market) and next Friday I have to listen to the score. There are two plays by you-know-who on my desk waiting to be read—and you *know* they are going to be CUTE instead of GOOD.[7]

In a letter to a friend telling him just how much and why he hated a particular script, he concluded:

> Now I will say something lofty. A show is not a toy, nor a series of gusts of saliva spray. It is some $400,000 worth of hard, sound business, all of it aimed at giving two and a half hours of continuous pleasure to its audience. True, it can and should reach into new, strange, and exciting resources toward the ultimate purpose. Resources themselves, however, should not be dumped on the stage like a paper bag full of rhinestones. They have to be mounted carefully in an appropriate design in solid gold.[8]

My father had a lust for knowledge that spread far beyond the music business. He enjoyed meeting and scheming with all kinds of people, from cabinetmakers to lawyers. Ad-libbing a deal over lunch was one of his favorite ways to do business, and on such occasions he amazed his associates with his quick and complex thinking, which often resulted in new ventures. His rules were simple: Be creative. Be clever. Make money.

So it didn't surprise anyone that Frank Music Corp., with its stable of first-class writers, got into the advertising business for a time. During lunch one day with an executive at Young and Rubicam, the subject of commercial jingles came up. "Jesus! What do you pay for that crap?" my father said. "I could provide you with writers who would knock your socks off, and you'd be paying them less than you pay those schlemiels you've got now—they're already working for me." A deal was struck. As Herb Eiseman remembers it, "Everyone was happy. We were able to deliver writers to the agency at a price much lower than they had been paying. The writers were happy because they were getting ASCAP performance income, we were giving them more assignments, and they were attracting attention."[9] FMC produced jingles for Sunkist Lemonade, Halo Shampoo, Newport Filter Cigarettes ("A hint of mint makes the difference"), Sanka Aroma Roast, and various (and very local) beers. My father just enjoyed it to tears.

In 1953, Frank Music Corp. was joined by Music Theatre International and, in 1960, by Frank Productions, Inc. Music Theater, a musical leasing company, buys the rights to lease shows after their initial runs. Customers range from amateur high school groups to professional regional theaters. Music Theater was the brainchild of orchestrator Don Walker, who noted that Tams-Witmark and Samuel French—the only companies at that time involved in secondary licensing—weren't doing a very good job of it. According to Allen Whitehead, president of MTI from its inception until his retirement in 1991, Dick Rodgers had asked Don Walker to reorchestrate a couple of numbers in *Pal Joey* for a revival. When Walker went to Tams-Witmark to pick up the original orchestrations, he was handed a small package wrapped in brown paper and tied with string. No one had checked it, and some material, including entire individual numbers, was missing. This meant that much of the show had to be reconstructed.

> That gave Don the idea of a company that really takes care of authors' works [Allen told me]—which should, after all, be

> preserved for posterity. He talked to Dick and Oscar about it, and he wanted to call it Music Theater.
>
> *Oklahoma!* and *South Pacific* and *Carousel* were about ready to go into subsidiary rights, which would be a good nucleus, and Don suggested that anything he orchestrated be brought into the company. Dick and Oscar loved the idea, and to make a long story short, they ended up loving the idea so much that they told Don to go screw, they would do it themselves, thank you very much.
>
> Well, Don still thought it was a good idea, and he and his agent thought about who else to approach. Don felt strongly about having an author be in on it—a natural source of material. He and Frank had been talking about *The Most Happy Fella.* He called Frank in California and Frank said, "Of course."[10]

Originally Music Theater was housed in the offices of Howard Hoyt, the leading agent in those days for Broadway musicals. The nucleus of properties was six shows from Hoyt's clients, including *Gentlemen Prefer Blondes, Call Me Madam,* and *High Button Shoes.* They added *Where's Charley?, Guys and Dolls,* and everything else my father wrote, and quickly developed a catalogue that is still going strong. Now owned by Fred Gershon, the list includes *Pajama Game, Damn Yankees, The Music Man, A Funny Thing Happened on the Way to the Forum, Candide, Fiddler on the Roof, The Fantasticks, Jesus Christ Superstar, Les Miserables, Miss Saigon,* and on, and on, and on.

Frank Productions was started up so my father could produce his own shows, beginning with *Greenwillow* in 1960. The company produced only a few works by others, notably a rather charming and original South African revue called *Wait a Minim,* which opened to pleasant notices in 1966 and ran a little over a year.

In New York my father's three businesses, which thrived on West 57th Street in the fifties and sixties, were known in the trade for their high ethics, for paying their bills on time, and for their class. Business associates were put up at the best hotels. Business lunches and dinners happened at the Russian Tea

Room across the street, or at the 21 Club, or Sardi's. Company executives traveled first class. The offices, while not opulent, were tastefully decorated and well appointed; the employees were chosen for their initiative and intelligence, and the majority of them stayed with the company for most of its life. As a former colleague puts it, "Frank's employees may not have been paid more than anyone else in town, but they had more fun."[11]

For two summers during high school I worked at my father's various offices in various capacities. I was a relief switchboard operator, a mailroom clerk, receptionist, and, after Cyd Cheiman sent me to secretarial school, a typist. I felt grown up and important and I kidded myself that my father's employees really thought of me as an equal. Oh, they liked me all right, and they were wonderful to me. But they were well aware that I hadn't come in off the street. I think we were all lucky that I wasn't a princess. I learned from them and I performed my assignments diligently. I loved it.

I loved it especially when I worked as a receptionist on the floor where my father had his office. It was the liveliest place to be, and I got to see my father almost daily. He used to stop by my desk and make fun of my long straight hair, which fell over my face, obscuring it stylishly.

"How the hell can you see where you're going?" he'd jibe. Or, "I guess you save time that way—you only have to put makeup on one eye." I, in turn, would tell him how awful he looked in his goatee, a recent acquisition.

Every day we'd go through this routine. He'd stand over my desk teasing me about my hair and I'd make cracks about his Alfred Drake beard. One day after his usual remarks he continued to stand there looking at me quizzically, beginning to make me uncomfortable. Finally he said, "Well?" And I looked up at him through my hair and said, "Well what?" And he said, "You haven't noticed?" And I said, "Noticed what?" And he stroked his chin. I said, "What, Pop? What is it?" And he stroked his chin again. His bare chin.

"Oh, Pop! You did it—you shaved it off! You look great! Really—Much better!" (I felt like an idiot).

"Sure," he said with an irritated little chuckle. "I can see what a big difference it makes to you." And I never felt right about complaining again when the goatee fancy struck him. He went through several Mephistophelian periods. I made a minimal fuss, and to be honest, I never noticed right away when he resumed shaving his chin.

Stuart Ostrow, Tony Award-winning producer of *M. Butterfly*, started out in the theater working for my father. They met when Stuart was in the Air Force during the Korean War, head of their Radio and Television department. He wanted to do a show like *Winged Victory*, and he wanted to get Frank Loesser to write the songs. The Air Force turned him loose and, surprising himself with his chutzpah, Stuart turned up one day at my father's New York hotel and sold him on the idea. On one condition. "I'll do your show," he said, "if you get Abe Burrows to write the book."

> I was in heaven. I called Burrows and set up a meeting that morning. I hadn't even shaved. I met him at "21." He said, "Yes, I'll do it."
>
> Well, here I had Frank Loesser and Abe Burrows. I went back to Washington and said, "Yup. Got 'em." And two days later I was summoned to a senator's office, and they started asking me questions: What political groups did I belong to, what affiliations did I have outside of college, and so forth. And suddenly I realized what was going on. This was the McCarthy era, and Abe had been blacklisted. I also realized that Frank had agreed to do this show to help Abe—get him identified with the United States Government. I thought that was the most remarkable thing. It didn't happen, though, because the government said no. And I had to go back to Abe Burrows and tell him the government didn't want him.[12]

My father suggested that Stuart call him when he got out of the service, so he did, and he was hired as a song plugger in New York. Then he was promoted to what my father called "Governor General" of the Los Angeles office. Later still, Stuart ran Frank Music in New York until he left to go out on his very successful own in the early sixties.

My father did not believe in pension plans. He didn't want employees sitting around waiting out their time until retirement. "If they're smart," he'd say, "they'll put the money aside and start their own pension plans." But he gave legendary bonuses. And he gave them at his legendary Christmas parties, extravagant affairs usually held at the Plaza or the Waldorf. Beginning with a luncheon for the two hundred or so employees, the party opened up late in the afternoon to include others in the music business—artists, songwriters, publishers, producers, lawyers, accountants, friends. And it went on until it felt like ending. People actually called two or three months in advance to ensure invitations to *the* Christmas party of the industry.

When Cyd Cheiman was hired as comptroller for the companies, she had a fight with my father about her salary. She won, but had to agree never to ask for a raise. "You'll get it when you deserve it," he said. "Don't ever ask me."

> And I never had to. He showered me. For instance, there was that Christmas party luncheon. It was Frank's habit to address the group just before dessert was served. One year, to my astonishment, he addressed his remarks to me—made it known to everyone how dependable I was. He said he knew I would show up at work every day of the year except for two days. One day would be Washington's Birthday, because he knew I was a true American and had respect for the father of our country. The second day would be Yom Kippur, because I was a good Jew. Since I was his first ten-year employee, he was giving me a special holiday trip to anywhere I wanted to go. And since he had been told that I enjoyed Las Vegas and loved to gamble, he was providing me with a dime a day figured out over a period of ten years, minus two dimes a year for the two yearly missing days. At which point the door opened and in walked two midgets carrying four heavy containers filled with dimes.[13]

(Why midgets? I heard about a party in California where he had a midget come running through the crowd scattering peanuts. Was it those Philip Morris commercials? Was it because little people were shorter than he was? Did everybody think midgets were funny in the old days?)

When my father cared about someone, he went out of his way for him or her, sometimes far out of his way. He gave his employees and associates generous, sometimes extravagant, presents. His lawyer, Harold Orenstein, once called him to ask the source of "All the Things You Are." The next day a complete set of *Best Plays* arrived with a note: "Don't bother me again." On another occasion he gave Harold the twelve-volume *Oxford English Dictionary*.

The day that ten major contracts for *How to Succeed* were to close, Harold's partner at the time, Allen Arrow, had to engineer the crucial meeting around a train strike and a two-foot snowstorm. He managed it, the contracts all got signed, and he was left sitting in his office, gazing out the window at the snow. The phone rang.

"How are you getting home?" my father asked.

"I was just wondering that myself," Allen said. "I might have to stay in town for the weekend."

"Just tell me when you want to leave. I'll take care of it." And at the appointed time a Rolls-Royce, driven by a chauffeur and accompanied fore and aft by two plow-equipped jeeps, pulled up to the building.

When his personal secretary, Mona Lipp, started taking piano lessons and asked him what kind of piano he thought she should rent, he bought a company piano and sent it to her house. When she left the company, he refused to take it back. She still has it.

Sometimes my father helped people in unexpected ways. When Henry Fanelli came to work at Music Theater in 1960, he brought with him excellent clerical skills, a love of the theater, a proficiency on the harp, and an introduction from me. We had met the summer we both apprenticed at Bucks County Playhouse. Henry wanted to write for the theater, and, having heard some of his songs, I thought my father might be interested.

He liked Henry very much and told him that if he wanted to be a writer he had to move into the city, see lots of theater, and write, write, write. He gave him a job at Music Theater writing letters and answering phones and filing. He gave him "a conducive environment, a small salary, and a lot of encouragement." But Henry just didn't have the energy to do much writing after a long day at the office.

> Music Theater was handling the score of *The Fantasticks* [Henry told me], and one day Frank said to me, "You play the harp, don't you? I can get you an audition at *The Fantasticks.*" I hadn't touched the harp in months. But I figured out something to audition with and found myself hired immediately as the standby harpist. After a year I took over as the main harpist. I gave up my job at Music Theater, and since then I've never had to work in an office again—I've always had a job playing the harp. In the last five years I've gotten every hit show's harpist position, and now I'm doing *Phantom of the Opera,* and this job could last me the rest of my career. And none of this would have happened if I hadn't met Frank.[14]

My father's personal office was a large room with a big desk, a grand piano, and a long, comfortable couch for his naps. He had a urinal installed in a closet so he wouldn't have to waste time going down the hall. He was particular and demanding. Pencils had to be plentiful and sharpened; the Kleenex supply for the cough and congestion that worsened over the years had to be inexhaustible; the yellow legal pads on which he composed lyrics, made notes, wrote memos, and produced his intricate doodles had to be ordered by the thousand. Coffee—brewed fresh and strong—was expected all day long, especially in the morning. Liquor, soft drinks, ice, and snacks were stocked in a refrigerator and crystal and china in a cabinet so that any type of meeting, from mainly social to strictly business, could be accommodated.

When my father summoned staff members, he expected an instant response. For a time he used an excruciatingly loud boat horn to get their attention. He also lost his temper and yelled at his employees regularly, but because he was as generous and charming as he was volatile, he kept most of them.

Sometimes the employees fought back. Mona once got real fed up. She felt that my father had been treating her like a servant lately, so she rented a French maid's costume—short skirt, black net stockings, little white apron and cap—and greeted my father at 8:00 A.M. with his steaming coffee in hand. The trouble was, he thought it was so funny that he had her serve drinks in the costume at a meeting that evening with some people from the West Coast, playing the scene completely straight until the end. "You couldn't top him," Mona says. "Frank would always do you one better."[15]

I wish I could say Mona refused to go along with the joke. Instead, I have to say that I understand perfectly well why she didn't. It was very hard to say no to my father. He was the boss, of course, and basically a good-hearted and generous boss whom people found easy to love. But he was also an immensely powerful presence with a maniacal drive and energy. Everybody wanted to please him, to amuse him, to capture his attention.

Including his daughter. I could not refuse my father, although I frequently failed him. I would be so flattered if he asked me to look something up for him, or tell him what I thought about something, or find him some obscure or rare or specialized item, that I would make every effort to give him what he wanted. And if my research was insufficient, or my opinion disappointing, or the item elusive, I suffered because, like everyone else around him, I wanted this fireball of a person to shine on me.

While I was in college at Bennington, my father employed me to scout for properties that I thought might be potential musicals. I was to write synopses and suggestions based on whatever I was reading for school or for pleasure. I earned a rather substantial allowance, dubbed by my father a retainer, but I never came up with a winner. The one suggestion I sent to which he responded positively was Anouilh's *Time Remembered,* a play he had been interested in for some time anyway. He talked to me at length about this play, explaining its attractions and problems, treating me like an equal. I was very flattered.

His birthday was always a challenge—what could I give that would surprise and delight him? One time I found him an antique pocket watch with an intricate enamelled face. He loved it, he said, and immediately went to work on it. He electrified it, cradled it in velvet, and crafted a gorgeous maple stand for it, completely dwarfing the original gift with his creative embellishments.

I remember this incident especially because it captures for me a kind of yin-yang, wonderful/terrible charm of my father. In his enthusiasm for life he couldn't resist the urge to take an idea and run with it like a kite, to see how much higher it could fly. People who worked for him and with him, or people whose creative lives intersected his in any way experienced this phenomenon. And for many it was inspiring. My cousin Ted Drachman, a lyricist, says my father brought out the best in him, that he always felt uplifted after being with him. My father's friend Cynthia Lindsay, a writer, said to me, "If he appreciated you, he made you the very best that you could be. He made people proud of themselves."

The flip side of this is, of course, that if you weren't real sure of yourself, he could make you feel inept, uncreative, pedestrian, boring, bush league. In many a conversation or correspondence, assignment or offering, solicited or volunteered, I felt as though I had presented him with a dingy old broken watch.

Perhaps my father's closest business associate was his attorney and friend Harold Orenstein. They met in 1951 when my father was "auditioning lawyers," as Harold puts it, to replace his current attorney, Francis Gilbert, who was dying. Harold worked with my father until his death and still represents our family in copyright and other legal matters. His crafty legal mind appealed to my father's love of scheming and wheeling and dealing. During their long association, Harold authored tough and creative contracts for my father, handled the businesses' legal affairs, drew up his divorce papers, formalized his

This is the only existing photo of Julia, Arthur, Grace, and my father all together. (*Mona Lipp*)

highly complicated will, and advised him on a great variety of ventures.

In all of this my father was, of course, actively involved. He was fascinated with law and liked to keep lawyers on their toes.

> Frank loved to tease lawyers [Harold told me]. And he was sharp. He familiarized himself with the *Meinhard v. Salmon* case (1928), which had to do with partnerships and joint ventures, and in the course of a negotiation he would throw the citation at the other lawyer, referring to it casually, as though everybody knew that case.[16]

Harold presented my father with a big old lawbook rebound in fine leather and retitled (in the fashion of ponderous legal tomes) *Loesser on Loopholes.* He kept it—prominently displayed—on his library shelves at home.

In the early 1960s a couple of books about emphysema also appeared on those shelves.

"Emphysema? What's that, Pop? What do you have books on that for?"

"It's a lung disease, and I've got it. That's why," he said, hacking his way through another Camel.

The books were medical treatises and hard for me to read, but I understood enough to know that my father's juicy, chronic cough was in fact a symptom of serious illness.

I was shocked. My father with his electric energy had always seemed invulnerable, his respiratory troubles mere sound effects, part of his fierce, explosive personality. Nothing to worry about. Only now I got worried.

He dismissed my concern as he dismissed everyone's. By then Jo was nagging him, begging him, yelling at him to stop smoking. Like Mark Twain, he quit hundreds of times. But the nicotine demon always won, and the cough that was his constant companion only got worse.

Although my father was always eager to find talented new writers and performers, he became increasingly impatient with modern trends in popular music, particularly rock 'n roll. In the fifties this irritation hardly mattered—Broadway was still in its prime, its theaters untainted by the brash young sounds of the teenagers my father called "pimplefarms." But by the mid-sixties, rock music—matured into a major musical force and enjoying a golden age of its own—began to invade the sacred prosceniums of Broadway. Suddenly rock became not just an irritant to my father but an affront, and, ultimately, a threat.

His staff of managers and song pluggers tried to encourage him to take on some of the newer singer-songwriters emerging on the music scene, but usually he balked. As Herb Eiseman put it, "He couldn't understand how these songs were being recorded and played on the radio. He was appalled by them. He used to say, 'They're just rhyming *sounds,* not words!' He was, I think, a little afraid. He saw the trend coming and didn't know how it was going to affect him and his kind of music."[17]

Indeed. It was a topic guaranteed to make him angry, on occasion inspiring contemptuous little ditties like this one, which he malevolently thrust into *Señor Discretion,* his last (unfinished) show:

I only know, Babe
I only know
I only know, Babe
I only know
I only know, Babe
I only know
Three chords on the guitar.

At the time, a large segment of rock music was evolving that went beyond simple, mindless lyrics and into lyrics of social protest and introspection. My father didn't like those songs, either. There was the time a young woman wanted to sell Frank Music her company and sign a songwriter's contract. My father asked his vice president, Milt Kramer, for an evaluation. And Milt, knowing his boss's difficulties with the woman's type of music, waffled. My father said, "I've got to tell you, I can't understand her goddamned lyrics—too complicated. Too modern. But if you want to do it, let's do it."

"It will cost us about a hundred grand," Milt said.

"Well, if it's a risk, I'd rather give the money to my family than to that lady and her lawyer."

So they didn't sign a contract with Janis Ian. Oh well, it could have been worse. It could have been Paul Simon. The only rock musician that Frank Music took under its wing was Loudon Wainwright III. And I remember how proud they were to have him and how lovingly they promoted him.

Meanwhile my father was, as ever, writing for Broadway. Writing for the Broadway that was not so slowly beginning to change—the Broadway that would soon betray him by embracing those very elements he detested.

My father's next show was to be a period piece, a costume piece, set in Russia at the court of Catherine the Great. He was going to dazzle them.

13

Pleasures and Palaces

Here's a musical comedy recipe: Imagine that when John Paul Jones goes to Russia in 1788 to fight the Turks for Catherine the Great, he becomes embroiled in a political and romantic intrigue. Catherine loves the devilish Potemkin, who adores the lusty, murderous Sura, who falls for the oh-so-Presbyterian Jones one minute, then into Potemkin's ready arms the next. Add a power struggle between Potemkin and his ministers. Allow Sura to simmer between lust and repentance. Make Catherine attractive and sympathetic. Flavor Jones with a charming mixture of youthful naivete, high moral standards, and heroic aspirations. Spice up Potemkin with a scheming, pragmatic outlook, a clever sense of humor, and a dashing, attractive personality.

Put it all together with Sam Spewack (who with his wife, Bella, wrote the book for *Kiss Me, Kate*) and Bob Fosse as director and choreographer. Garnish with Robert Randolph's gorgeous sets and Freddy Wittop's lavish costumes.

Hold dress rehearsals, get encouraging feedback from your peers, and take the show on the road.

Die in Detroit.

Alfred Urhy had suggested the idea. When my father said

he might be interested in writing something about the era of Catherine the Great, Urhy said, "Well, you know there's this play by Sam Spewack called *Once There Was a Russian.*" This 1961 effort had run for exactly one night on Broadway. My father read the comedy and thought it might redeem itself as a musical. So did Sam Spewack. So did Bob Fosse, who liked the idea of having some Russian-style choreography to play with. The three of them began work in the fall of 1963, my father writing music, lyrics, and, with Spewack, the book. Once they had a working script (which they inexplicably called *Ex-Lover*) and my father had most of the songs in varying stages of completion, the problem—and it was a problem—was casting.

For some reason they wanted British actors to play Potemkin and Catherine—to give them a European sound, I suppose. Initially they thought Richard Harris would make a wonderful Potemkin. Fosse and my father went to London to see Harris, who arranged to meet them at the Connaught Hotel. As Gwen Verdon remembered it:

> There's a grand staircase that comes down into the lobby of the Connaught. Frank and Bob were sitting in the lobby when Harris made his entrance down the stairs. He did scenes from *Richard III,* bits and pieces of every Shakespearean role he'd ever played. He sang Irish songs—all in the stuffy lobby of the Connaught Hotel. Harris was terrific; Frank and Bob were glued to the spot. I said, "Weren't you embarrassed?" and they said, "Oh no, we loved it."[1]

Despite their enjoyable meeting, they didn't end up with Richard Harris. For one thing, at that time he had a reputation for being unreliable. For another, he didn't really want the part. Instead they hired Alfred Marks, a British actor well known in London's West End. Marks was not particularly dashing, more of an off-beat character actor who could sing, but they hoped he would be a fresh new personality on the Broadway stage. For Catherine they chose Hy Hazell, who had recently enjoyed great success as Mrs. Squeezem in a period musical called *Lock Up Your Daughters* that had run for years in London and in Sydney, Australia.

Back in New York, they cast Phyllis Newman as Sura and John McMartin as Jones.

All during 1964 they worked on the show. Bob Fosse had a wonderful time with the choreography, Gwen Verdon told me:

> The Bolshoi had just appeared in New York for the first time. They did so many tricks that Frank and Bob decided that they should come up with something in response. So Bob made all kinds of jokes. One man did a great big jumping split—at which point, with sound effects, his pants would rip. Another man would do a cartwheel and his hairpiece would come undone. We didn't have enough men, so after various protests, they finally dressed the girls up like men and put mustaches on them. Kathryn Doby taught them how to do kazatskies.[2]

In January 1965 Alfred Marks and Hy Hazell arrived and rehearsals began. Before they all left for Detroit in early March, they invited colleagues to see a couple of dress rehearsals and to give advice. Apparently the response was enthusiastic, although today, safe in the luxury of hindsight, practically everyone I've talked to says something like, "I told them it wasn't working," or "I told them I didn't think much of it."

So off to Detroit they went, opening on March 11 at the Fisher Theater, and from that moment on everybody worked desperately to hold the show together and make it come to life.

They rehearsed all day, performed all evening, rewrote all night. They cut scenes, they added lines. The atmosphere was tense, nobody was getting any sleep, and Alfred Marks was afraid of heights.

> Alfred had to make an entrance from the top of the staircase [Gwen Verdon remembered]. They put so much glow tape down that the people in the balcony could see it. Frank, who was in the balcony for one of the performances, came running down to Michael Sinclair, the stage manager. "What's all that glow tape up there for?" And Michael, who was very British, said, "That's so Mr. Marks won't be nervous before his entrance, because he's up in the air and he's afraid of heights." Frank said, "But you can see all that tape from the balcony!" And Michael said, "Yes, sir. I know. It looks like Kennedy

> Airport." Frank just loved that. Any anger he might have had dissolved. From that point on he'd say, "Let's take it from the Kennedy Airport entrance of Mr. Marks."[3]

Eventually—well, sooner than eventually—they let Mr. Marks go. Potemkin was meant to be romantic, something of a swashbuckler, if a rather conniving and dastardly one, and Marks was too much of a character to be a rake.

They called the Coast and made a deal with Jack Cassidy, who arrived a couple of days later with fifteen suitcases, and, as Gwen Verdon says, "all those teeth." He was very dashing and he improved the part. Unfortunately, Potemkin was only one element among many that needed improvement.

My father's manuscripts for this show span a period between October 1963 and March 1965, the last ones written as they withered in Detroit. There are a total of fifty-five numbers, twenty-two of which were actually used, ranging from lyrical ballads through specialty comedy songs to, hopefully, show-stopping production numbers. The manuscripts are annotated with instructions, queries, comments, opinions, and anxieties about key, performers' ranges, and orchestrations.

A marginal note on "Ah, to Be Home Again," a ballad for Jones and men's chorus, reads, "In this key, or near this key, there seems to be no way to write a decent or proper bass line for voice. Even an exceptional bass might do it, but succeeds in making the piece *heavy* instead of *plaintive.* Is it legitimate or effective to put the true bass part in the orchestra? I have heard it work for GIRLS' voices." One fragment of composition, which he apparently found suspiciously familiar, is signed "Loesser-Bizet." "Barabanchik," a production number featuring Bob Fosse's hi-jinks, has a two-bar pause for which my father's note reads: "Breathe, you buggers!" "Far, Far, Far Away," a sad and beautiful ballad, is labeled "A Slightly Modal Yodel," and queried: "Any pop possibility?" I wish I could print the haunting tune. The words are very simple:

> Far, far, far away
> Sails my love tonight.

Far, far, far away
All my heart's delight.
Cold, cold, cold this room
Long each hour's flight
While far, far, far away
Sails my one true love tonight.

"Truly Loved," a ballad for Catherine, also has a lovely tune and simple lyrics:

I know that I am truly loved
And that every moment
The man is all mine.
I know that I am truly loved
And the very knowing
Makes every moment shine.

And then there are the funny songs, like "Foreigners."

Foreigners—
I do not like foreigners.
Oh why is the world so full of foreign foreign foreigners?
And why do they not reform
Their queer manner of living?
When they don't adopt mine,
There's cause for misgiving.
(Americans take baths!)
Foreigners—mysterious foreigners,
Those obstinate people who perversely choose to be
To be—well, to be different,
Suspiciously different,
From plain simple huitieme arrondissement me.

And "To Your Health," for the British and German admirals, which begins with a musical repartee in which each man reveals his strategy for staying out of battle. The chorus:

To your health, to your health,
May it ever continue the best.
To your health, to your health,
May it never be put to the test.
May your drive to survive
Keep you far from the firing line.

May your belly get shot full of nothing
Stronger than fine Rhine wine.
May no strife mar your life
May no swordplay cut short its design.
May your throat feel the tickle of nothing
Sharper than fine Rhine wine.

There are fragments, variously titled "Stick This Up Your Fez," "Anything Turkish or Playable about This?," "Partial Martial," "Turk a Chance," "What Does Bobby Want?," "Sura the Coloratura," and "MUSTAFA KEMAL: I've Been Smoking All Morning and I Still MUSTAFA KEMAL."

I'm sure he MUSTAFAD many Camels. The show would not come together. But the reviews did, unanimously. The *Detroit News* called it "lesser Loesser." The *Detroit Free Press* said, "It's a Rolls-Royce of a show, a magnificent combination of artful scenery, lively choreography, and engaging people. But there's no gas in the Rolls-Royce tank." *Variety:* "The spirit and the resolution which produced one of the great rallying cries in history ["I have not yet begun to fight"] are urgently needed by Frank Loesser, Sam Spewack, and Bob Fosse, who are principally responsible for the disappointing launching at Detroit's Fisher Theatre of a new musical, *Pleasures and Palaces.*"

Jo came out to Detroit, saw how poorly the music came off, and suggested they change the orchestrations. My father thought that the orchestrations were the least of it. Everybody worked, in Allen Whitehead's words, "like slaves. People came in—Cy Feuer, Abe Burrows—but that just added more confusion. Every time we fixed something, that would leave a hole somewhere else." They stayed in Detroit about six weeks. Bob Fosse wanted to put his own money into the show and take it on to Boston. He was convinced they could make it work, but my father was just as convinced they couldn't. It was his decision to close it, and *Pleasures and Palaces* hasn't seen the light of day since.

The title of the show is taken from John Howard Payne's 1823 song, "Home, Sweet Home." ("'Mid pleasures and palaces though we may roam, be it ever so humble, there's no place like home.") True enough. Returning from Detroit exhausted and disappointed, my father was happier than ever to spend long weekends in his country house on Long Island.

After renting beach houses for several years, he and Jo had decided to buy their own. In 1963 they found a large white clapboard house in Remsenburg, a little hamlet near Westhampton, right on Moriches Bay. They had a dock built, then bought a flat-bottomed pontoon boat, a bargelike thing with benches and a sun canopy, in which he and Jo and Hannah and anybody else who was visiting tootled around the bay. After a summer of tootling, my father felt sufficiently expert to trade in the floating front porch for a Boston whaler. As Jo says, "He always thought he was quite something, driving a boat. But actually he was never very good at it."

My brother spent a lot of time with him at sea:

> He would create these incredibly complicated ways to moor the boat, which only he could figure out and which made very little difference to the stability of the boat. Sometimes he'd let me take the wheel, but he'd sit there and backseat drive the whole way.
>
> He liked navigation. He liked to figure out how to get from point A to point B on a map. He had lots of maps. He'd find a buoy on a map and then we'd go out to find it in the bay. But first he'd spend hours plotting a course to it, even though it was only about a hundred yards away. It wasn't a natural thing for him to be out on the water, but he loved it.[4]

My father and my brother had a troubled relationship. They loved each other intensely, yet each was disappointed in the other.

Johnny was a dreadful student. We were all sure the book *Why Johnny Can't Read* was about him. He was usually in trouble at school, could never bring himself to study, must have repeated the sixth grade three times. His poor performance was a thorn in my father's side, and he wasn't very sensitive to Johnny's feelings when he talked to him about it. Mostly he yelled at him. At one point he tried to tutor him, a project that drove them both nuts. I think my father was disappointed because Johnny showed no inherited genius, or even the family's celebrated intellectual curiosity. He did not see himself in his son. It wasn't that Johnny had better things to do. He wasn't writing poetry or mastering chess in his spare time. He just goofed off. He was indifferent to school and quietly resistant to any proffered guidance. Our mother, although concerned about his lack of performance, was no model of studious perseverance, and was in any event generally absent by virtue of being asleep during most of our waking hours.

Eventually, to our pleased surprise, Johnny did rather well at a boarding school in Connecticut, where he excelled in soccer and passed most of his courses. At his ninth grade graduation, which my father attended, he got a leadership medal. After the ceremonies, as they were getting into the car, my father said, "You know, Hitler was also a leader."

Was he consciously being vicious? Or was he making a wisecrack about the notion of leadership awards generally, aiming to entertain, instead of praise, his son. Maybe he thought that Johnny should accept his award the way he accepted his "Putziller." Maybe he took it for granted that Johnny would get an award, not noticing that, to him, it represented a kind of recognition and encouragement that would have been deliciously sweetened by a father's acknowledgment.

Johnny knew early on that he wanted a career in the theater. He knew he would prove to be no rival of his father, and he never tried to compete with him. He wanted to be left alone, to bide his time, to squeak through school any way he could, and as soon as possible to go out into the world of schmooze. He has come a long way since his school days. As executive director of a succession of performing arts centers all over the country, the former truant has even taught a couple of college courses in theater management. He deals, he wheels, plots and plans and makes things happen. He is well known and respected in his trade, and he schmoozes with the best of them.

My father and Johnny in Remsenburg.

My brother enjoyed a good part of several summers in Remsenburg, and there, in the relaxed country setting, where school wasn't an issue, the two of them did much better together. Of course, in that environment my father was as mellow as he ever got.

Before Remsenburg, he was fond of quoting Harry Kurnitz, who, when asked what he would do with a twenty-acre woodlot, said, "I'd pave it." But Remsenburg brought out the latent nature lover in my father, or perhaps it might be more accurate to say, the latent country squire. This Broadway-bred urban sophisticate developed interests in the most unlikely pursuits. In his words:

> I never thought of myself as a mensch who would concern himself with the *weather.* For me weather was something said to be happening outside somewhere—among *others,* like ships at sea, or race tracks, or people with precious marijuana crops.
>
> But weather in Remsenburg is now *my* subject. More ab-

sorbing than birds or woodwork or musical comedy. That's because it has not rained decently here in four weeks, and the lawn and shrubs are drying up. I have to water very sparingly or we will run out of house water or else draw in brackish water from the bay. (Why do they call it BRACKISH when they mean DRECKISH?)

Anyway, I now own a wallful of impressive-looking instruments—a hygrometer, a thermometer, a barometer, a tide clock—and if I owned the *Mona Lisa* I wouldn't know where to put her.

The birds don't seem to mind. They are all back, being spoiled by my sunflower seeds. Also there are my special shore birds—a kingfisher and a green heron. Both are marvelous fishermen. One dives and catches, the other wades in with great stealth and pokes.[5]

He loved the birds. So, of course, he quickly became knowledgeable about them and creative in his appreciation. He built bird houses and bird feeders; he had several bins of different sorts of bird seed that he referred to collectively as his "birdyteria." Like all backyard birdwatchers, he became obsessed with keeping squirrels away from his feeders. But unlike most backyard birders, he came up with his own devices to keep them (and "bad" birds) away.

One of his more elaborate ones was a balloon attached to his window feeder and connected to a blowpipe on his side of the window. He would sit in his office behind the one-way glass (yes) and watch for marauding squirrels and jays and starlings and pigeons. When one landed on the feeder, he would inflate the balloon from his battle station and scare the critter off. He rigged up a system on another feeder that would deliver a mild electric shock to anything bigger than a cardinal. (He especially admired a pair of resident cardinals whom he named Claude and Claudia.)

The other enemies in the bird world were the gulls, who took a scatalogical liking to his new dock. John Steinbeck, well versed in such bucolic irritations since he had been summering in Sag Harbor for years, had given him a plastic owl for just such an emergency. My father wrote a thank-you note:

I would have gotten this off to you a while back, but we have been having the painters—or maybe, by strange good luck you *don't* know, so I will tell you that the classic truth of the matter is that the painters have been having us.

They are a strong union here around Moriches Bay—and if you tell them off about slapdash work, they scream back at you and continue to give you more of the same. And if you try to walk up and confront the boss on the subject, he and the others haul ass to some other job, jeering as they go.

It is a sort of family Mafia or Cosa Nostra organization—certainly not AFL-CIO—named after their founder Longipennes (I looked it up), who became famous for his knack of eating shit and then shitting calcimine.

The present organization are all cousins, representing two descendent families, Larinae and Laridae (I researched that too), and I suppose this tight breeding accounts for the fact that they have no bridges to their noses. In fact they have no noses. As I watch them work—they are still here—I think to myself how a little I.L.G.W.U. blood could have helped.

Well, they showed up the other day, right after we had our dock put in for the season, and began to paint it. Now, the work would have been okay if they had brought along rollers and done a quick over-all job with no holidays. Jo walked out toward the dock, took one look at the work, and gave them a mezzo-forte mew (not unlike the one in *Most Happy Fella*): "He's an old man, an old man—I don't want him leaning all over me!" Only Jo didn't say "leaning," and all she got for her effort was a raucus Laridae laugh and a spackled left shoulder.

After I helped her change—with a pair of scissors—she went back and tried an appeal in low-register pop style, explaining (I thought winningly) that she herself had started as a chorus gull, but had taken a tern for the better and now shit Charlotte Rousses in cellophane into individual egg cups at twelve-inch altitude, and why couldn't they try to improve themselves along those lines? She finished with an affectionate "mwa!" like Dinah Shore, even.

I observed all this from under our big lawn umbrella, and I can tell you that nothing helps. The Larinae work from posts and do all the striped work, while the Laridae favor a streak technique from overhead in full flight—something like

Dufy. The younger members of both families (it's a featherbed union) are strolling pointillists.

There are barnacles on the submerged sections of the posts, and there are jellyfish clearly visible in the water. Also there are clusters of weeds sticking up, and on occasion a floating beer can. ALL GOOD TARGETS. SPORTING. PROPER. Right? You'd think these birds would pick out a jellyfish or a seaweed clump to shoot for. Alas, no.

They want to *paint.* Paint people's docks, people's boats, and—whenever possible—people.

About the middle of the day I'm reporting on, they flew off to eat more so they could make more paint. It was then that I thought of the owl you gave me. Steinbeck's remedy!

I got a foot length of pipe and threaded an end (cutting my hand a little), then put the pipe in a flange, got some nails and a hammer, grabbed your owl and walked out on the dock to install him. I *walked.* I should have hop-scotched. As a result I slipped (jarring my butt) but recovered and proceeded more circumspectly to just the right post. There I nailed in the flange (hammering my thumb twice) and stuck your owl on the pipe, where he sort of jiggled and twirled in the wind—I thought ominously.

But I am no Longipennes. Or even a kittiwake. Those birds came back and scared your owl so bad that HE started shitting.

And now we have got a Jackson Pollock dock.

With the possible exception of Jerry Lewis, the hardest thing in the world to get off the boards is gullshit. Rain helps but it's too slow. Garden hosing is too gentle. The stuff has to be cracked and pounded and scrubbed off, and even then some of it sits forever in the open grain of fir planking.

People have been saying all sorts of prayers for countless centuries: prayers for rain, for bringing the dead to life, for going to heaven, for peace, etc.

I suppose it is out of a sense of the decent or fastidious that there is nowhere on record a prayer for the cleansing away of tern turds.

Until now, John. I am sitting here (on a soft pillow), changing the bandaid on my right wrist and soaking my left thumb in hot bicarb, feeling myself all over for broken promises, looking out the window at the goddamn dock, and—first time on record—*PRAYING FOR HAIL.*[6]

My father had everything he wanted out in Remsenburg, including a second woodworking shop in the extensive basement where he spent much of his time making things: a large picture frame, an armoire, a plant stand, a weathervane in the shape of a hula dancer with pingpong ball breasts that bounced furiously in the breeze.

I loved to visit them in Remsenburg. The house was so lovely and comfortable, my father's office always had a new gadget (acquired or invented) to admire. Usually there were other guests or neighbors contributing to the entertaining atmosphere.

One exceedingly hot day comes to mind. Besides me and my soon-to-be husband, there were a couple of other guests (probably Howie and Lela Wilson). We had gone clamming off the dock, but the bay water was tepid and the sun unmerciful, so we retired to the shady porch and drank Bloody Marys and waited for lunch. There was no air conditioning—usually there was no need—only a few days a year were this hot. Everyone, including my father, moved in slow motion. We languidly assembled in the stifling dining room for lunch. Philip, the butler (so elegant he intimidated me), brought out a cold soup and iced tea, and as the sweat rolled down our faces, we sipped desultorily and mopped our brows.

Suddenly, my father sprang to his feet, stomped over the radiator, and started kicking it, roaring, "Goddammit—what's wrong with this fucking thing? Where's the heat?"

We'd go to Westhampton Beach and swim in the ocean, or we'd go clamming off the back yard, or out for a spin in the boat. And there were big parties and small gatherings—at the Steinbecks' in Sag Harbor, or at Nancy and Ernie Martin's in Westhampton, or at the Fishers' in Southampton (Jack Fisher was Jo's decorator; his wife, Shirley, was John Steinbeck's literary agent. They were both gay. She played the bagpipes and she flirted with me.) The Steinbecks, the Martins, Cy and Posey Feuer, Bob Fosse and Gwen Verdon were among many summer residents of the Hamptons who socialized with my father and Jo.

John and Elaine Steinbeck, and Frank and Jo Loesser. In the center are Eddie Condon and an unknown friend.

Gwen Verdon remembers a Fourth of July party to which John Steinbeck brought his (very real, working) cannon and my father came in costume: American-flag shorts, tails, a bow tie and a top hat. He had stuffed wads of paper money (also real and working) into every pocket, his hat band, the fly of his shorts, the knot of his tie. He was totally covered in money, and he said, "This is my recognition of this great country. Only in America could a schmuck like me make this kind of money."[7] (Now why does this make me think of Arthur? I wasn't at that party, but I think I would have cringed.)

There was one party where John and Elaine Steinbeck brought their new dog, an English pit bull named Angel. Angel looked like a white pig. He was the first pit bull I had ever seen, and I was fascinated. He was sitting quietly beside John when I came over and sat by the dog, petting him and asking John the usual "Is it a pig or a dog" questions, which John answered with tolerant patience. Angel was very docile, but not overly friendly. Hoping to capture his interest, I proffered an hors d'oeuvre, which he took daintily from my fingers. Whereupon John struck him across the face with an extraordinary combination of alacrity, force, and coolness. "He has to learn not to take food from strangers," John explained to me. "It could save his life some day." I don't know how many training sessions it took before Angel got the point. It only took me that one time. Since then I don't feed people's dogs without asking.

My father, who was quite fond of animals, as long as they were someone else's responsibility, was very taken with Angel, and shortly after they met he wrote him a long letter:

Dear Angel,

Meeting you again last night was a fine experience as always. But, as always, it left me with the feeling of something unsaid and unsolved (at first, anyway.)

(Members of my breed characteristically want things said and solved, and I am no exception. Like other people I get little satisfaction out of the simple spirit and smell of something—but at once proceed to bombard it with notions about cause and effect. This human process has many names: drama, mathematics, recipe, research, logic, and *worry.* You dogs are smart enough to know that *worry* is something you do with a bone, and let it go at that. Even Pavlov couldn't do any more than prove that your brain is in your gut—something that *you* knew all the time. My breed insists that the brain is in the head, and that is what *we* worry.)

Now, since meeting you several times in mixed company, I've felt a constantly sharpening uneasiness about the inevitable resort to cheap memory-simile-symbolism that bounces around the room every time:

"HE LOOKS LIKE A PIG"

Now, Angel, you must excuse people for that. They have manufactured the phrase "looks like" to complicate their senses with. This is a process which escapes your understanding, so I won't labor it further—except to say it is a sickness, and a pitiable one. I have had it, and your father has it, and please be sorry for us.

Your father has another sickness. Remember last night how he rolled you over and showed me your underside? You know what he said? He said (showing me some negligible gray spots): "Some dalmation origin."

He is a dramatist-historian (incurable) and felt compelled to report on who made buckety with who around what town pump to produce your great-uncle Rover.

I am not a dramatist-historian, but a popular poet. I deal in sounds. You know, like "Let's go Mets." (That isn't one of mine.) I string sounds together. But to string them I have to remember a bunch of old ones I heard somewhere and then juggle them into a new rhythm and shape. Where you will be satisfied with the concept, "I see the cat," I juggle it into "Hello Dolly" (Not one of mine either. Shit!). I supply the cat's name, imply that it's at least a second meeting, and a pleasant one. I do this to please people, not dogs, so don't give it another thought. But do please let me explain about the juggling process that produces a new and qualified version of "I see the cat."

We have learned to call it word association. One word reminds us of another word or name. Then this leads us to another reminder. With me it's like this: I see a tree; I notice it's a maple; maple sounds like Mabel. Mabel hasn't been used in a song since—let me remember—oh yes, nineteen twenty-nine. That was the year of the crash. Christmas eve I waited, *freezing*, on line in the street to draw what I could out of my deposits in a busted bank. No gloves! Blue hands—and I'd have to write my signature in a minute—hence:

"BABY IT'S COLD OUTSIDE" (Mine! Mine! Mine!)

Note how narrowly I escaped writing a *Mabel* song or (God forbid) one called "BLUE HANDS."

You, my dear Angel, wouldn't torture yourself this way. You'd see a *tree,* and without remarking on its being a maple or reminding you of anybody would know exactly what to do about it.

Me, I'm complicated. But it's a living, I tell myself. Also, every once in a long while this disease manages to produce a fine and beautiful truth—as (they say) some oyster illness makes the wondrously perfect pearl.

Well, last night and this morning my unrelenting tendency to invent has led me to one of those rare, fine, and beautiful truths! Remember when we wagged tails goodbye last night? (I was trying to squeeze into the seat of my small but exquisite car.) At that moment, while having a last look at your lovable face, I said to myself: "MRS. WEISSBERG."

And my wife and I drove off.

I hasten to tell you that you don't look at all like Mrs. Weissberg. But I would like to tell you who she is, or was, and what that leads to.

Mrs. Weissberg owned the candy store on our block when I was a little kid. I supposed my feeling of fondness for you reflected a feeling of fondness for her, which I now recollected. It was a different *kind* of fondness, of course. I wouldn't have wanted to rub her belly, for instance. I was about five; just old enough to be allowed to go alone with my nickel to Mrs. Weissberg's for a cone (yes, Angel, a giant cone was once a nickel).

Last night, in the car, I found myself remembering those walks around the corner, and how I savored the new independence, the first solo flights without big sister or Mama. (Remember no-leash?) The pride of it tasted almost better than ice cream. Almost.

But there were still some curbs and heeling. My mother, like other mothers, used to have a notion that kids' treats were full of harmful poisons—notably artificial coloring or the paraffin they use to harden chocolate against the New York summer, or saccharine, which was dirty-trick sugar and not really edible. My mother may have been right in principle, but out of her suspicions came the conclusion that the *whiter* something was, the *purer* it had to be. So, although the walks were my own, the choice of flavors was not. I was limited, alas, to *vanilla*.

Vanilla was, and I guess still is, a fighting word to a kid. Even French vanilla, which is the same thing with dirt spots. If mothers could have a dopey credo about purity, kids certainly were entitled to believe that *no color* implies *no flavor.* So with me, the joy of those walks was imperfect. I wanted chocolate, strawberry, pistachio!

Then one day something wonderful happened. Mrs. Weissberg knew Mama's rules, but she had two very fine Jewish qualities. She knew about *compromise* and she had a soul full of *compassion.* (These are not exclusively Jewish characteristics, but the Jews have an exclusive way of putting them together.) So after having held back tears of pity for almost a whole year, Mrs. Weissberg just couldn't stand it any more—hearing me ask for vanilla while gazing wistfully into one after another can of rich and flamboyant ice creams. I guess I must have been good at wistful gazing back then. I'm not any more. We all get over it. Remember how you got trained out of table begging?

Anyway, she said, knowing her duty, "Vanilla I got to give you." Then she added, singsong talmudic:

"BU—UT . . . ."

[high note] [low note] [diminuendo]
[portamento]

Out of nowhere—HOPE! Bu—ut what? What?

Mrs. Weissberg's hand was mashing the big ball of vanilla into my cone. Now it swept over to the big can of strawberry. There was the strawberry scoop, nestling in the pink and clustered generously with what I had not learned to call residuals. Even one real quarter of a strawberry was stuck in the edge of the scoop.

Up it came, the giant number two scoop, and onto my vanilla. And then Mrs. Weissberg—artist that she was—performed a historical collage, mashing first concave, then sliding convex, until there it was, without losing a crumb: my first almost strawberry cone. Now it was in my hand and I was staring at it.

"Walk slow," said Mrs. Weissberg, "and leck off all the pink before you get home." (Only at a distance would anyone mistake it for plain vanilla.)

That was the first of many many strawberry tainted vanilla cones. The ritual lasted until I was old enough to order crumbled butter pecan or cherry-fudge-walnut or anything else I wanted.

Well, that's why I said to myself, "Mrs. Weissberg" last night. And this morning. Angel, you do NOT look like a pig. That is cheap and over-convenient imagery, and lousy songwriting.

YOU LOOK LIKE VANILLA ICE CREAM DRESSED UP WITH THE STRAWBERRY SCOOP. And I'm the one who knows it.[8]

Another Long Island party memory: Nancy Martin asks me what I'm up to and I tell her I'm going to get married next spring. She looks at me with her shrewd and amused eyes and says, "I think it's a very good idea to marry your first husband when you're very young. That way you get done with it early and have lots of time to find the right one."

I was terribly indignant. Peter and I loved each other. How could Nancy be so sure we would fail? How could she be so cynical? Just because I was nineteen? Just because my parents had divorced? Just because of her own experiences? Maybe all of the above. As it turned out, she was right on the money.

Jo was eight months pregnant with their second child at my first wedding in May 1965. I had wanted to get married at their house, but I knew my mother would be hurt, so we had the wedding in her West Side apartment. I remember few of the details, but I can see from what's left of the pictures that virtually all my relatives were there, including both grandmothers; that Peter's elegant family felt somewhat uncomfortable with my mother's dramatically casual hospitality; that Jo was in charge of Johnny and his boutonniere; that Abe and Carin Burrows were there and that Carin was gazing out of the window during the ceremony.

My mother kept us all waiting while she put on her makeup. My father walked me to the fireplace where the judge married us and read some Edna St. Vincent Millay (badly). Jo and my mother behaved like good old friends, which they invariably did when they found themselves together socially, although I can imagine how my mother must have felt, seeing Jo so pregnant and my father so jovial. To her credit, she didn't tell me, although it was always clear enough to me that she had lost her world when she lost her man.

By now, most of their friends had become his friends, and my mother's social life was shrinking. She began to have additional health problems, and her general decline (which would end with her death in 1986 at seventy) was well underway. She would end her days as a sickly and bitter recluse who took no responsibility for her fate. But at the time of my first wedding she was still a lively character, loud and boisterous, hanging on to the past with one hand while reaching for a future with the other. The past was gone, and the future would prove barren.

At my first wedding.

While awaiting the new baby, my father and Jo debated names.

> Nicholas is a final name in a progressive series [he wrote]. As an infant and small child he'd be Nicky—then among his cronies, age seven to ten, he'd be Nick. Now Nick has a sharp sound—peremptory and biting—and by the time he's twelve that tone will have been resorted to by Jo and me often enough (NICK! Whatever it is you're doing, you MUSTN'T! NICK! DO YOU HEAR ME?) so that Nicky will fall into desuetude except maybe among young and amorous ladies when he's eighteen. Nicholas will appear on diplomas (if any) and that's about all till he has his own chain of clothing stores, or whatever—or if he doesn't make what he considers the proper status—he may adopt Nicholas (as well as a homburg hat) to give himself some dignity.
>
> But to quote my late colleague Mr. Hammerstein, SUPPOSING IT'S A GIRL!!![9]

Emily was born in June 1965. As a toddler, she looked like a Japanese doll with her dark bowl of straight hair and her almond eyes. She was a bright, happy, and fearless child, and she and Hannah further delighted my father that summer as he counted his birds and his blessings, entertained weekend guests, worked on his carpentry projects, explored Moriches Bay, and commuted to New York and his office, whence he corresponded with friends and associates while looking for the next project.

He was in touch with his old and dear friend Bill Schuman, who, as one of America's most prestigious classical composers had also come a long way from peddling his songs to Leo Feist. My father had apparently made some disparaging remarks about the newish Lincoln Center, and it was in his capacity as president of the arts complex that Bill dropped my father a line:

> Since you accuse me of being a stuffed-shirt statesman, I will play the role and call you an artist. As an artist, which you certainly are, your cavalier dismissal of our enterprise rather shocked me. The fact that you have never been to Lincoln Center is to me appalling and should be changed immediately. I want you to see the Center, but more, I want you to understand it. Its program should claim your support. I am sending

My father with Hannah on his lap and Jo with Emily on hers.

On his dock in Remsenburg. The gull carvings didn't scare the real ones away any better than the owl did. (*John Loesser*)

you a publication which may tell you something about the Center that you did not previously know.[10]

My father wrote back:

Dear Billy,

Answering yours of August 13, lissen [*sic*]:

I did not accuse you, but merely remarked on your guise as statesman. *You* supplied the word stuffed-shirt . . . I don't particularly *take pride* at not having been at Lincoln Center. I simply was reporting on the fact that I knew very little about it, but that thus far I was impressed the wrong way chemically.

Anyway, I have read the literature you so kindly included. When we meet in the fall, I will have made it a point first to have visited Lincoln Center. I'm sure I will have seen nothing *evil* in it, any more than I do in the type faces used in your giant brochure. But I will want some definitions from you. For instance, the words:

ARTISTIC
DEVELOPMENT
ENCOURAGING
EDUCATION
etc., etc.

And another definition I will want will be yours for *THE* PERFORMING ARTS. I seems to me that your prospectus does not include a few of the performing arts, for instance:

PROFESSIONAL WRESTLING
BULL FIGHTING
AUTO RACES
BURLESQUE COMEDY
RADIO & TV ANNOUNCING, NEWS & WEATHER REPORTING
POLITICAL DEBATE
RELIGIOUS ORATORY
FIGURE SKATING
STRIP TEASE
DIVING
AUCTIONEERING
STILT WALKING
JUGGLING
RESTAURANT GREETING AND SEATING

MARCHING AND DRILLING EXHIBITION
etc., etc., etc.

Please, Billy, don't suppose that I am pushing for a more vulgarian tendency in your program. I am pushing for nothing, but simply pointing out that THE PERFORMING ARTS ARE NOT NECESSARILY THE NIFTY PERFORMING ARTS, or THE DIVINE PERFORMING ARTS, or THE ACCREDITED PERFORMING ARTS. Let me submit that Hemingway—a high-class fellow—found something *noble* in bullfighting; that Fred Allen, the much esteemed wit, started as a juggler; that Victor Moore, who gave such a sensitive performance as Gramps in *Borrowed Time,* learned his craft in Burlesque; that Billy Graham is more effective as an actor than Sir Laurence Olivier; that the Indianapolis Speedway has a bigger and more avid audience in one day than do the combined performances of LA TOSCA in this country over a ten-year period—even though both audiences are there enjoying the smell of imminent death; that there is an abiding thrill for millions in the performance of those boys marching across the field at West Point; and that sky writing, parachute jumping, and fireworks (all performing arts) make one look up in awe and wonder. But what I have just reported I don't mean as corrective criticism. It happens that I myself prefer ballet, drama, opera, and musical comedy—and not too many other kinds of performance. I am not proposing that you include Billy Graham or Manolete (this dates me) in your programs. A sneaky thought reminds me that I would indeed like fireworks emanating from your real estate. But skip it, until you run short of plays.

What I really have a sense of dismay about is that there is a *center* of anything. I think maybe Cleveland can use one. Also possibly Los Angeles needs informed cultural guidance and a place to go get it. But not New York. New York *is* a center, a world's fair, and a den of thieves, and a house of miracles. Sometimes I like my hot dogs at Nathans, sometimes the gentile kind at ball games. Sometimes I go to one stadium, sometimes the other. (Sometimes with my wife and children, and sometimes with a man I'm trying to sell something.) Sometimes I like my opera at Asti's and sometimes at the Met, and sometimes on records at home and sometimes at a funny place in Brooklyn. I walk in Central Park and also on Madison Avenue, and sometimes around in circles in my

> study—and when I read, sometimes it's the *Herald Tribune* and sometimes the Talmud and sometimes your Lincoln Center brochure. In short, I have lots of places to go. It isn't that one is *better* than the other, but simply that it is *different* from the other.
>
> Now all this reflects on a chemical preference, and a very private one. Remember, about thirty-six years ago you and I met a girl named ___________? She was symmetrical and well spoken. Not only that, but her father owned a chain of liquor stores, and she was reported as conveniently nymphomaniacal. Yet, as I recall, neither you nor I especially wanted her phone number. Maybe she was too wondrously neat, or maybe she was too predictably available, or maybe she gave the impression of being so vastly prized that we couldn't prize her at all. Anyway, we agreed on that one. On the present lady we don't agree. But *you're* married to her and *I* have to go by whatever my antenna tells me, and, admittedly, by my built-in prejudices.[11]

But Bill had the last word:

> Just as I always suspected, at heart you are a professor. Okay—we'll change the name to Lincoln Center for Some of the Performing Arts.[12]

That month my father read a short story by Budd Schulberg (*What Makes Sammy Run, On the Waterfront*) called *Señor Discretion Himself.* He had found his next project.

14

Señor Discretion Himself

Schulberg's story, "Señor Discretion Himself" features a short, ill-tempered, disheveled baker, Alfonso (Pancito) Perez, who owns the "smallest, poorest and most bedraggled bakery in the small Mexican town of Tepalcingo." Pancito, an illiterate widower who tends to drown his perpetual sorrows in the neighborhood cantina, has four daughters. The youngest, Lupita, is a precocious fifteen-year-old who, as the story opens, is being courted by Hilario Cortez, the flashy proprietor of a modern, neon-lit bakery four times the size of Pancito's. When Pancito catches Hilario in his kitchen talking to his beautiful daughter, he flies into a rage and throws the rival baker out of his house. He then hires Martinez, the local schoolteacher/public stenographer, to send Hilario such a threatening letter that "the big, self-important Don Juan of a baker would never dare to come near Pancito's prize little guava again."

Maestro Martinez is horrified by the letter Pancito dictates. Under the guise of retyping it, he composes a carefully worded, diplomatic entreaty in its stead, which Pancito unwittingly signs. The next day, amazed to run into a friendly and gracious Hilario, Pancito goes back to the schoolteacher and dictates an even more violent diatribe. And the day after that Hilario is not only friendly but calls Pancito the wisest man in Tepalcingo. Renaming him Señor Discretion, he invites him to a drink at the most respectable café in town. Pancito, mystified but flattered, spends a companionable evening with Hilario, who persuades him that they should become partners.

Five years into their merger, Pancito is a changed man. Cheerful, well-dressed, and with a full-fledged reputation for giving wise counsel, he manages both bakeries while Hilario spends his time expanding their business. For the grand opening of their modern chrome and plastic coffee shop at Cuernavaca, the two partners find themselves in the plushest hotel in town, relaxing on their balcony. Hilario, who has kept Pancito's letters all this time, takes the first one out and reads it to Pancito as a sentimental prelude to his formal request for the hand of Lupita, now that she is of marriageable age. Pancito, concealing his delighted surprise at hearing his own wise words, agrees wholeheartedly to the marriage. Lupita, on the other hand, does not. Rather than Hilario—an old man (he is forty) who lost her respect when he was so easily scared off by her father—she has chosen Maestro Martinez. Martinez has also kept Pancito's letters—the original versions—and now threatens to reveal the identity of the real Señor Discretion if Pancito fails to bless their union. So Pancito offers Hilario one of his older, plain-faced daughters, Hilario graciously accepts, and all ends happily.

Schulberg's agent, H. N. Swanson, sent the story to my father with a note asking if he'd be interested in adapting it for Broadway. My father replied almost immediately, saying he would. Whereupon "Swanie," who obviously didn't know my father very well, wrote back to say that he intended to bring a well-known TV producer, Bob Banner, into the project. Could Banner and Loesser get together to "discuss a possible collaborative production"? My father replied by return mail:

> Your letter of September 14 appalls me. If I had any idea that you intended to select my producer for me, I would not have communicated as I did. It is not at all likely that I would have read Budd Schulberg's story even once, much less several times.
>
> I wish you would quickly tell Bob Banner that I don't wish him to communicate with me on this. I hasten to add here that this is not based on any lack of regard for Mr. Banner's work in the past or his qualifications for Broadway producership. Let's just say that things have to be written before they get produced, and as far as I'm concerned, *all* my bedfellows are *my* choice . . .
>
> The only thing I can suggest is that I (or this company [Frank Productions]) acquire the basic rights for a long enough time to let me try a hand at the musicalization and some songs. Possibly alone. Possibly with someone else. The only way I can commit this to actual production is by liking the *result* well enough.
>
> If the above sits well with Budd, let me know. If, however, Budd feels that he'd rather do it himself out West, I will of course understand. If after he accomplishes any adaptation without songs, he wants to shoot it to me, I would be very much pleased, but only if there are no commitments with producers, directors, and others beforehand.[1]

He sent a copy of his letter to Schulberg with a cover note:

> I imagine you won't want to trust me with the whole thing. I'll feel bad about that because for the last week there has been a notion smoldering in my belly button about how to do it quite richly.[2]

Both Schulberg and his agent replied positively. Schulberg wrote:

> Since geography is a problem for us, and I fully agree that collaboration cannot be a long-distance affair, it seems to me that the happiest arrangement might be for you to take over the story for some specified period. When I have a story I like, as I do this one, I don't usually feel this way. But in this case I have enormous faith in your talent and also feel you would be unusually sympatico with this material.[3]

My father's notion was to make the adaptation "abundantly musical." "I would relate it to a work of mine, *The Most Happy*

Fella, with respect to the almost operatic (I shudder at that word) quantity of music. But I expect this one to be much more gay and to include a good deal more choreographic material and bouncing stage activity."[4]

At this point, it was important to my father to keep the project a secret until he had a viable product, and he and Schulberg agreed that they would not discuss it with anyone. In November 1965 a three-and-a-half year option on the story was negotiated and my father began work. In March 1966 he informed Schulberg that "things are coming along—although there have been some delays and obstacles. But I am indeed working, and so far I like the results pretty well."[5]

He elaborated the plot, adding three priests who are disheartened by the boring, repetitive nature of the daily confessions and by the few and paltry offerings in their Sunday collections. Longing to make their little town (now called Tepancingo—probably because it is easier to sing) famous, they pray for a local miracle so they can have a little shrine of their own. The transformation of Pancito, of course, turns out to be their miracle.

Lupita has but one older sister, Carolina, verging on spinsterhood and in love with Hilario. Hilario lives up to his name—he is rather a buffoon—an outrageously dressed dandy who, it turns out, is actually an escapee from a mental institution. Scenes were added wherein both officials and inmates from the institution come seeking Hilario, whose real name is Ricardo Levine. There's a running joke about beans and who will buy them, a lot of business with the priests, and a complicated scheme engineered by our hero Pancito to marry Hilario to Carolina—thereby saving the former from being reincarcerated, the latter from an old maid's fate, and paving the way for Lupita and Martin (who has lost his "ez") to wed.

Martin, a lovable, handsome, extraordinarily sloppy and absent-minded character, has his own quest. He wants to pursue his study of world peace and earn a professorship at the university in Mexico City. Thanks to Hilario's financial support (Hilario wants to keep him away from Lupita), he indeed goes, only to be expelled in the first semester for his lack of neatness. Returning home defeated and ashamed, he gets uncharacteristically drunk and reveals the truth ("*I* am the virgin of Tepancingo"). But all ends happily when it is discovered that since Pancito has been treated as a wise man, he has actually become one. His discreet "better wisdom," at first dictated by Martin and Lupita, has become his own. Carolina gets Hilario, Lupita gets Martin, and Pancito keeps his good friend and partner.

My father fastidiously researched many aspects of this project: Mexican currency, the look of a public notary sign in Mexico, the laws regarding Mexican mental institutions (consulting two Mexican attorneys and amassing a small file of information in the process), and especially the specific sounds and rhythms of Mexican music. He wrote to Don Walker, asking him to orchestrate the show:

> Without knowing the precise dates I can't, of course, ask my office to negotiate a contract with you at the moment, but consider yourself invited by me to join this project. When I see you next Monday (I hope) I will be asking you about religious processional music in small Mexican towns; the size of low-range marimbas; the use of a small diatonic harp (I have heard vaguely of such); instrumentation of mariachi music in the section two hundred miles south of Mexico City; etc., etc. Bring a pencil and give me a good hour.[6]

Two weeks later:

> In addition to all the other things, please find out for me what sort of music is played by marching bands in Mexico. I do not mean military or patriotic, but more the stuff that a carnival parade would use. If there are any recordings of such things please get them for me, along with other material.[7]

He sent Abba Bogin, who was working with him once again, on a partially paid vacation to Mexico. Abba was to immerse himself in the local music for consultations upon his return.

At first he had a very good time with the writing. The few manuscripts for this show include plenty of his characteristic witty annotations. For instance, on the eighth and last version of "Compañeros":

Some parts of vocal should be sung Rubato Mexicano, sometimes known as "Hey Rubato." The technique consists of a *lazy* sort of push and delay. This style should *not* be attempted when a vocal duet or in ensemble unless all the people were born and raised together in Tehuantepec. This includes our Jewish conductor.

We are henceforth and forever
Compañeros, compañeros
In whatever we endeavor
Compañeros, you and I.
Arm in arm we will walk
Heart to heart we will talk
Eye to eye we will see
What a team
What a team we will be.
Like a big and little brother
Compañeros, compañeros
A companion for each other
Plus a partner, plus a friend
Compañeros—to the end.

Written on the manuscript of "Padre, I Have Sinned," a half-sung, half-spoken confessional scene: "The intention is to create a 'funny' Religioso sound via odd instrumentation and brittle awkward voicing. AY CALAMIDAD! I COULD BE WRONG!!"

A solo comedy number for a minor character in which Martin is warned of the dangers in Mexico City is set contrapuntally against a sweetly-singing chorus:

Ensemble: Hasta la vista
Negrin: Don't drink the bottled water
Ensemble: I will see you soon again
Negrin: No matter what you do
Ensemble: Hasta la vista
Negrin: They boil it and they strain it
Ensemble: God be with you until then
Negrin: Which is very bad for you
Ensemble: Hasta la vista
Negrin: Don't drink the bottled water
Ensemble: Though you journey far away

Negrin: It will thin you out the blood
Ensemble: Hasta la vista
Negrin: No color and no flavor
Ensemble: Is a happy thing to say
Negrin: And the bottom got no mud

Each part is a complete song with an independent tune.

"I Cannot Let You Go" is the big love song for Lupita and Martin:

I cannot let you go
I cannot let you out of my arms
Now that your lips are warm upon mine
And eagerly my fingers caress your hair
I cannot let you go
Without the sudden feeling of doom and despair
To think of losing you,
Losing you only for a little while
Chills my heart
And I cannot smile and be brave
I am both captor and slave
I say the word goodbye
But I can hear my soul crying no
I cannot
I cannot ever
Let you go.

Despite the secret nature of the project, word inevitably got out. In July 1966 my father wrote to Schulberg: "Leonard Lyon's column spilled the beans about the identity of our musical. I called him and asked him how he had come by the information, and of course he announced in a righteous tremolo that to reveal a source is to commit a mortal sin." The pressure was now on for them to formally announce the project, and by December they agreed that the beginning of the new year would be the right time. On February 5, 1967, Lewis Funke wrote in the *New York Times:*

> Those of faint heart who have given up the theater for dead, please note: already the 1967–68 campaign looks good. This morning's optimism is based on the news that two of the

> theater's major guns are ready again to take their turns on the line: Arthur Miller and Frank Loesser, the playwright with *The Price,* his first drama since *Incident at Vichy,* the composer with a still untitled work based on a story by Budd Schulberg, "Señor Discretion Himself" . . . Mr. Loesser, as he has done in the past with such as *The Most Happy Fella,* expects to be responsible for the book and lyrics along with the music. As of the moment, the book is just about finished, Mr. Loesser contending that his first interest is in developing a valid play. The music will not be troublesome. He already has spotted the places for the songs. "You have to know where the song rises out of the action. And you want to know something? That's one of the problems playwrights have when they try writing for the musical stage. There are certain laws of gravity in this business, and unless you understand them, you're heading for trouble." Plans call for a production in the fall.[8]

By the end of that month my father had a "jumbo pre-first draft" to which he appended "The Optimist Manifesto, or Ground Rules for the Reading of [it]," a lengthy memo that instructs the reader in great detail just how to read and comment on the draft:

> This will be tedious going. There are some 242 pages to read carefully. In the event that you believe you are up against the new Parsifal, I hasten to assure you that I have done some rough timing with generous allowance for songs and choreographic and pantomime passages—and that this show is at the moment no more than twenty-five minutes longer than what is considered normal. The extra jazz that stretches this manuscript to its present length consists of detailed visualization of the specific ACTION, MANNER, and PHYSIQUE of the show, as I imagine it at this moment.
>
> If it seems to you that I itch to usurp the functions of director, choreographer, scenic designer, costume designer, makeup man and coffee girl, please take comfort in my assurance that I simply want these people to *improve* what I have written. Let's call this form of script a challenge—an invitation to my cohorts to amend, correct, excise or clarify—and generally make what is there more effective. But at least there *is* something there—and you are stuck with the job of absorbing it. . . .

Brace yourself for many of the locutions. My intention is that this entire show be played with a distinct Mexican accent. Please try to get used to "I go tomorrow to the house of my uncle" as opposed to "I'm goin' to my uncle's house tomorrow." If you doubt that all the performers can master the accent, consider that anybody who can say CHUTZPAH can also say CHAVE JOU MET MY SEESTER? . . .

And now, the big big demand on you: I want negative criticism only. Here are some examples:

"I hate the whole thing."

"On pages x, y, and z the intention seems to be to get laughs. It's not funny to me."

"The quotation on page 606 sounds like an infringement."

"This and this line is uncharacteristic of the character speaking. He is reversing himself."

"On page ABC you are informing the audience for the fourth time that the cat has fleas."

"I don't have a clear notion of Nebenzahl's attitude."

"How did Orville know Wilbur could be at Kitty Hawk at such an ungodly hour? Hmm?"

WHAT I DON'T WANT is for you to run with the ball, for the time being. I will give you some examples of what to *avoid* telling me:

"If the boy's part were changed to the part of the girl and she came on stage two scenes later with a parasol it would make much better sense."

"I have a much more literate ending for your song JADA."

"It would be much more logical to have a table fifty-three inches long instead of fifty-four."

"Hire at least two Negroes."

"If Pferdfus is a backward child, why doesn't he come in backward?"

"This play should be narrated by a sort of master of ceremonies. This would shorten your exposition. Incidentally, my cousin Selig, who looks Mexican. has put in a great and long apprenticeship at the Concord."

"When the leading lady cries, she should wave an American flag so we know how she feels."

"I have a much dirtier way of telling that joke: The lady walks into the saloon with one of her—"

. . .

> Finally, I beg you to return the script promptly without having made notes on it or marking it in any way. Your copy may very well be the one intended for the eyes of a prospective director or choreographer or even investor, and should remain pristine. In passing, let me state that I have used pristine for years and find that while it indeed closes my mind, it does open my sinuses.[9]

He had a grand vision of the show, and he invented staging, costumes, sets, props, and something he called the "Synchronous Fluid Multi-Stop Iris:"

> What I expect is that the Iris will become a *constant* of the show, not only to close (black) over concluded scenes, but when closed or partially closed, to serve as an actual reasonably decorative scenic background for certain shallow scenes.
>
> With regular light on it I see the Iris to be a framed velour thru-traveler plus header—of the same brown color as the Franciscan habits. The mechanical construction is such that it creates *variously shaped* apertures on closing and opening. It's use dictates a certain amount of downstage central staging, as well as certain specific use of light from the foots. I don't mean footlights as such, but small pre-set spots.
>
> This leads me to another *constant* I visualize, and that is the use of ultraviolet. With the iris set 6 or 7 feet up from the apron, there are possibly 3 or 4 lines available downstage of it. I see these as hung with flat scenic elements or symbolic designs painted for ultra violet projection during and after the black closings, and then necessarily fading as ordinary light hits the closed iris . . .[10]

And on he went at length, not only about the use of ultraviolet light but also about the uses of magic and Mexican colors and patterns. He dictated the exact measurements of certain scenic elements to be used for very specific effects. The script is loaded with detailed descriptions of these effects—as well as detailed descriptions of the characters. Hilario, for example:

> HILARIO is middle-aged, tall, robust, and wild-eyed with uncanny mischief but not villainy. He can be Mastroianni, he can be Cesar Romero with eyes like Robert Newton. Or George Irving or possibly Terry-Thomas, or a large Leo Carillo. Or have you ever met Vernon Duke? Judging from his

> make-up, carriage, and manner of speech he thinks himself both handsome and dashing. His mind darts from subject to subject without benefit of sequitur. In short, he is a nut, if not a complete madman. Nevertheless there is no doubt that he is masculine. He had also better be one hell of a baritone.

He sent the manuscript and its ground rules to several of his colleagues, including John Steinbeck, Cy Feuer, Don Walker, and Abba Bogin. Those who read it were more impressed with his reach than his grasp. The scenic and lighting elements, the costumes, the specifications for each prop, the characters themselves were all highly entertaining to read about, but the actual script, when disentangled from the rest, was found disappointing. My father, unhappy with his work almost as soon as the ink was dry, began making revisions even before he solicited advice.

Schulberg had read much but not all of the script by then. At the end of March my father wrote to him, "There is no point in my sending you the script, of which you have already read part. Having finished it I immediately found fault with it in many areas and am now busily rewriting as well as cutting." In May he wrote again, at length:

> The reason I haven't sent along the script is that it is simply not good enough. I don't mean this only as a matter of degree. It is un-right, so please forgive me for not showing it.
>
> . . . The play in its present condition is terribly diffuse. It lacks concentration on a prevalent rooting line, and I must supply that. My difficulty for the last month or so has been in deciding what line to follow. You read about three quarters of it some time back, so I think you will understand specifically what I mean.
>
> For instance, there is a strong opening scene that presents a small problem of the clergy about no cojones in the confessions. The *problem then disappears* as a larger and more exciting one is assigned to Hilario. We then introduce Pancito and his problems as the town's drunken reprobate. But he shortly finds this *problem ended* by virtue of his quasi canonization through Hilario, who in turn *abandons his own purpose* of seeking nookie with a fifteen-year-old. The happy coalition of the two bakers provides Lupita with a *release from her status*

anxieties. This leaves us Martin, who has a clear-cut purpose which continues although I propose no interesting or entertaining penalty for failure in his professorship examinations. We are also left with Carolina as the standard old maid who continues to pray for a husband. Along with this I suppose we must consider the trio of priests as exerting a continuous drive toward putting their town on the religious map.

Well, I have never considered constructing the play as the story of Martin, or the story of Carolina, or the story of the three priests. But that is what the present script leaves me with, and in all honesty I don't believe any audience would stand for such stakes after careful presentation of at least three others as being our big principals. . . .

To put it very briefly, I have asked for a rooting section at a ball game which gets rained out in the second inning; then begged them to travel to another field where darkness shortly stops the game; invited them on a bus ride which takes them around in a circle; and then coaxed them off the bus for a supper of chicken noodle soup, only to serve it in bowls with holes at the bottom.[11]

Schulberg replied: "I think, Frank, the kind of severe self-criticism you apply to your work is courageous and deeply creative. At the same time I wonder . . . whether you are not driving your criticism too far."[12]

My father struggled with the show throughout 1967. In the fall of that year his first collaborator and good friend Irving Actman died suddenly at sixty. This was a hard blow for my father to take, and it was the first of several. Suffering through this loss did not help him in his work on *Señor Discretion,* which he finally gave up in March 1968. He wrote Schulberg:

A sad time has come. I find myself obliged to report to you that I don't know how to budge my version of *Señor Discretion* in any further direction or into any other shape. I have begun to remechanize the poor thing in several different ways, only to find the results deadly dull—and with not at all the feeling I had wished for it.

I think I have already told you that I went to the three theatrical writers I consider most valuable in the musical comedy field—and offered each the job of doing a new book. In each case I got some friendly words, but neither Abe Burrows nor Doc Simon nor Joe Stein came anywhere near considering my offer.

And now finally I must confess that I have grown cold on the subject. Not cold *to* it. I feel sure there is someone in our business who will know how to write a good adaptation but that someone is not me or any of the people I trust, and so I have told the company not to take advantage of its option which comes up in May, but to return it with regret to you.

I feel confident that you understand me and that my decision to quit is one I simply had to make after all this time. Also I feel sure that this will not change what I think is a happy regard you and I have for each other.[13]

15

The Last Year

My father did not write from that time on. Letters—wonderfully clever letters—he tossed off effortlessly. But no lyrics, no music, no books. At the time I was living in Germany with Peter, who was working for the Motion Picture Export Association. This was (and probably still is) the European branch of Jack Valenti's Motion Picture Association, primarily concerned with the promotion and protection of American movies abroad. Most of Peter's colleagues were in their forties and fifties: very formal, very correct, very German. They were probably very nice, too, but we were in our bratty early twenties, very American, very out of place, and very filled with ourselves, so we didn't notice. We lived in a kind of cultural and social limbo while we were there, spending most of our time with people who did not interest us, doing grown-up things like attending cocktail parties and movie openings, knowing almost no one of our own age and background. We shouldn't have gone there. (We shouldn't have gotten married in the first place, which we were beginning to realize.)

My main source of happiness in Frankfurt was the unwitting mailman. Through the kitchen curtains I would stealthily watch his approach every morning and listen for the sound of letters from home being slipped through the slot in the front door. I would scoop them up, devour them, and write back by return mail. My father was one of my most loyal correspondents. He wrote often, especially in response to various Germanic goodies we would send him:

> And now about the LEDERHOSEN. They were a hilarious surprise on my birthday. I didn't want to audition them in mixed company (we had guests) so I waited until next morning to try them on. It was about 4:00 A.M. and I think I almost laughed the neighborhood awake. *Yes, they are a trifle big.* So I stuck out my gut to keep them on—over my otherwise naked body—and paraded up and down past the mirror—reflecting that if Germany had engaged a Yiddishe Gauleiter or two in every hamlet they could have gotten rid of the entire male Jewish population via CHAFE and saved GAS and their own world image as well. There is a limit to how long one can distend the middle section artificially—especially with raw bleeding thighs. So I figured I would support the narcissistic experience with BEER. This swells the belly real good—and is of course in the right tradition.
>
> So I marched (YES) to the fridge where I had a moment of pause in realizing it was *Danish* beer, but presently got some moral comfort out of the realization that we Germans are liberal and international—also out of the fact that I was now negotiating a tour of the downstairs floor without any effort in keeping the pants up. I remembered I had a hat, shaped (vaguely) in the Tyrolean manner. I found it and put it on. True, it is made of *straw,* and the hatband says LET'S GO METS—but I squinted that away and went happily on with my goose-step. It was now full daylight and I swear all the grackles, cardinals and bluejays I have been watching were out there on the other side of the window WATCHING ME! It is an odd experience, I can tell you, and very disconcerting. So I lowered the blinds and tried some mountain climbing over Jo's pink living room furniture—humming snatches of the Horst Wessel song to myself as I went.
>
> Presently I realized I had to take a leak. (This is a fairly common sensation among beer drinkers.) I got down off the arm of the sofa and made for the bathroom—proceeding to undo the fly. What fly? There are *two* of them. Like on sailor pants, only zippered. *European* zippered yet, which is always a problem. But on heavy leather!!! Anyway, the fly wouldn't open. So I rushed to undo the belt. The belt wouldn't budge. I should have known. I was once locked in a pair of French

> swimming trunks for three days in Antibes. Well, there I was with this now exaggerated urgency to piss. So I decided to go out on the lawn, dress right and piss down one leg, then smartly dress left and dribble down the other. It occurred to me that there might be some soothing balmlike effect on my SPARTANISCHEN BEINEN—and if it worked, I might bottle the stuff—sell millions of gallons of it to alpine guides and retire (with the profits) to Bad Homburg. I prepared for squirt number one—adopting the position known fondly here as the EMILY AKIMBO. The grackles seemed to find it quite natural and didn't remark much as they watched. But I myself was overtaken by the sudden thought that this whole thing was quite childish. I told myself (aloud) to be aware that I was now FIFTY-EIGHT YEARS OLD!!—and a voice answered mine:
>
> "You don't look it."
>
> It was Conzetta (our sometimes maid) who often comes out on the lawn early mornings to kick mushrooms.
>
> Then she added "Happy Birthday," helped undo the belt (she worked for a locksmith once), and rushed me solicitously to the bathroom, where I made it just in time.
>
> Look, I hope you kids won't mind if I don't put the lederhosen on again. Even when my legs get their skin back. Also I hope you won't think me ungrateful if I don't run them up the flagpole—because ours isn't strong enough. What I'd like to do is take the pants to Abercrombie and Fitch and see if I can trade them in on a beartrap.[1]

Lots of funny letters, some with not-so-funny parts: "You can judge that I have been a busy bee, making things in the basement. That is mostly because I have not *written* anything. Yes I have, but what I write turns out to be SCHIDT as the Germans put it. And they sure know how to put it."[2] Or, in August of that year, "Well, I have caught you up on my interests and activities. You have already deduced that I am writing NOTHING. GAR NICHTS—or like my father used to say, KEINE SCHPOOR" [Keine Spur: "not a trace"].[3] And in September:

> In some ways I am starting to dodder. My memory is sloppy and so is my cabinetwork. And I resist sailing into a new writing project for fear nobody else will like it (I've never

Nana.

been that way before). Also, I find myself glued to the TV more and more. And more and more tolerant of Ed Sullivan.[4]

I returned home in January 1969 to find that my father had been hospitalized twice for tests the previous fall, which failed to determine the source of his "aching gut" and his weight loss. He looked tired and drained.

On January 5 Arthur died of a heart attack while sitting in the car in his driveway. A surprise, although he was seventy-four. My father was shaken and depressed by the news. There was a memorial service in Cleveland, which my father, Jo, Nana, Johnny, and I attended (Grace and her husband were abroad). I remember only fragments—Nana, now eighty-eight and suffering from phlebitis and grief, was sadly regal, sadly resigned at outliving her favorite if not her biological child. (I had finally come to appreciate my grandmother and feel some affection, if not deep love, for her. While I had lived in Germany the two of us had carried on a correspondence in German, and while she was exacting and rigorous in her critiques of my letters, she was also clearly proud of me and interested in my life. And it pleased me that she was. We both had enjoyed that interlude and now I could see a softness in her, in her sorrow, and I could feel for her.)

My father was subdued, in a dark suit and a quiet tie, thin and weary but still in charge of our mournful little group. A long (or so it seemed) concert at the Cleveland Institute of Music, and a longer (or so it seemed) visit with my Aunt Jean, Arthur's widow, sitting on uncomfortable furniture, waiting for it to be over.

Not three weeks before, John Steinbeck had died. Unlike Arthur's death, John's was expected—he had been failing for some time and had chosen to come home from the hospital to die in his own bed. But expected or not, the loss was an unacceptable cruelty for my father. He had spent a great deal of time visiting John in his last weeks—trying to believe, and trying to make John and Elaine believe, that the doctors were wrong, that John would live. And when he didn't, my father was inconsolable. When Elaine asked him to serve as a pallbearer at the funeral, he told her he simply couldn't do it. "I would fall down in the middle of the church," he said. But then, realizing that it was the last thing he could give his beloved friend, he served. Elaine told me she had never seen anyone suffer as much at a funeral.

Illness and death were suddenly my father's main preoccupation. He was often angry, off-balance, intolerant. His personal pain was not eased by current events in the winter of 1969. The Vietnam War was changing the way people led their lives, changing attitudes and priorities and culture. Music and theater were by no means immune, and my father took these changes as personal insults.

For me, returning to the States that January was like waking up from a long, dim dream. In the time I had been away, the war had escalated to such a pitch that even I had to take notice. In Germany I was so homesick I actually experienced a lump in my throat at the sight of my flag. Hearing about people burning American flags only irritated me. For news from home I listened to the Armed Forces Network, the war news providing a sort of unfocused background rumble from which a jolt of headline material emerged from time to time, like the Chicago riots and the assassinations of Robert Kennedy and Martin Luther King. Now that I was home the background rumble became clear.

I went to see *Hair,* that season's Broadway musical smash. I was amazed. Thrilled. Shocked. Smitten. Then my friend Janet turned me on to Crosby, Stills, Nash, and Young, the Moody Blues, The Stones, The Doors, Jimi Hendrix, marijuana. My friend Linda educated me about the immorality of the war to which I had paid so little attention. It didn't take me long to begin sporting headbands and tie-dyed T-shirts and, belatedly, adopting the attitudes and tastes of my suddenly aroused generation.

My father was as appalled by the changes around him as I was excited by them. The man who had written "Praise the Lord and Pass the Ammunition" for a relatively popular war whose issues were clear-cut did not appreciate the hairy hippies' message. In *his* war, a war in which his talent thrived and matured, the goals were simple and unarguably righteous. Now, young people were smoking pot and raising hell and singing songs that my father refused to understand or even listen to. The popular music coming out of this war could have come from another planet, so far as he was concerned. He was sick and his friends were dying. Vulnerable and irritable, he was less interested in whether the Vietnam War was misguided than he was affronted by a counter-culture that he found ugly and stupid.

He was heartbroken by that time. He couldn't write, and what he saw being written and being fancied had nothing to do with his tastes or concerns or talents. The world was racing past him, the younger generation nipping at his heels as it went by, and drawing blood.

As sick and as angry as he felt, he was still a man of flamboyant tastes and colorful words. He still wore his wonderful loud ties and still roared his opinions. He could still be funny and charming. He still even jumped up and down occasionally. But there was a new edge of defiance in his style, as if he knew he was fighting for his life (which I think he did know, before anyone else). "I'm gonna live to be a hundred and three," he said often and fervently in his last year. "Don't mess with me, 'cause I'm gonna live to be a hundred and three."

Bob Wright and Chet Forrest described a poignant encounter with my father that winter:

> The last time we saw Frank, we ran into him on 57th Street. He put his arms around us and said, "What are you doing? Come on over and have some caviar. I'm eating nothing but caviar these days." We went over to the Russian Tea Room and sat down and ate nothing but caviar with Frank Loesser.[5]

Late that winter my father felt worse and went back in the hospital for more tests. He was clearly seriously ill now. My father—the raging Rumpelstiltskin, the fiercely funny ball of fire, the driven genius whose energy knew no limits—had suddenly become frail and shaky and old at fifty-eight. The transformation was nearly impossible to accept, so fast, so fundamental it was. We forced an attitude of optimism, and so did he. The doctors would find the source of his mysterious infirmity and he would get well, and everything would be all right. It just couldn't go any other way.

By spring he was having trouble eating, losing weight rapidly, in worse pain. One of his doctors thought he might have pancreatitis. He operated, found and removed a small node, and put my father on a fat-free diet. I remember Jo grilling chicken breasts for him until they were dried-up shards, the skin removed, the meat carefully separated from any fleck of fat. But he couldn't get them down. And it wasn't because he had no appetite or because his pancreas was malfunctioning. The lung cancer that the doctors couldn't find had by then invaded his esophagus, and he was unable to swallow properly.

His daily life became more limited and more labored. Going out to dinner was impossible. So was going to the theater. His memory faltered; he couldn't walk unassisted. Hannah and Emily, now seven and four, too young to be aware of his suffering, would try to climb on him as little kids do, teasing him for hugs and games, and he could only weakly rebuff them. He still loved to watch the birds and went to Remsenburg and spied on them from behind his one-way window until he got too weak to make the trip.

In June he was back in the hospital for the last time. His new doctors took new X-rays, and they found the cancer. They told Jo, but I don't know if they told him. They didn't tell me. He didn't tell me. I didn't tell him. But he knew, and I knew. Everyone knew. Everyone knew and was afraid to say the deadly word.

We visited. Jo was there all day every day. I came more and more often as he dimmed faster and faster. On one visit he asked me where Peter was. "We're living separately," I said. "We're going to get divorced."

"Is it that bad?" he whispered. "I always thought you could have done a lot worse."

"I'm gonna do a lot better, Pop."

He smiled but made no further comment, leaving me wondering what he really thought.

We brought him a cake on his fifty-ninth birthday. It was one of his bad days, and we sat around his bed forcing it down our throats while he dozed restlessly. Nana was there, trying not to believe her eyes.

Abe and Carin Burrows came to visit him, and Abe, all jolly and nervous, suggested he keep a diary of the silly things that happen in the hospital, "so when you get out of here you'll have some good laugh material for your next show." My father's cabinetmaker friend Tom from Remsenburg visited often, talking with him about woodworking projects, making drawings and plans. Harold Orenstein was a mainstay. Allen Arrow, who came several times, was not the only one who provided him with the cigarettes he still craved so badly. My mother didn't come, although she wanted to. She still loved him and always would. I think she had realized he was dying long before the rest of us, having divined the truth from the bleak bulletins my brother and I delivered at frequent intervals.

The day before my father died, a man unfamiliar to me suddenly appeared in the room. He must have been an acquaintance, because my father, who had been drifting in and out of consciousness, responded by trying to sit up, to shake hands, to remember the name—to be the gracious, ebullient host. He failed on all counts, and the man retreated, aghast.

That is my last memory of my father, a picture so vivid that for many years I could not conjure up any other one. He died very early the next morning—his time of day.

He had left a letter of instruction with Harold Orenstein:

> Beyond the time necessary for medical and legal confirmation of the fact that I have indeed departed this life, I wish my remains viewed by no one—and that includes family members. Immediately upon becoming officially dead, I would like my remains turned over to an organization licensed to cremate. The ashes are to be disposed of by the cremators in any way that they may see fit, providing that under no circumstances they place them separately in any urn or vessel or in any spot of ground or other identifiable place. I would prefer that what is left of me be commingled with other refuse so that it is in every respect untraceable.
>
> I wish there to be no ceremony of any kind marking the event of my death, nor any gathering of people pertinent to the occasion of my disappearance. There will, of course, have to be the official brief death notice in the daily newspapers. However, under no circumstances is anyone or any company or organization left behind to place any form of commemorative or mourning notice or advertisement as sometimes seen in *Variety* and other such trade papers. This last applies at the time of my death, as well as to subsequent anniversaries of same and to any other later time.
>
> I am deeply grateful that you have agreed to do whatever you can toward carrying out the above requests. I realize, however, the possibility that you might, at the time, not be close at hand or indeed available to carry out everything. In that event, I trust that you will assign someone else the job of

> doing away with a body without benefit of ceremony, religion, speech-making, coffin-selecting, flower-sending etc. This person should be someone who isn't an old buddy or relative but is simply efficient and cold to sales talks about real silver casket handles.[6]

The cremators flew my father's ashes over Moriches Bay and scattered them therein. The pilot's name was Red. A simple but colorful name. The name of a local hero, perhaps. A no-nonsense type just doing his job—without ceremony, but with style. We all thought my father would have enjoyed the casting.

Try as he did, my father didn't prevent the front page obituary in the *New York Times* the next day, or the loving eulogy that Abe Burrows wrote for the following Sunday's Arts and Leisure section of the *Times*. I don't remember any death notices. I didn't read them back then.

Since there was no funeral or other formality, many people gathered spontaneously at my father's house, and some gathered at my mother's. Johnny and I trudged back and forth from the East to the West side, sort of like at Christmas time, only it wasn't fun. The days blurred into weeks and we drifted back into our day-to-day lives. But things weren't the same. The great fiery comet who had been my father had burned himself out, and it took us all a long long time to stop looking for his light.

Epilogue

That fall the Mets won the World Series, so in a sense they were gone too. No more hilarious fumbles and endless losing streaks. Baseball lost its family significance as our lives went on. After my father's death, Jo ran the business, going in to the office daily. But it wasn't for her, the life of a businessperson, so after a few years she sold Frank Music and Music Theatre and dissolved Frank Productions. She resumed her singing career, developing a cabaret act of Frank Loesser songs, keeping his work and his name in the public eye as much as one woman with one act could. Not that his music wasn't performed elsewhere. *Guys and Dolls* was put on every year by countless college and amateur groups, summer stock theaters, and professional companies all over the world. (Of particular note was the London revival at the National Theatre in 1982, starring Bob Hoskins. It ran for a season and was so successful it reopened and then moved to the West End in 1984.) It was even revived on Broadway once, briefly, in an all-black production. The other shows, too, were performed consistently, except for *The Most Happy Fella,* which presented musical and logistical challenges to most amateur or stock companies, and was rarely put on. The old movie songs could still be heard in the old movies on late-night television. Many of his tunes, disguised in Muzak format, accompanied supermarket shoppers and annoyed people on hold on the phone.

But for twenty years, although his music was out there, his name and his fame diminished steadily. Only my stepmother, with her little cabaret act, and a very few other old timers celebrated his musical genius, or even mentioned his name.

And then, as this manuscript was taking shape, so was a

veritable Frank Loesser renaissance. I started hearing his songs on prime-time television and in current movies. In 1989 when Stuart Ostrow accepted the Tony for M. *Butterfly,* the first person he thanked on nationwide TV was Frank Loesser. In the spring of 1991 the Goodspeed Opera Company produced a two-piano version of *The Most Happy Fella,* which was so enthusiastically received by Frank Rich and other critics that it came to Broadway. The current spectacular success of the Broadway revival of *Guys and Dolls* has firmly restored his name to the prominence it deserves. (When I wore my *Guys and Dolls* T-shirt to my aerobics class—a place where generally I speak to no one and no one speaks to me—a young woman pointed excitedly at my chest and said, "Wasn't it fantastic? Wasn't it great?" When I went to an eye doctor recently for a checkup, the receptionist saw my name and said, "Oh yes. As in Frank Loesser. Any relation?" Just like the old days.)

Four new Frank Loesser albums have been released: the two cast albums from the Broadway revivals; *Loesser by Loesser,* a couple of dozen songs performed by Jo, Emily, and Don Stephenson, Emily's husband; and *An Evening with Frank Loesser,* in which you can hear my father singing demos of two of his scores. If you knew him, you'll see his wonderful, expressive face as he sings to you, loud and good and clear and strong. You'll see the twinkle in his eyes and the furrows of his brow and the crafty smile, full of life.

If you didn't know him, I hope you can imagine Frank Loesser as you enjoy his songs. He didn't intend to write for posterity, it is true. But even so, his work is now being discovered by a new generation, and I think he would, despite his protestations, be tickled.

Notes

CHAPTER ONE

1. Grace Drachman, personal reminiscences.
2. From Arthur Loesser, "My Brother Frank," in *Notes,* March 1950, Vol. VII, No. 2, p. 217.
3. Letter, Henry Loesser to Arthur Loesser, December 3, 1912. From the Arthur Loesser collection in the International Piano Archives at the University of Maryland.
4. Letter, Henry Loesser to Arthur Loesser, February 14, 1914. From the Arthur Loesser collection in the International Piano Archives at the University of Maryland.
5. William Schuman, personal interview.
6. Letter, Frank Loesser to Arthur Loesser, undated. From the Arthur Loesser collection in the International Piano Archives at the University of Maryland.
7. Lynn Loesser, unpublished memoir.
8. Ibid.
9. Ibid.
10. William and Frances Schuman, personal interview.

CHAPTER TWO

1. Various letters, Frank Loesser to Lynn Loesser, May–July, 1936.
2. Letter, Frank Loesser to Arthur Loesser, April 27, 1936, from the Arthur Loesser collection in the International Piano Archives at the University of Maryland.
3. Letters, Frank Loesser to Lynn Loesser, September 23 and October 3, 1936.
4. Burton Lane, personal interview.
5. Ibid.
6. Lynn Loesser, unpublished memoir.
7. Letters, Frank Loesser to Lynn Loesser, July 3 and July 10, 1937.
8. Burton Lane, personal interview.
9. Lynn Loesser, unpublished memoir.
10. Letter, Frank Loesser to Lynn Loesser, September 9, 1937.
11. Ibid.
12. Letters, Frank Loesser to Lynn Loesser, August 1937.
13. Miriam Call, personal reminiscences.
14. Letter, Frank Loesser to Lynn Loesser, June 26, 1939.
15. Burton Lane, personal interview.
16. Jule Styne, personal interview.
17. Ibid.
18. Letters, Frank Loesser to Lynn Loesser, July 18 and July 19, 1940.

19. Letters, Frank Loesser to Lynn Loesser, November 6 and December 8, 1941.

CHAPTER THREE

1. David Ewen in *Theater Arts Magazine,* May 1956.
2. Letter, Frank Loesser to Lynn Loesser, March 12, 1942.
3. Letter, Frank Loesser to Lynn Loesser, April 18, 1942.
4. Mary Healy, personal interview.
5. Jule Styne, personal interview.
6. Milton DeLugg, personal interview.
7. *Chicago Times,* March 20, 1946.
8. Letter, Frank Loesser to Lynn Loesser, April 18, 1945.

CHAPTER FOUR

1. Lynn Loesser, unpublished memoir.
2. Benay Venuta, personal interview.
3. *New York Times,* December 22,1980.
4. Lynn Loesser, unpublished memoir.
5. Ibid.
6. Ibid.
7. Margaret Whiting, personal interview.

CHAPTER FIVE

1. Brooks Atkinson in *New York Times,* October 12, 1948.
2. Richard Watts in the *New York Post,* October 12, 1948.
3. Ward Morehouse in the *New York Sun,* October 12, 1948.
4. Cy Feuer, personal interview.
5. Lynn Loesser, unpublished memoir.
6. Cy Feuer, personal interview.
7. Lynn Loesser, unpublished memoir.
8. Cy Feuer, personal interview.
9. Ibid.
10. Arthur Loesser, "My Brother Frank," in *Notes,* March 1950, Vol. VII, No. 2.
11. William and Frances Schuman, personal interview.
12. Cynthia Lindsay, from the Introduction to the *Frank Loesser Songbook,* New York: Simon & Schuster, 1971.

CHAPTER SIX

1. Goddard Lieberson in *The Saturday Review,* December 30, 1950.
2. Michael Kidd, personal interview.
3. Cy Feuer, personal interview.
4. Carin Burrows, personal interview.

5. Letter, Frank Loesser to Robert Anders, June 14, 1961.
6. Cy Feuer, personal interview.
7. Ira Bernstein, personal interview.
8. Carin Burrows, personal interview.
9. Richard Watts in the *New York Post,* November 25, 1950.
10. Alvin Colt, personal review.
11. Michael Kidd, personal interview.
12. Jule Styne, personal interview.
13. Michael Kidd, personal interview.

CHAPTER SEVEN

1. Sylvia Fine Kaye, personal interview.
2. Farley Granger, personal interview.
3. Farley Granger as quoted by A. Scott Berg in *Goldwyn, A Biography,* New York: Alfred A. Knopf, 1989, p. 463.
4. Letter, Emily Preyer to Frank Loesser, undated.
5. Sylvia Fine Kaye, personal interview.
6. Elaine Steinbeck, personal interview.
7. Letter, John Steinbeck to Frank Loesser, September 9, 1958.

CHAPTER EIGHT

1. Elliot Norton in *The Boston Post,* February 6, 1949.
2. *Time* Magazine, February 28, 1949.
3. Samuel Taylor, personal interview.
4. Ibid.
5. Jo Loesser, personal interview.
6. Ibid.
7. Susan Johnson, personal interview.
8. Lynn Loesser, unpublished memoir.
9. Ibid.
10. Abba Bogin, personal interview.
11. Ibid.
12. Ibid.
13. Joseph Anthony, quoted in Martin Arthur Mann, *The Musicals of Frank Loesser,* City University of New York Ph.D. Thesis, 1974, p. 109.
14. Susan Johnson, personal interview.
15. Arthur Rubin, personal interview.
16. Arthur Loesser in *The Cleveland Press,* June 2, 1956.

CHAPTER TEN

1. Robert Willey, personal interview.
2. Letter, Joy Chute to Frank Loesser, May 22, 1957.
3. Letter, Paul Osborn to Frank Loesser, undated.

4. Letter, Frances Goodrich and Albert Hackett to Frank Loesser, December 28, 1958.
5. Abba Bogin, personal interview.
6. Ibid.
7. Allen Whitehead, personal interview.
8. Abba Bogin, personal interview.
9. Terry Little, personal interview.
10. Abba Bogin, personal interview.
11. George Roy Hill, personal interview.
12. Ibid.
13. Abba Bogin, personal interview.
14. Ellen McCown, personal interview.
15. George Roy Hill, personal interview.
16. Ibid.
17. Kenneth Tynan in *The New Yorker,* March 19, 1960.
18. Jo Sullivan, personal interview.

CHAPTER ELEVEN

1. Cy Feuer, personal interview.
2. Elliot Lawrence, personal interview.
3. Charles Nelson Reilly, personal interview.
4. Cy Feuer, personal interview.
5. Rudy Vallee, in *My Time is Your Time,* New York: Ivan Obolensky, Inc., 1962, p. 233.
6. Cy Feuer, personal interview.
7. Ibid.
8. Gwen Verdon, personal interview.
9. *Village Voice,* October 26, 1961.
10. Jo Loesser, personal interview.
11. Frank Loesser, notes to performers.
12. Allen Arrow, personal interview.
13. Theodore Loesser Drachman, personal interview.
14. Letter, Frank Loesser to Susan Loesser, undated.
15. Letter, Frank Loesser to Susan Loesser, undated.

CHAPTER TWELVE

1. Herb Eiseman, personal interview.
2. Robert Wright and George Forrest, personal interview.
3. Richard Adler, personal interview.
4. Ibid.
5. Mark Bucci, personal interview.
6. Alfred Uhry, personal interview.
7. Letter, Frank Loesser to Susan Loesser, undated.
8. Letter, Frank Loesser to Cliff Ferré, June 27, 1962.

9. Herb Eiseman, personal interview.
10. Allen Whitehead, personal interview.
11. Allen Arrow, personal interview.
12. Stuart Ostrow, personal interview.
13. Cyd Cheiman, personal interview.
14. Henry Fanelli, personal interview.
15. Mona Lipp, personal interview.
16. Harold Orenstein, personal interview.
17. Herb Eiseman, personal interview.

CHAPTER THIRTEEN

1. Gwen Verdon, personal interview.
2. Ibid.
3. Ibid.
4. John Loesser, personal interview.
5. Letter, Frank Loesser to Susan Loesser, undated.
6. Letter, Frank Loesser to John Steinbeck, undated.
7. Gwen Verdon, personal interview.
8. Letter, Frank Loesser to Angel Steinbeck, undated.
9. Letter, Frank Loesser to Susan Loesser, undated.
10. Letter, William Schuman to Frank Loesser, August 13, 1965.
11. Letter, Frank Loesser to William Schuman, August 18, 1965.
12. Letter, William Schuman to Frank Loesser, August 20, 1965.

CHAPTER FOURTEEN

1. Letter, Frank Loesser to H. N. Swanson, September 20, 1965.
2. Letter, Frank Loesser to Budd Schulberg, September 20, 1965.
3. Letter, Budd Schulberg to Frank Loesser, September 24, 1965.
4. Letter, Frank Loesser to H.N. Swanson, September 24, 1965.
5. Letter, Frank Loesser to Budd Schulberg, March 11, 1966.
6. Letter, Frank Loesser to Don Walker, November 28, 1966.
7. Letter, Frank Loesser to Don Walker, December 12, 1966.
8. Lewis Funke in *The New York Times,* February 5, 1967.
9. Frank Loesser, "The Optimist Manifesto, or Ground Rules for the Reading of the Jumbo Pre-First Draft of *Tepancingo.*"
10. Frank Loesser, draft script for *Señor Discretion.*
11. Letter, Frank Loesser to Budd Schulberg, May 22, 1967.
12. Letter, Bud Schulberg to Frank Loesser, June 20, 1967.
13. Letter, Frank Loesser to Budd Schulberg, March 19, 1968.

CHAPTER FIFTEEN

1. Letter, Frank Loesser to Susan Loesser, undated.
2. Letter, Frank Loesser to Susan Loesser, undated.

3. Letter, Frank Loesser to Susan Loesser, undated.
4. Letter, Frank Loesser to Susan Loesser, undated.
5. Robert Wright and George Forrest, personal interview.
6. Letter, Frank Loesser to Harold Orenstein, April 23, 1962.

Index